Robert E. Howard: A Closer Look

ROBERT E. HOWARD:
A Closer Look

Charles Hoffman and Marc Cerasini

Hippocampus Press

New York

Dedicated to the new breed of Howard scholar: Fred Blosser, Rusty Burke, Frank Coffman, Bobby Derie, Mark Finn, David Gentzel, Charles Gramlich, Leo Grin, Chris Gruber, Mark Hall, Scotty Henderson, Don Herron, Morgan Holmes, Jeffrey Kahan, Patrice Louinet, Gary Romeo, Jeffrey Shanks, David C. Smith, Steve Tompkins, and other esteemed peers.

Special thanks to Rusty Burke for his invaluable assistance in bringing this project to fruition, and to Torin Mizenko for his careful proofreading.

Copyright © 2020 by Charles Hoffman and Marc Cerasini
Originally published in 1987. Expanded and updated edition copyright © 2020 Hippocampus Press.

Published by Hippocampus Press
P.O. Box 641, New York, NY 10156.
www.hippocampuspress.com

All rights reserved.
No part of this work may be reproduced in any form or by any means without the written permission of the publisher.

Cover art and frontispiece copyright © 2020 by Rick McCollum.
Cover design by Daniel V. Sauer, dansauerdesign.com
Hippocampus Press logo designed by Anastasia Damianakos.

First Edition
1 3 5 7 9 8 6 4 2

ISBN 978-1-61498-311-8 (paperback)
ISBN 978-1-61498-260-9 (e-book)

Contents

Introduction 7
   I. Howard's Life, Career, and Legacy 13
   II. Bran Mak Morn 49
   III. Solomon Kane 65
   IV. King Kull 99
   V. Conan 127
   VI. Other Fantasies 196
   VII. Horror Stories 217
   VIII. Other Prose and Poetry 237
   IX. Conclusion 255
Works Cited 265
Bibliography 269
Index 293

Abbreviations:

B1	*The Best of Robert E. Howard, Volume 1* (2007)
BCC	*The Bloody Crown of Conan* (2004)
BMM	*Bran Mak Morn: The Last King* (2005)
CCC	*The Coming of Conan the Cimmerian* (2003)
CSC	*The Conquering Sword of Conan* (2005)
CL	*Collected Letters* (2020)
CP	*The Collected Poetry of Robert E. Howard* (2008)
HS	*The Horror Stories of Robert E. Howard* (2008)
IMH	*The Collected Letters of Doctor Isaac M. Howard* (2011)
K	*Kull: Exile of Atlantis* (2006)
PO	*Post Oaks and Sand Roughs* (2019 ed.)
ST	*The Savage Tales of Solomon Kane* (2004)
WT	*Robert E. Howard's Western Tales* (2013)

INTRODUCTION

In a meteoric career spanning little more than a decade, Robert E. Howard (1906-1936) produced hundreds of vivid and gripping stories for the pulp fiction magazines of his day. He wrote historical epics for *Oriental Stories* and *Magic Carpet*, westerns for *Argosy*, adventure stories for *Top-Notch*, boxing stories for *Action Stories* and *Fight Stories*, and horror stories and fantasies for *Weird Tales*. It was in the pages of *Weird Tales* that the heroic fantasies for which Howard is best known first appeared. Here were the tales of Bran Mak Morn, king of the Picts of ancient Britain; Solomon Kane, deadly seventeenth-century swordsman; and King Kull, ruler of a mysterious realm that was old when Atlantis was young. But towering over them all was Conan, the giant barbarian warrior from the bleak northern wilderness of Cimmeria who sought adventure in the colorful lands of the lost Hyborian Age.

Howard was a born storyteller plying his trade during the 1920s and '30s when the pulp magazine industry was at its zenith. Pulp fiction has frequently been dismissed as cheap entertainment of the tawdriest sort due to its often lurid and sensationalistic content, but like any sort of fiction it can be done well or poorly. The pulp magazine was the descendant of the dime novels and penny dreadfuls of the nineteenth century, but pulp fiction at its best could be considered a twentieth-century successor to nineteenth-century Romanticism. "Philosophically, Romanticism is a crusade to glorify man's existence," Ayn Rand duly noted; "psychologically, it is experienced simply as the desire to make life interesting" (Rand 109-10).

This Romantic yearning for more out of life—more excitement, more meaning—was something that Robert E. Howard, living in a small town in semi-rural Texas, grasped instinctively. When the editor of *Weird Tales* requested some biographical information about the young author, Howard wrote in response:

> Like the average man, the tale of my life would merely be a dull narration of drab monotony and toil, a grinding struggle against poverty . . . I've picked cotton, helped brand a few yearlings, hauled a little garbage, worked in a grocery store, ditto a dry-goods store, worked in a law office, jerked soda, worked up in a gas office, tried to be a public stenographer, packed a surveyor's rod, worked up oil field news for some Texas and Oklahoma papers, etc., etc., and also etc.

Howard was moved to conclude, "And there I believe is about all the information I can give about a very humdrum and commonplace life" (Robert E. Howard [hereafter REH] to Farnsworth Wright, c. June-July 1931; CL 2.225-27).

Many years later Mark Schultz, illustrator of a collection of the Conan tales, recalled:

> I discovered Robert E. Howard's Conan in 1969, when I was 13 years old. I read the stories then for their incomparable high adventure and mind-blasting horror. It wasn't until much later that I realized they hit so hard and stayed so timeless because Howard's feverish, passionate writing was a crystal clear reflection of a young mind in turmoil, fighting to be free of the limitations of his physical surroundings. (Schultz 2)

Howard's writing derives much of its power from the intensity of this longing for liberation from the banality of everyday life. The most heartfelt conviction of the working-class man is that he is capable of *more*. As an author, Howard sensed that his readers benefited in some way from seeing their struggles reflected on a higher level. He understood that consumers of narrative art have an innate hunger to identify with characters placed in extreme circumstances. Well in advance of writers like Mickey Spillane and Ian Fleming, Howard was crafting sexy, violent entertainment. Unusual situations, intense moods, and heightened emotional states, prominent features of Romanticism and its Gothic subgenre, are also boldly displayed in his writing.

If indeed the lot of the average man is one of drab monotony and toil, it falls to the storyteller to furnish needed refreshment for tired minds. As a storyteller, Robert E. Howard was more than a pulp fiction virtuoso. Both a knowledgeable history enthusiast and a gifted poet, he shared a spiritual kinship with the bards and skalds of old. As such, he sought to resurrect the heroic saga where it had long been lost.

When America declared its independence from the Mother Country, it was also bidding farewell to St. George and King Arthur. No comparable myths grew up to take their place. The new folk legends that appeared in the wake of the Industrial Revolution celebrated laborers and producers of goods. Today everyone has heard of Paul Bunyan, John Henry, and Casey Jones, yet no one really cares about them. "Tall tales" of how hard some guy worked were a poor substitute for the epic sagas of Odysseus, Siegfried, Roland, and Beowulf. That tedious labor, no matter how useful, was not enough to fill a man's heart was something Robert E. Howard understood only too well.

Howard also understood clearly that he had to do more than simply mimic the old-time epic saga; he had to bring it up to date. He wrote for the American working class of the early twentieth century. His readers were widely separated by time, distance, and upheaval from the myths and legends that had enthralled their ancestors in the Old World. They lived in a world rocked by cataclysm, no less than the fictional Hyborian Age of Conan had been. In 1906, the year Howard was born, the world was ruled by kings, dukes, emperors, sultans, kaisers, and czars. Twenty years later, they were all gone. The slaughter of the First World War and the lawlessness of the Roaring Twenties were followed by the malaise of the Great Depression.

Writing before Carl Jung was well known in America, before Joseph Campbell's work had appeared, Howard possessed an instinctive grasp of mythic, archetypal figures—king, warrior, magician, femme fatale. He knew that the ancient figure of the warrior would resonate on a deeper, more subconscious level than the cowboy, the detective, and other familiar heroes of pulp fiction. Yet he also knew that he could not present sword-wielding warriors as they had appeared in legends from long-past eras when people lived, thought, and felt differently. He realized that a hero backed by a patron deity and gifted with magical weapons would impress struggling Depression-era readers far less than one with only his own craft, guts, and sinews to rely on.

Robert E. Howard also broke with the effete fantasy tradition in English literature that began in the Victorian era. Howard was not an upper middle-class professional like William Morris, definitely not a clergyman like George MacDonald, nor an academic like C. S. Lewis or J. R. R. Tolkien, much less a titled aristocrat like Lord Dunsany. As a working-class writer of popular fiction, Howard's fantasies were harder, tougher, grittier, bawdier, and at times more cynical. In place of elves we find stunted, freakish troglodytes. Instead of ogres, there are monstrous carnivorous apes. In lieu of dragons, gigantic venomous fifty-foot serpents. No enchanted princesses here; in their stead we meet alluring slave women, lusty wenches, bold lady pirates, and seductive femme fatales.

Conan himself could be considered a precursor to the modern action hero. When a trembling naked woman gasps that a monster Conan has just killed must be the devil, the Cimmerian nonchalantly quips, "'Then hell needs a new devil'" (CCC 265). This sort of dry wit is typical of more contemporary heroes like James Bond, Dirty Harry, and *Die Hard*'s John McClane. Prominent heroes of the pulp era such as The Shadow and Doc Savage were essentially supercops, maintainers of the status quo. Robert E. Howard had something different in mind when he conceived of Conan. His giant barbarian is an outlaw, a sword-for-hire, basically out for himself, yet still retaining a certain knack for doing the right thing. Conan is not a preserver of order; he is a rebel, a brawler, a mover and shaker, the whirlwind at the center of momentous events.

Though created in 1932 and popular with contemporary readers of *Weird Tales*, Conan really broke big in the later, more raucous decades of the 1960s and '70s. Sadly, however, his creator did not live to see this triumphant resurgence. Subject to severe bouts of depression, Howard took his own life during a particularly troublesome phase. His works fell into a decades-long period of obscurity. During this time, the pulp magazine was gradually replaced by the mass-market paperback book. It was here that Conan would live again. In 1966, Lancer Books began issuing a series of paperback collections of the Conan stories. These featured eye-catching cover paintings by Frank Frazetta. Frazetta's vivid paintings were the perfect visual counterpart to Howard's vigorous prose. A marriage made in heaven, Howard and Frazetta helped raise each other's profile.

A new generation of readers picked up those Conan paperbacks, liked what they read, and wanted more. Kull, Solomon Kane, and Bran Mak Morn soon followed Conan back into print. The demand for REH's bold storytelling remained unabated. Howard's lesser-known characters and work in other genres—horror stories, westerns, historical tales—all eventually appeared in mass-market paperbacks.

Howard's gripping, intense sagas resonated with modern readers in a way that the more conventional adventure fare of Sir Walter Scott, Rafael Sabatini, and H. Rider Haggard could not. The knights in Howard's historical epics were grim, violent men rather than the flower of chivalry. Likewise, the gunfighters in his westerns were taciturn loners. Howard tempered Romanticism with realism, just as iron is tempered with carbon to make steel. In this manner he satisfied his readers' Romantic longing for color and excitement in a way that rang true. This gritty realism extends even into his most fantastic works. Howard considered Conan the most realistic character he ever created.

Howard's heroic fantasies are anchored by the humanity of his protagonists. Bran Mak Morn will go to any lengths to save his dying race from the encroachment of the world's mightiest empire. The dour Puritan Solomon Kane is driven by the demands of his rigorous and demanding faith to seek out evil and give battle. Kull strives to bring order and justice to a decadent kingdom infiltrated by monsters. Conan is the consummate self-determining man, alone in a hostile universe.

Conan's universe—and Howard's—is a hostile one indeed. Violence and bloodshed are commonplace facts of life. Hatred and vengeance are omnipresent and can lead to bitter blood-feuds. The monsters and horrors in Howard's fiction are the symbolic physical manifestations of all that is utterly destructive and evil. Modern existential thought is also reflected in Howard's work in the sense that no triumph is permanent or has any meaning in the vast cosmos-at-large. History is cyclic; civilizations rise from barbarism, decay, and are swept away by new waves of barbarians. Bleakness, futility, and the inevitable passing of all things are part of the worldview of Robert E. Howard.

All this makes for compelling reading and gives Howard's work a gravitas found in few of his contemporaries. It could be said that many readers *come to* Robert E. Howard for the action, adventure, thrills and horror to be found in his stories, but they *stay for* the dark, turbulent undercurrent that runs just beneath their surface. It is this dark undercurrent that gives his work its lasting appeal and makes Robert E. Howard an author worthy of a closer look.

I. Howard's Life, Career, and Legacy

Robert Ervin Howard was born on January 22, 1906, the only child of Dr. Isaac Mordecai Howard and Hester Jane Ervin. The Howards at that time resided in the tiny hamlet of Dark Valley, Texas, populated by a mere fifty souls. Dr. Howard took his wife to the larger community of Peaster, thirty-five miles west of Fort Worth, to give birth. Though the family moved away from Dark Valley when Robert was just a baby, REH always claimed to remember it as a somber, gloomy place:

> Man is greatly molded by his surroundings. I believe, for instance, that the gloominess in my own nature can be partly traced to the surroundings of a locality in which I spent part of my baby-hood. It was a long, narrow valley, lonesome and isolated, up in the Palo Pinto hill country. It was very sparsely settled and its name, Dark Valley, was highly descriptive. So high were the ridges, so thick and tall the oak trees that it was shadowy even in the daytime, and at night it was as dark as a pine forest—and nothing is darker in this world. The creatures of the night whispered and called to one another, faint night-winds murmured through the leaves and now and then among the slightly waving branches could be glimpsed the gleam of a distant star. Surely the silence, the brooding loneliness, the shadowy mysticism of that lonesome valley entered in some part into my vague-forming nature. (REH to H. P. Lovecraft, c. October 1930; CL 2.120)

While the family still dwelt in Dark Valley, Hester Howard suffered a miscarriage and so Robert remained an only child.

In 1908, the Howard family relocated west to Seminole before moving on again in 1909, and yet again in 1910. In all, the Howard family relocated ten times before finally settling in the town of Cross Plains, located in the flat, dry "post oaks" country of central Texas, in 1919. Dr. Howard's ambition led him to follow various oil and agricultural booms as he searched for opportunities in newly prosperous areas. It has been speculated that being uprooted so often during his formative years could have had a detrimental effect on Robert's emotional well-being. In any event, it is interesting to note that many of Howard's characters—Solomon Kane, Steve Costigan, Turlogh O'Brien, and Conan—are wanderers.

At the time of Howard's birth, the West was still a wild and open place, many thousands of square miles of territory remaining much as before the coming of the Europeans. The populace was only a generation or two removed from the frontier, and Howard informed a correspondent that "I've had kin in nearly every movement of conquest and colonization from the Revolution on—War of 1812, Gold Rush of '49, Civil War, settling and developing of West Texas, Apache uprising in New Mexico, settling of the Indian Territory, etc." (REH to Wilfred Blanch Talman, September 1931; CL 2.277).

Hester Jane Ervin, Howard's mother, was born in 1870, three years before the last Comanche raid in central Texas. As a young girl, she was acquainted with many settlers who bore scars from fierce battles with the Comanches, including one man who'd been scalped and survived. Howard made mention of his mother's intense hatred of Native Americans, as well as her habit of drawing the curtains of a lamp-lit room after dark, which Howard described as "an involuntary relic of the old days when it was not wise for any man to give his enemies such a clear shot at him" ("The Wandering Years" 9).

Dr. Isaac Mordecai Howard, Robert E. Howard's father, was the son of a '49er headed for the gold fields of California who was halted in his trek by a cholera epidemic that decimated his party and so weakened him that he was unable to continue further westward. Isaac Howard was born in Holly Springs, Arkansas, in 1871. He grew up to become one of the pioneer physicians of central Texas and married Hester Jane Ervin in 1904.

Howard himself grew to manhood in the post oaks country and witnessed the final phases of the settlement of the lower Rio Grande valley and the early oil booms that so altered the geography and social landscape of Texas. Young Robert, however, was something of a misfit among the simple, pragmatic, hard-working, God-fearing farmers, cattlemen, and oilmen he grew up around. He later alluded to being bullied to a certain extent during childhood. Given his introverted personality and intellectual leanings, this was to be expected. The problem could have only been exacerbated by the fact that his family moved from town to town every six to twelve months during the first nine years of his life; he would have always been "the new kid." During this period, Howard's mother read to him for hours at a time, endowing him with a love of literature, especially poetry, that would remain with him long after he overcame his bullying peers.

In boyhood Howard's imagination was fired by accounts of ancient history that he read in such books as he could obtain in that isolated region. His introverted personality, intellectual pursuits, and rejection by his peers no doubt contributed to the feelings of alienation that he experienced, but it was something even deeper and more basic to his nature that made Howard an outsider. From the beginning, it was clear that his inmost longings lay far from his native milieu:

> I have lived in the Southwest all my life, yet most of my dreams are laid in cold, giant lands of icy wastes and windswept fens and wilderness over which sweep great sea-winds, and which are inhabited by shock-headed

savages with light fierce eyes. With the exception of one dream, I am never, in these dreams of ancient times, a civilized man. Always I am the barbarian, the skin-clad, tousle-haired, light-eyed wild man, armed with a rude axe or sword, fighting the elements and wild beasts, or grappling with armored hosts marching with the tread of civilized discipline, from fallow fruitful lands and walled cities. This is reflected in my writings, too, for when I begin a tale of the old times, I always find myself instinctively arrayed on the side of the barbarian, against the powers of organized civilization . . . (REH to H. P. Lovecraft, c. January 1931; CL 2.176)

It is evident from this passage that Howard's sense of kinship with vanished peoples and remote epochs was not the result of personality quirks acquired through unpleasant experiences in childhood or adolescence; rather, it was rooted in the core of his being.

Despite the vividness of his dreams and imaginings and the intensity of his identification with men of ancient times and places, Howard was not oblivious to the world around him. Statements to the contrary have been made by critics with a superficial understanding of Howard's complex personality. According to his father, Howard was "very realistic . . . The neighborhood news and happenings of the narrow sphere in which he lived was of interest to him, just like it was to the slow plodding folks around Cross Plains . . . He was keenly interested in the pageant of both nation and state in which he lived. At election time I've known him to sit by his radio far into the night listening to election returns" (Dr. I. M. Howard to E. Hoffmann Price, 21 June 1944; *IMH* 204).

In addition, Howard was steeped in his frontier heritage, was knowledgeable concerning the details of the lives of his pioneer ancestors, and took considerable pride in being a Texan. His wealth of knowledge concerning feuds, gunfights, Indian attacks, and range wars, as well as the more mundane aspects of frontier life, would stand him in good stead when he later wrote his many westerns. Additionally, Howard's letters speak of the exploits of such forefathers as

G. W. Ervin, the Confederate colonel; William Benjamin Howard, the '49er; and Jim Henry, an early pioneer. But more distant ancestors held a much stronger grip on Howard's imagination, folks like the Martins of Galway, the Dano-Irish O'Walsers, and the O'Tyrells of Connaught. Howard's ancestry was a mixture of English, Danish, Irish, and Scottish strains, and he felt an uncommonly strong sense of kinship with his remote ancestors.

His lifelong fascination with his Celtic progenitors, for instance, manifested itself in a bitter resentment of Britain's transgressions against the Irish, in his tales of such characters as Cormac Mac Art, Cormac Fitzgeoffrey, and Black Turlogh O'Brien, and in his endless discussion and speculation concerning the Celts in letters to friends and colleagues. The extent of Howard's knowledge about Celtic history, lore, archaeology, and anthropology revealed in these letters is little short of amazing, considering his circumstances.

Howard's formal education was typical of his time and place. In the 1920s, the public school system in Cross Plains went only through the tenth grade and, in the agricultural regions, summer vacations lasted six or seven months. Howard's knowledge of literature and many other subjects beyond the basics was the result of his own initiative, though he was to some extent handicapped by the scarcity of reading material in his remote, rural region. Howard sometimes gained permission to read the contents of the libraries of various country schools. He told a correspondent that, failing this, he would break into the buildings, fill a flour sack full of books, and ride away on horseback, always taking care to return the books when finished with them. Howard once wrote, "In my passionate quest for reading material, nothing could have halted me but a bullet through the head" (REH to H. P. Lovecraft, c. July 1933; *CL* 3.81–82). Howard's favorite writer was Jack London. He also expressed admiration for Edgar Allan Poe, Rudyard Kipling, Mark Twain, Sir Walter Scott, Harold Lamb, Talbot Mundy, H. Rider Haggard, Robert W. Chambers, Jim Tully, and H. P. Lovecraft.

Such formal education as Howard did receive was not to his liking. As he matured, Howard grew from a lonely outsider into a militant nonconformist. Throughout his life, he harbored a strong resentment of authority that first manifested itself during his school days:

> I hated school as I hate the memory of school. It wasn't the work I minded; I had no trouble learning the tripe they dished up in the way of lessons . . . I wasn't at the head of my classes—except in history—but I wasn't at the foot either. I generally did just enough work to keep from flunking the courses, and I don't regret the loafing I did. But what I hated was the confinement—the clock-like regularity of everything, the regulation of my speech and actions; most of all the idea that someone considered himself or herself in authority over me, with the right to question my actions and interfere with my thoughts . . . (REH to H. P. Lovecraft, 6 March 1933; CL 3.31)

Although his individualism—and perhaps his eccentricities—increased as he got older, Howard ceased to suffer abuse for it due to a rigorous program of bodybuilding he undertook while still a boy. This regimen included calisthenics, bag-punching, and weight-lifting. Howard informed his father that "I intend to build my body until when a scoundrel crosses me up, I can with my bare hands tear him to pieces, double him up and break his back with my hands alone" (Dr. I. M. Howard to E. Hoffmann Price, 21 June 1944; *IMH* 207).

By the time he entered Cross Plains High School, Howard was a large, powerful young man. As an adult, Howard stood 5 feet 11 inches and weighed 200 pounds, most of it solid muscle. Howard's colleague, H. P. Lovecraft, remarked that with his Celtic features, dark hair and complexion, blue eyes, and "the massive build of a born fighter," Howard "suggested more than casually his own most famous character—the intrepid warrior, adventurer, and seizer of thrones, Conan the Cimmerian" ("In Memoriam: Robert Ervin Howard" 126).

I. Howard's Life, Career, and Legacy

Howard decided at an early age to become a writer. He wrote his first story at age nine and began to write professionally at fifteen. His decision coincided with his first purchase of *Adventure* magazine. He was generously endowed with the raw talent essential to distinguishing himself in this profession, but other prerequisites for a career as an author, such as education, training, and opportunity, were different matters. As Howard himself observed:

> It seems to me that many writers, by virtue of environments of culture, art and education, slip into writing because of their environments. I became a writer in spite of my environments. Understand, I am not criticizing those environments. They were good, solid and worthy. The fact that they were not inducive to literature and art is nothing in their disfavor. Never the less, it is no light thing to enter into a profession absolutely foreign and alien to the people among which one's lot is cast; a profession which seems as dim and faraway and unreal as the shores of Europe. The people among which I lived—and yet live, mainly—made their living from cotton, wheat, cattle, oil, with the usual percentage of business men and professional men. That is most certainly not in their disfavor. But the idea of a man making his living by writing seemed, in that hardy environment, so fantastic that even today I am sometimes myself assailed by a feeling of unreality. Never the less, at the age of fifteen, having never seen a writer, a poet, a publisher or a magazine editor, and having only the vaguest ideas of procedure, I began working on the profession I had chosen. (REH to H. P. Lovecraft, c. July 1933; CL 3.81-82)

His early attempts at fiction were primarily action and adventure tales, which were consistently rejected. Three years would pass before, at the age of eighteen, he would break into print in a professional publication. During this period, Howard also toyed with thoughts of a musical career, taking violin lessons from local musicians. In the meantime, he completed his education at Brownwood High School, which he attended after finishing the tenth grade at Cross Plains. In the fall of 1924, he enrolled in the academy of Howard Payne College in Brownwood, where the eighteen-year-old took shorthand, typing, and other courses he felt would advance his writing career.

During his high school years, Howard roomed at a boarding house with a close friend, Lindsey W. Tyson. Here Howard exhibited a behavior that might be regarded as an early sign of self-destructive tendencies; he was a chronic sleepwalker and once even walked out a window. Since his room was on the ground floor he was not badly hurt, and afterwards he tied one foot to the bedpost to prevent further mishaps.

While in Brownwood, Howard made his first professional sales to *Weird Tales*. Alongside *Black Mask*, which first published Raymond Chandler and Dashiell Hammett, *Weird Tales* is today considered one of the finest pulp magazines of the era. It commenced publication in 1923, and its editor, Farnsworth Wright, purchased three of Howard's early efforts: "Spear and Fang," "The Lost Race," and "The Hyena."

"Spear and Fang" appeared in the July 1925 issue of *Weird Tales* and another story, "In the Forest of Villefere," appeared the following month. It was the editorial policy of *Weird Tales* to pay for stories upon publication rather than upon acceptance, and these two stories netted Howard $24 in his first year as a "pro." It would be some time before Howard's writing career got off the ground.

At the end of the spring semester of 1925, Howard left the academy in Brownwood and returned home. An oil boom hit Cross Plains that year and Howard, unable to sell more of his writings, worked at a number of jobs, including picking cotton, branding calves, hauling garbage, working in a grocery store, and writing oil field news for several Texas and Oklahoma newspapers. Howard was finding the workaday world no more to his liking than he had previously found public school:

> I tried working in a post office but couldn't get along with the postmaster, so that venture was out. Next I worked a while in a gas office, but lost the job because I wouldn't kow-tow to my employer and "yes" him from morning to night. That's one reason I was never very successful working for people. So many men think an employee is a kind of servant. I'm good natured and easy going, I detest and shrink from rows of

all sorts, but there's no use in a man swallowing everything . . . (REH to Wilfred Blanch Talman, September 1931; CL 2.279)

Howard worked as a private secretary for a short time and tried to establish himself as a public stenographer. A few years later, he wrote an autobiographical novel titled *Post Oaks and Sand Roughs*, apparently inspired by Jack London's *Martin Eden*. Though the names of people and places were changed in order to fictionalize real events, it is notable as a heated recollection of the young Howard's experiences between the ages of eighteen and twenty-two. He bitterly recalls his brief time as an office worker:

> At last he got a position in an oil office as a stenographer and office man. His employer was a fellow who had suffered the most extreme poverty until chance, as it often works in the oil fields, had made him wealthy. A natural boot-lapper himself, he demanded the utmost servility from all people who happened to be less prominent or wealthy than he. Steve [Howard's fictionalized alter ego] resented this as only an artistic savage can resent arrogance. The kow-towing attitude of the rest of the office help nauseated him. He knew that they had families depending on them, and the thought that the food of women and children rested entirely on the dexterity in which one lapped the boots of an ignorant and arrogant swine filled him with a cold hatred of the whole system. (*PO* 148)

Even though another story, "Wolfshead," appeared in the April 1926 *Weird Tales*, this was the last story Howard was to sell for two years. At this point, "depressed and discouraged," Howard temporarily abandoned writing and took a job in the local drugstore. "The manager was no Santa Claus," Howard recalled, "but we got along alright after I offered to tie my right hand behind me and beat his head off with my left" (REH to Wilfred Blanch Talman, September 1931; CL 2.279). Though employed as a soda jerk, Howard held down the entire store most of the time. Because of the oil boom he had to work long hours, from 9:30 in the morning until after midnight, often till two or three A.M., seven days a week.

This pace proved grueling, especially as he was "going at high speed most of the time" (REH to Wilfred Blanch Talman, September 1931; CL 2.279). In his thinly disguised autobiography, he recalled:

> He did not read or write, scarcely had time to answer his correspondence. He had absolutely no time for recreation or even rest. All during the day he would dash back and forth behind the fountain which he had grown to hate, serving drinks and waiting on customers, doing many things for which he was not paid to do. At night he staggered home to fall into his bed and sleep the sodden sleep of utter exhaustion. He went to bed fatigued and he awoke fatigued. (PO 172)

In addition to fatigue from chronic overwork, he felt humiliated at being relegated to a low-prestige service job that others, notably the burly oil field workers, tended to look down upon: "A man who works all day or all night swinging a heavy sledge, clambering about on an eighty-foot rig, and in general doing work suitable for a giant, has scant respect for one who makes his living by doling out soft drinks" (PO 170).

Drugstore customers also included "whores, bootleggers, gamblers, dope fiends, and yeggs, besides the general riff-raff of drillers, tool dressers, and roustabouts" (PO 172). Overwork was taking its toll on his body, but "Worse still was the mental effect of taking orders and occasional insults from the scum of the earth" (PO 172).

Eventually Howard suffered mental and physical exhaustion so acute that he was forced to quit. The whole bitter experience prompted him to remark, "I'll say one thing about an oil boom: it will teach a kid that Life's a pretty rotten thing about as quick as anything I can think of." (REH to Farnsworth Wright, c. June–July 1931; CL 2.226).

It was during these boomtown days that Howard found a way to let off steam by participating in amateur boxing matches. Since Cross Plains lacked a regulation boxing ring, bouts were held at a local icehouse. On sweltering summer nights, surrounded by an audience of cheering, jeering oil field roughnecks, Howard duked it out with various ranch hands, farm boys, and oil workers. He battled hard and bled, but found it to be an exhilarating, transcendental experience, as portrayed in his autobiographical novel:

> Steve reeled, the blood gushing from his mouth to mingle in the sweat on his chest. And in that fleeting instant before they began the combat again, Steve knew Life, fierce, red and vibrant. God, but this was his element! To fight, to kill or be killed, here in this Hell-hot, smoke-laden atmosphere, with a gang of roughnecks screaming oaths and obscenities and shouting for his slaughter. (PO 180)

And afterwards, "Steve felt jubilant in a strange manner. His mind was clear now and the blood raced through his veins. He felt no bad after effects from his terrific battle . . . He sighed deeply and with relish, glanced up at the stars which seemed somehow less cold and more friendly" (PO 181).

In the autumn of 1926, Howard returned to the academy at Howard Payne College to study bookkeeping, rooming once more with Lindsey Tyson. The relaxed atmosphere of academic life proved beneficial in many ways. While recovering from the rigors of his drugstore job, Howard was able to associate with other young people who shared his artistic and literary leanings. He contributed to amateur journals and began to write poetry.

Though he sold a few poems with eerie or supernatural themes to *Weird Tales*, he knew he had little chance of seeing most of his verse published. Nevertheless, in the next few years Howard would compose hundreds of poems, only a fraction of which would be appropriate for *Weird Tales*. In composing his poetry, Howard seems to have allowed himself to write solely for self-expression, a luxury he denied himself in his other literary efforts.

Howard completed his studies in August 1927 and returned to Cross Plains. Although he tried for a time to get a bookkeeping job, his heart was not in any such endeavor, and he knew it never would be. Howard's pride and individuality were such that he felt writing was the only profession he was suited for:

> I could have studied law, or gone into some other occupation, but none offered me the freedom writing did—and my passion for freedom is almost an obsession. I honestly have paid the price of freedom by living with Spartan simplicity and doing without things I really wanted . . . Personal liberty may be a phantom, but I hardly think anybody would deny that there is more freedom in writing than there is in slaving in an iron foundry, or working—as I have worked—from twelve to fourteen hours a day, seven days a week, behind a soda fountain. I have worked as much as eighteen hours a day at my typewriter, but it was work of my own choosing and I could quit any time I wanted without getting fired from the job . . . (REH to H. P. Lovecraft, c. July 1933; CL 3.80)

In 1928 Howard promised his father that if he failed to make his mark as a writer within a year, he would settle down in some steady, conformist occupation. Such a promise was based on sheer faith on Howard's part, for his future as a writer did not look promising. Only one story and two poems had appeared in *Weird Tales* in 1927, earning him a total of $37.50. A collection of poetry entitled *Singers in the Shadows* failed to find a publisher, as did his autobiographical novel *Post Oaks and Sand Roughs*. His efforts to break into such diverse pulp markets as *Adventure*, *Argosy All-Story Weekly*, *Liberty*, *Ghost Stories*, *True Stories*, *Romance*, and *Thrills of the Jungle* continued to go unrewarded.

Soon, however, Howard was to taste both artistic and commercial success. The cover of the August 1928 *Weird Tales* spotlighted his story "Red Shadows." This marked the debut of Solomon Kane, the first of Howard's heroes to be introduced to the reading public. A year later, Howard was a regular in *Weird Tales* and would remain so for the rest of his life.

The turning point in Howard's career came in 1929 when he began to sell to markets other than *Weird Tales*. A boxing enthusiast,

Howard started writing prize-fighting stories for the sports pulps of the day. His own firsthand ring experience stood him in good stead, and these stories met with unprecedented success. Howard earned $772.50 during 1929 and was able to support himself solely by writing from that point on.

At twenty-three, Robert E. Howard had arrived as a successful writer. His income topped $1000, and it reached $1500 the following year. At that time, $1000 was about the average annual income. The Great Depression that began in 1929 would not affect Howard's finances for several years. Howard's fiction appeared in *Fight Stories, Action Stories, Magic Carpet, Top-Notch*, and other magazines, but *Weird Tales* remained his most dependable market with more than a third of his fiction published in it during his lifetime. Howard had now all but ceased to write poetry, save to revise some earlier works, in order to concentrate on his expanding markets.

Concerning his work habits, Howard wrote, "I work in bursts and spurts. I may turn out a month's output in a few days, and then loaf for weeks" (REH to H. P. Lovecraft, week of 10 August 1931; *CL* 2.264). This afforded him ample time for leisure activities. He enjoyed watching football and boxing. He owned a car and traveled widely throughout the Southwest, visiting historical sites and making occasional forays into Mexico. Though he professed an aversion to tobacco and coffee, Howard did enjoy the consumption of alcoholic beverages, mostly beer and occasionally tequila, mescal, and Spanish wine for variety's sake.

Sometimes friends such as Truett Vinson and Tevis Clyde Smith would accompany him on his excursions, and they would ride off into the country to guzzle bootleg liquor and raise hell. Despite his enjoyment of drinking, Howard rarely got drunk, nor was he known to get into fights, though possessed of a quick temper. L. Sprague de Camp, a Howard biographer, felt that brawls and similar fracases hinted at in Howard's letters were exaggerations or fabrications, but added, "On the other hand, the sprees are mostly said to have taken place away from Cross Plains. Possibly, in deference to his religious parents, Howard led a sober life at home and went on a tear abroad" (de Camp, *Literary Swordsmen and Sorcerers* 144).

Few facts are available concerning Howard's sex life. His interest in the opposite sex was normal enough, despite aspersions cast on his heterosexuality by some. For much of his life Howard was shy in approaching women and doubtless experienced difficulty finding a woman with whom he shared common interests in the narrow environment of Cross Plains. In their biography of Howard, *Dark Valley Destiny*, L. Sprague de Camp and Catherine Crook de Camp express the belief that Howard most likely died a virgin. The basis of the De Camps' conjecture is that Howard would have avoided the sexual outlet available to him in the form of prostitution.

Howard would have had access to prostitutes in travels throughout the Southwest and in Mexican border towns like Piedras Negras. The de Camps believed that Howard adhered to the clean-living values of his parents, despite his consumption of alcoholic beverages at a time when they were illegal. More convincingly, they cite Howard's scorn for the loose women who congregated in Cross Plains during the oil boom.

Probably Howard's attitude towards prostitutes, like that of most men, was ambiguous. But this would not necessarily have deterred him from availing himself of their services. Evidence that he did indeed patronize them on occasion exists in the form of two poems recounting visits to a brothel. That these were not positive experiences are indicated by lines such as "I left a thousand misty dreams / In the cavern of her womb" and "I was brood of the jackal's brood, / Gorging on common flesh" (*Collected Poetry* 414). It seems reasonable to assume that Howard did not habitually indulge in such activity, but rather had occasional recourse to prostitutes when his sexual tension became unbearable.

I. Howard's Life, Career, and Legacy

In addition to his circle of friends in Cross Plains and Brownwood, Howard corresponded with a number of literary colleagues such as August Derleth and Clark Ashton Smith. However, his most voluminous and significant correspondence was exchanged with the twentieth century's grandmaster of horror fiction, H. P. Lovecraft.

Howard's correspondence with Lovecraft began in 1930, soon after he read Lovecraft's Gothic masterpiece "The Rats in the Walls" when it was reprinted in *Weird Tales*. The story reaches its climax as the narrator descends into madness, regressing backwards in time along his cursed family line:

> Curse you, Thornton, I'll teach you to faint at what my family do! . . . 'Sblood, thou stinkard, I'll learn ye how to gust . . . wold ye swynke me thilke wys? . . . *Magna Matar! Magna Matar!* . . . *Atys . . . Dia ad aghaidh's ad aodann . . . agus bas dunach ort! Dhonas's dholas ort, agus leat-sa!* . . . Ungl...ungl . . . rrrlh . . . chchch . . . (H. P. Lovecraft, "The Rats in the Walls" 396)

At the time of the story's composition, Lovecraft wryly observed that "the only objection to the phrase is that it's *Gaelic* instead of *Cymric* as the south-of-England locale demands. But as—with anthropology—details don't count. Nobody will ever stop to note the difference" (Lovecraft to Frank Belknap Long, 8 November 1923; *Selected Letters* 1.258). However, someone eventually did note the difference, and that someone was Robert E. Howard when the story was reprinted six years later. Howard wrote a letter to *Weird Tales* editor Farnsworth Wright praising the story, but felt moved to add, "And I note from the fact that Mr. Lovecraft has his character speaking Gaelic instead of Cymric, in denoting the Age of the Druids, that he holds to Lhuyd's theory as to the settling of Britain by the Celts." (REH to Farnsworth Wright, c. June 1930; CL 2.47). Wright forwarded Howard's letter to Lovecraft, who got in touch with Howard.

So began a lively exchange of letters—many running to dozens of pages—that lasted until Howard's death. The robust Texan and the cerebral New Englander—the original Odd Couple—discussed and debated, often heatedly, such topics as history, literature, anthropology, contemporary politics, and much more. It makes for reading no less compelling than their fiction. Howard and Lovecraft's joint correspondence has now been published and fills two large volumes.

As an adult, Howard was moderately successful in a profession of his own choosing. He had won his cherished freedom from the drudgery of working for others. He could travel about alone or with friends whenever he wished and had to answer to no one. Through correspondence, he could exchange ideas with intellects as keen as his own. "The Eyrie," the letters section of *Weird Tales*, brought him the praises of a growing legion of fans. He often had a great deal of fun and his life was well rounded, combining both physical and mental activity. Yet there was something wrong. Howard would often grow moody, sullen, somber, depressed.

Basically an introvert, he did have a number of friends, but he was, like many of his characters, the prey of powerful emotional forces. Howard was buffeted by wild mood swings, and today he might be diagnosed as bipolar or even mildly schizophrenic. Howard's father recalled that "He was so sensitive to things of a depressing nature that his mother and I never mentioned anything of a depressing nature in his presence. It has been thus with him since childhood" (Dr. I. M. Howard to E. Hoffmann Price, 21 June 1944; *IMH* 205). Aware to a certain extent of his own emotional instability, Howard occasionally alluded to his spells of gloom and deep melancholy: he was wont to attribute them to the blood of his Celtic ancestors.

In 1930, Howard was plunged into the deepest despair by the death of his dog, Patch. Years later, his father informed E. Hoffmann Price that "His dog died when he (the dog) was 12 and Robert 24. He raised the dog from the time he was a wee thing, before his eyes were barely open, through the life of the dog. The dog was an inseparable companion to Robert." Concerning the occasion of the dog's death, Dr. Howard recalled:

> Robert knew his dog was going to die. He packed his grip, opened the gate, walked out, and said, "Mama, I am going." He went to Brownwood [and] stayed until his dog died, which was two or three days. But each morning he phoned and asked his mother if Patch (that was the dog's name) was still alive . . . After the fourth day when his mother told him the dog was going, he never inquired anymore; he knew the dog would soon die. Therefore he never spoke of him again. I had the dog buried in a deep grave in the back lot, then had the lot plowed deeply and then had them take a big harrow and harrow it deeply all over to destroy every trace of the grave, so sensitive [was he] to the loss of the dog. (Dr. I. M. Howard to E. Hoffmann Price, 21 June 1944; *IMH* 205)

Getting back to work, Howard produced historical adventures, boxing stories, horror stories, and fantasies throughout 1931. Late in the year, he sold two stories to a new pulp magazine, *Strange Tales*, a short-lived competitor to *Weird Tales*. These sales netted him enough cash to take a winter vacation in February 1932. He spent a few weeks in southernmost Texas, a semi-tropical region near the Gulf Coast roughly the same latitude as Fort Lauderdale, roaming the border towns of Mission and McAllen.

This venture proved fortuitous so far as Howard's creativity was concerned. He composed a poem, a pastime he now indulged in only infrequently, titled "Cimmeria"—"Written in Mission, Texas, February, 1932; suggested by the memory of the hill-country above Fredericksburg seen in a mist of winter rain" (CCC 1). A rare but effective use of blank verse by Howard, "Cimmeria" is presented as the memory of a previous incarnation in which the orator recalls the gloomy, heavily wooded wilderness of his birth. There are parallels with the Dark Valley of Howard's own infancy, as recalled by Howard. But he was just getting started. It was also during this sojourn that Howard conceived of what would become by far his most renowned literary creation, the indomitable barbarian warrior Conan. Howard later asserted that "Conan simply grew up in my mind" while "stopping in a little border town on the lower Rio Grande" (REH, quoted in Perry 66). He unfortunately did not specify the town by name as Mission, McAllen, or elsewhere. Since Howard made Conan a native of a gloomy northern wilderness called Cimmeria, the poem or Howard's conception of it played a role in his conceptualization of the character as well.

Returning to Cross Plains, Howard busied himself writing the first of Conan's adventures throughout the spring of 1932. That spring was marred by a bitter disappointment, however. H. P. Lovecraft had been traveling throughout the South and had arrived in New Orleans. Unfortunately, Howard was by then low on funds, without a car, and therefore unable to join him. Lovecraft had nearly exhausted his travel budget and could not travel further west. Thus, two of the twentieth century's greatest fantasists never met face-to-face.

Howard was also beginning to suffer the loss of some markets due to the Depression. To alleviate his financial difficulties, he engaged fellow pulp writer Otis Adelbert Kline as his agent early in 1933. He continued to sell directly to *Weird Tales*, his most reliable market, but by now checks were often overdue. In an effort to remain solvent, Howard attempted to find new markets by working in previously untapped genres. At his agent's behest, he tried his hand at detective stories. Unfortunately, Kline managed to place only one story for Howard during the entire year. In 1933, Howard's income plummeted to below $1000 for the first time since 1929.

Adding to his misfortunes, Howard himself was injured and nearly killed in an auto accident during the Christmas holidays. On the rainy, foggy night of December 29, while driving through the nearby town of Rising Star, he collided with a flagpole set in the middle of the street due to poor visibility:

> The night was rainy and there was a steel flagpole in the middle of the street. I rammed it head-on. The fellow on the seat with me went through the windshield and I went partly through it, being checked by the steering-wheel which was bent double on my breastbone. He got a bad gash on his head and I got my jaw ripped open. A little lower and it would have been my jugular. But what kept me from writing for so long, was the fact that my hands were cut up, too ... (REH to Clark Ashton Smith, c. January 1934; CL 3.196)

On a more promising note, Conan stories had been appearing regularly in *Weird Tales* throughout the year, prompting enthusiastic letters from readers clamoring for more.

Howard's markets began to expand once again in 1934, and his income increased substantially. Howard had turned more of his attention to writing westerns and early in the year created a series concerning the humorous exploits of Breckinridge Elkins of Bear Creek, Nevada. The Elkins stories appeared in every issue of *Action Stories* until after Howard's death. In the meantime, Conan appeared in ten issues of *Weird Tales*. Howard's earnings for 1934 nearly doubled those of the previous year, making his income quite enviable by Depression standards. However, his good fortune was offset by another major disappointment: Howard had been commissioned to write a full-length fantasy novel for a British publisher, but the company went bankrupt before the book was issued. The novel was *The Hour of the Dragon*, and Howard salvaged it by selling the serial rights to *Weird Tales*.

At about this time, Howard, now in his late twenties, was regularly dating a young schoolteacher named Novalyne Price. They had been previously introduced by a mutual friend, Tevis Clyde Smith, early in 1933 and became reacquainted when Novalyne took a teaching position at Cross Plains High School in the fall of 1934. An English teacher, well read and with literary ambitions of her own, she sought out the only person she knew in town who shared her interests.

Feisty and intelligent, Novalyne proved to be a congenial companion for Howard. Their dates often consisted of long drives through the Texas countryside, during which they carried on spirited discussions. Unfortunately, basic incompatibilities undermined their chances for a more permanent relationship. Howard was awkward in social situations, making it unlikely that he would be accepted by Novalyne's family and peers. Moreover, like many another young man, Howard was ambivalent when it came to making a firmer commitment to the relationship.

Although his income remained stable in 1935, Howard found himself burdened with heavy expenses from a serious operation performed on his aging mother early in the year and her subsequent hospitalization and treatment. This placed him under considerable financial stress. Howard's father was a respected physician, but his patients were mostly rural and often paid him in farm produce. Howard was the only family member bringing in actual money. To make matters worse, lateness of payment from *Weird Tales* worsened as the Depression wore on.

On May 6, 1935, Howard wrote to Farnsworth Wright pleading for money already owed him. The letter makes for painful reading:

Dear Mr. Wright:
  I always hate to write a letter like this, but dire necessity forces me. It is, in short, an urgent plea for money . . .
  My expenses for the past month have been great. My mother was forced to have her gall bladder removed, a very serious operation, especially for a woman of her age and state of health. She has been almost an invalid for years . . . But for the professional discount on the operation, my father being a physician, I do not know how we would have been able to meet the expenses. As it was they were great . . . Whether my mother ever recovers or not possibly depends on the kind of care and attention I am able to give her, and that in turn depends on the money I am able to earn.
  And that brings me to the matter at hand. For some time now I have been receiving a check regularly each month from Weird Tales—half

> checks, it is true, but by practicing the most rigid economy I have managed to keep my head above the water; that I was able to do so was largely because of, not the size but the regularity of the checks. I came to depend upon them and expect them, as I felt justified in so doing. But this month, at a time when I need money so desperately bad, I did not receive a check. Somehow, some way, my family and I have struggled along this far, but if you cut off my monthly checks now, I don't know what in God's name we'll do. (REH to Farnsworth Wright, 6 May 1935; CL 3.306-7)

Possibly Wright had been "robbing Peter to pay Paul." If so, "Paul" may have been Seabury Quinn, another *Weird Tales* mainstay and prolific author of the popular adventures of occult investigator Jules de Grandin. Howard continues:

> I do not feel that my request is unreasonable. As you know, it has been six months since "The People of the Black Circle" (the story the check for which is now due me) appeared in Weird Tales. Weird Tales owes me over eight hundred dollars for stories already published and supposed to be paid for on publication—enough to pay all my debts and get me back on my feet again if I could receive it all at once. Perhaps this is impossible. I have no wish to be unreasonable; I know times are hard for everybody. But I don't believe that I am being unreasonable in asking you to pay me a check each month until the accounts are squared ... (CL 3.307-8)

Howard was moved to conclude, "A monthly check from Weird Tales may well mean the difference between a life that is at least endurable—and God alone knows what" (CL 3.308).

Angry over being reduced to begging for money that was rightfully his, Howard complained bitterly to his agent, Otis Adelbert Kline:

> I wrote Wright, telling him the trouble I'd been in, and explaining my desperate need for money, and up to now he's coolly ignored my letter. No check—and not the slightest word of explanation. The case is simple enough: Weird Tales owes me over $800, some of it for stories published six months ago. I'm pinching pennies and wearing rags, while my stories are being published, used and exploited. I believe Wright could pay me every cent he owes me, if he wanted to. But now, when I need money worse than I ever needed it in my life before, he refuses to pay me any-

> thing, and ignores a letter in which I beg him to pay me even a fraction of the full amount. What's his game, anyway? Is Weird Tales still a legitimate publication, or has it become a racket? (REH to Otis Adelbert Kline, 13 May 1935; CL 3.308-9)

Wright did eventually respond with a portion of the money, but at the time of Howard's death thirteen months later, *Weird Tales* still owed him $1,350.00.

On July 22, Howard sent Wright the manuscript for "Red Nails." This story was the final appearance of Conan and ostensibly marked the end of Howard's career as a fantasist. He later informed Lovecraft, "I would hate to abandon weird writing entirely, but my financial needs are urgent, immediate and imperious. Slowness of payment in the fantastic field forces me into other lines against my will" (REH to H. P. Lovecraft, 11 February 1936; *CL* 3.414).

It was also in July that Howard broke up with Novalyne Price. Their parting was not a pleasant one, although they did later reconcile and resume a cordial friendship. It was Howard who ended the relationship, accusing her in a bitter letter of dating their mutual friend, Truett Vinson, behind his back.

Alone once more, Howard returned to his work. This now consisted mainly of westerns, both humorous and serious. Howard stories appearing in *Weird Tales* had been written some time previously. Howard made it clear in his letter to Wright that he felt a certain amount of sentiment and loyalty toward the magazine that had given him his start. Still, economic necessity was hard to ignore, and other markets, notably those for western fiction, offered steadier work at higher pay. They were altogether a much more reliable source of income and, moreover, were easier to produce for. The Breckinridge Elkins series was still going strong in the spring of 1936, so when John F. Byrne, the editor of *Action Stories*, moved to *Argosy*, he asked Howard to begin a new series similar to the Elkins series. Howard sold three stories about a character named Pike Bearfield to *Argosy*, as well as creating yet another humorous western hero, Buckner J. Grimes, for Street and Smith's *Cowboy Stories*. "If I can get a series running in *Argosy*, keep the Elkins series running in *Action Stories*, now a monthly, and the Buckner J. Grimes yarns in *Cowboy Stories*, I'll feel justified in devoting practically all my time to the writing of western stories," wrote Howard in 1936 (REH to H. P. Lovecraft, 13 May 1936; CL 3.461–62).

By early 1936, Howard's sales were at an all-time high. His markets were steadier and more dependable than ever before. He was on the verge of becoming a regular in *Argosy*, a high-paying, widely read magazine that had existed prior to the pulps and would survive their demise. Still, Howard was dissatisfied with what he was doing. He still felt moved to express himself through fantasy and wrote the reincarnation tale "The Thunder-Rider" in the spring of 1936. His last story, "Nekht Semerkeht," written within a month prior to his death, was also a fantasy.

Such career matters, however, were overshadowed by imminent tragedy. Howard's mother lay on her deathbed. Hester Jane Ervin Howard never fully recovered from her operation of the previous year. Her physical condition continued to deteriorate and trips to the hospital were frequent. Mrs. Howard had a long history of tuberculosis, which may have been complicated by cancer. Despite his utmost efforts to provide the best of medical care, Howard knew that his mother was dying. Early in June, Howard wrote to Otis Adelbert Kline in Chicago to instruct him on the handling of his literary estate in the event of his sudden death.

On the morning of June 11, 1936, Howard's mother was sinking deeper and deeper into her final coma. Upon learning that she would never regain consciousness, Howard went to his car, got in, and shot himself fatally through the head. A little over two weeks later, Howard's father wrote to H. P. Lovecraft recounting the grim sequence of events:

> My Dear Mr. Lovecraft:
> It is barely possible through some other source that you may have heard of the death of Robert E. Howard, my son. If not, I will say that after three weeks of vigilant watching at his mother's bedside, on the morning of June 11, 1936, at eight o'clock he slipped out of the house, entered his car which was standing in front of the garage, raised the windows and fired a shot through his brain. The cook standing at the window at the back part of the house, saw him go get in his car. She thought he was fixing to drive to town as he usually did, when she heard the muffled sound of the gun, she saw him fall over the steering wheel. She ran in the house and called the physician who was in the house. The doctor was taking a cup of coffee in the dining room and I was talking with him. We rushed to the car and found him. We at first thought it was a death shot but the bullet had passed through the brain. He shot himself just above the temple, just above and behind the left ear. It came out on the opposite side. He lived eight hours and never regained consciousness. (Dr. I. M. Howard to H. P. Lovecraft, 29 June 1936; *IMH* 63)

Dr. Howard and a physician friend, Dr. Dill, carried Robert back into the house. Both medical men instantly realized that the wound was fatal. Howard lingered until about four that afternoon. Commentators have surmised that Howard must have possessed exceptional physical vitality to have survived so long following the passing of a bullet directly through his brain. Dr. Howard somberly concluded:

> Lest I worry you with this I will close, but will say in conclusion, Mr. Lovecraft, that Robert was a great admirer of you. I have often heard him say that you were the best Weird writer in the world and he keenly enjoyed corresponding with you. He often expressed hope that you might visit in our home some day, so that he, his mother and I might see and know you personally . . .
> Yours very truly,
> Dr. I. M. Howard
> (Dr. I. M. Howard to H. P. Lovecraft, 29 June 1936; *IMH* 65-66)

Howard's mother lingered until the next day, dying without ever regaining consciousness or knowing her son had preceded her in death. On June 14 Robert E. Howard and Hester Jane Howard were buried in Greenleaf Cemetery in Brownwood.

When Howard was examined, the following couplet was found on his person:

> All fled—all done, so lift me on the pyre,
> The feast is over and the lamps expire.

This couplet was long thought to be a paraphrase of a line in the fourth stanza of the Decadent poet Ernest Dowson's famous poem "Non Sum Qualis Eram Bonae sub Regno Cynarae," which reads in part: "I cried for madder music and for stronger wine, / But when the feast is finished and the lamps expire, / Then falls thy shadow. Cynara! The night is thine . . ." However, research by Rusty Burke has proven beyond all reasonable doubt that the actual source was a more obscure poem, "The House of Cæsar" by Viola Garvin. Each of the five stanzas ends with the refrain, "The Feast is over and the lamps expire!" The third stanza concludes with, "All fled, all done—a Cæsar's brief desire— / The Feast is over and the lamps expire!" The final stanza ends with, "All dim, all pale—so lift me on the pyre— / The Feast is over and the lamps expire!"

Troubled, frustrated, unhappy, and unstable, Howard had resolved not to bear the loss of the person he felt closest to. Howard's critics have made much of the author's suicide on the occasion of his mother's imminent death, choosing to regard it as evidence of an "Oedipus complex." But in *Dark Valley Destiny*, the de Camps point out that "the determinants of Howard's behavior were deeper and older than his grief over his mother's impending death and . . . her passing became the occasion for, not the cause of, his suicide" (*Dark Valley Destiny* 10-11).

It is also worth mentioning that a number of factors were in play that would have further undermined Howard's emotional stability. He had felt compelled to abandon his favored means of creative expression because he was losing money writing for *Weird Tales*. His one romance had ended on a sour note. Throughout late 1935 and into 1936, as his mother's health deteriorated, Novalyne Price noticed him exhibiting quirky behavior and eccentric dress, such as a Mexican sombrero. Mental health professionals sometimes see such behavior as a cry for help. During his final days, he was under considerable stress as the caregiver of a sick, elderly person—a very demanding responsibility, as anyone who has ever assumed it will attest. In their biography, the de Camps note that toward the end Howard ate very little, was severely sleep-deprived, and consumed great amounts of coffee, a beverage he did not normally drink. It could be said that a perfect storm had been gathering that hindered Howard's ability to resist the urge to self-destruction.

H. P. Lovecraft astutely observed:

> I suppose that, in the last analysis, his desperate reaction to his grief came from the selfsame endowment of sensitiveness and imagination which made his stories stand out so. He saw everything in the heightened light of its dramatic relationships to things behind and around it, and subjectively felt the events of history, and the spirit and overtones of scenes and personalities, as very few are able to see and feel. Turned on the sorrow in his immediate life, this faculty must have given things an intolerable aspect and precipitated the fatal act. One could wish that, for once, he had been less of a sensitive artist! (H. P. Lovecraft to E. Hoffmann Price, 5 July 1936; *Selected Letters* 5.276)

L. Sprague de Camp once remarked, "In assembling Howard, the gods somehow left out the cog-wheel that furnished love of life" (*Literary Swordsmen and Sorcerers* 184). Howard was obsessed by death and the inevitable end that eventually comes to all things. As an abstraction, this finality recurs as a consistent literary theme and his poetry is suffused with it. The facets of Howard's personality that led to his self-destruction at age thirty can be better understood after the various pieces of his heart and soul revealed in his writings have been examined. For now, a simple observation that Howard himself once made will suffice: "Every now and then one of us finds the going too hard and blows his brains out, but it's all in the game I reckon" (REH to Farnsworth Wright, c. June–July 1931; CL 2.226).

During his lifetime, Howard was one of the more popular pulp authors. His popularity among readers of *Weird Tales* was matched only by that of Lovecraft and Seabury Quinn. Readers consistently voted his stories their favorites for the issues in which they appeared. His work was also well received in virtually every other pulp magazine to which he contributed. Other writers, mostly fellow contributors to *Weird Tales*, also expressed their appreciation of his better tales.

H. P. Lovecraft, who would himself perish only nine months later, composed a moving obituary, "In Memoriam: Robert Ervin Howard." Originally published in *Fantasy Magazine* (September 1936), it contained an insightful appraisal of Howard's literary gifts:

> The character and attainments of Mr. Howard were wholly unique. He was, above everything else, a lover of the simpler, older world of barbarian and pioneer days, when courage and strength took the place of subtlety and stratagem, and when a hardy, fearless race battled and bled and asked no quarter from hostile Nature. All his stories reflect this philosophy, and derive from it a vitality found in few of his contemporaries. No one could write more convincingly of violence and gore than he, and his battle passages reveal an instinctive aptitude for military tactics . . .
>
> It is hard to describe what made Mr. Howard's stories stand out so sharply, but the real secret is that he himself was in every one of them . . . Not only did he excel in pictures of strife and slaughter, but he was almost alone in his ability to create real emotions of spectral fear and dread suspense . . . That such a genuine artist should perish while hundreds of insincere hacks continue to concoct spurious ghosts and vampires and space-ships and occult detectives is indeed a sorry piece of cosmic irony. (125)

Clark Ashton Smith, August Derleth, E. Hoffmann Price, and the young Robert Bloch also praised aspects of Howard's works. Some of Howard's colleagues preferred his less famous fiction. Bloch left himself open to verbal assault by *Weird Tales* readers when he suggested that the Conan series consumed too much of Howard's writing time. E. Hoffmann Price was one of the few professional writers actually to meet Howard and was more impressed with the man himself than his work.

Howard appreciated comments and criticism from his fellow writers. His spirits were also buoyed by the *Weird Tales* readers. He once informed Farnsworth Wright that "the praises the readers have been kind enough to give me in 'The Eyrie' have given me an immense amount of sincere pleasure" (REH to Farnsworth Wright, c. June-July 1931; CL 2.227).

Undoubtedly this praise helped keep Howard writing, since, unfortunately, most of his personal acquaintances believed that his writing was junk. Novalyne Price, an English teacher, felt his work was lurid, escapist fare. Truett Vinson, Howard's best friend, regarded Howard's fiction as a waste of his talent and considered him something of a commercial "sellout" for not devoting his life to the pursuit of aesthetic perfection. Howard's literary acquaintances from Howard Payne College concurred with Vinson's opinion and cited F. Scott Fitzgerald and Sinclair Lewis as appropriate role models for the young author.

After Howard's death, his work was seldom seen except for backlog stories and an occasional reprint. For years he was all but forgotten, save by a small cadre of hardcore fans, primarily the admirers of Conan. In 1946, ten years after Howard's death, Arkham House, under the editorship of August Derleth, published a collection of Howard's fantasy and horror tales, *Skull-Face and Others*. This was followed in the 1950s by a series of hardcover collections of the Conan canon. The Gnome Press Conan series was edited by L. Sprague de Camp. In 1957 Arkham House released the first collection of Howard's poetry, *Always Comes Evening*, compiled by Glenn Lord. De Camp and Lord, then the executor of Howard's estate, are primarily responsible for the resurgence of interest in Robert E. Howard's work.

De Camp reprinted the Conan stories that had appeared in *Weird Tales* twenty years before and unearthed those rejected by Farnsworth Wright. The Conan series as published by Gnome Press formed the basis of the Lancer Books paperback editions ten years later, and with them the revival of interest in Howard's writing truly began.

Unfortunately, de Camp and later Lin Carter, Bjorn Nyberg, and a host of others were tempted to add additional tales to the Conan series in an effort to "fill gaps in the saga." This regrettable practice diluted the effectiveness of Howard's original saga and did nothing to enhance Howard's reputation among serious readers.

For a long time, Howard's reputation in academic circles was a dubious one at best. *Skull-Face and Others* was reviewed by the *New York Times Book Review* but, not surprisingly, it was panned. Howard's tales seemed to have fallen victim to the general prejudices of the critical establishment against works of fantasy, fiction that appeared in the pulps, and writing that is deliberately commercial. Howard was for the most part ignored by critical and academic circles and, when noticed, dismissed as a mere adventure writer.

However, while ignored by critics and scholars, Howard's work has always been warmly received by new generations of writers and artists. Fritz Leiber expressed his admiration for Howard's work, as have notable writers such as John Jakes, Michael Moorcock, and Harlan Ellison. Ellison once even contemplated writing a novel based on Howard's life, tentatively titled *RIF*. According to de Camp, J. R. R. Tolkien once remarked that he enjoyed Howard's Conan stories despite the fact that they differed greatly in theme and tone from his own writings. Artists such as Frank Frazetta, Roy G. Krenkel, and Barry Windsor-Smith have based some of their greatest works on Howard's images.

By the mid-1970s, the Howard revival was in full swing. A vast quantity of his fiction from the pulps, as well as hitherto unpublished material, was unearthed and rushed into print in both hardcover and paperback editions. Zebra Books offered an extensive array of Howard's fiction in mass-market paperback books with lush, dramatic cover paintings by Jeff Jones. Often lesser-known Howard characters like Cormac Mac Art and El Borak would be published in hardcover collections from small specialty publishers such as Donald M. Grant and FAX Collectors Editions, then subsequently be reprinted in mass-market paperbacks by well-known houses such as Ace, Bantam, and Berkley. These were the years of the "Howard boom," spanning the period from the publication of the Lancer paperback *Conan the Adventurer* in 1966 until around the time of the appearance of the Ace paperback *The She Devil* in 1983.

This renewed interest did bring about a flood of Robert E. Howard "criticism," but it consisted primarily of the same sort of thing said about his work a generation before, i.e., that he was a great adventure writer and nothing more. The decade of the 1970s was the era of the Howard "fanzine"; a number of small, limited print-run magazines devoted to Howard and his fiction cropped up around the United States. While these periodicals sometimes offered a genuine new approach to Howard criticism, most concerned themselves with textual problems (the proper order of the Conan series, etc.) or general articles comparing Howard's work with that of others in the adventure and fantasy genres. Such figures as Robert Weinberg, Wayne Warfield, and Karl Edward Wagner did contribute some valuable new insights into Howard's work, but the field was still dominated by the L. Sprague de Camp view that, in effect, Howard was nothing more than an entertainer.

The later 1970s saw several attempts to define the totality of Howard's fantasy fiction. Robert Weinberg's rather ambitious attempt at undertaking this task resulted in *An Annotated Guide to Robert E. Howard's Sword and Sorcery*, which, while at times competent, too soon degenerated into a mere synopsizing of the canon with few critical comments, most of which were concerned with whether a story succeeded or failed as entertainment. Darrell Schweitzer's *Conan's World* repeated all the basic fallacies concerning Howard, while offering uninformed opinions and no new insights; even the author subsequently expressed dissatisfaction with it.

In 1983 Howard criticism came full circle with the publication of the first full-length biography of Robert E. Howard, *Dark Valley Destiny*, by L. Sprague de Camp, Catherine Crook de Camp, and Jane Whittington Griffin. Packed with facts about Howard's life, times, and background, it is the result of extensive correspondence and interviews with dozens of Howard's contemporaries. Howard's family history is detailed, and chapters are devoted to each of his parents. The events of Howard's early life are reconstructed, and his adolescence in a boom town is explored. Howard's one great love affair is recounted in some detail, and his professional career is examined.

Unfortunately, de Camp's belief that Howard's work is mere entertainment, albeit of a high quality, is reasserted throughout *Dark Valley Destiny*. Like de Camp's previous work, *Lovecraft: A Biography* (1975), it is long on facts and short on insights. However, a wealth of biographical information is presented, allowing readers to form their own conclusions. If other writers in the future are able to see farther than de Camp and his collaborators, it is because these authors have laid invaluable groundwork for future Howard studies by interviewing parties personally acquainted with the Howards before this generation passed on.

De Camp subsequently took some flak from Howard enthusiasts who found fault with his research methods and criticized his editing of the Conan stories for book publication. However, de Camp's reputation was particularly besmirched by his controlling interest in Conan Properties, a corporate entity formed to control the publishing and licensing of the Conan character. As a result of legal wrangling, attempts by publishers to issue an edition of Howard's Conan stories, free of de Camp's editing and additional stories, were quashed. Ultimately, Howard's original Conan stories became unavailable throughout the 1980s and '90s, even as an endless torrent of Conan pastiche novels by other writers flooded bookstores.

By 1984 the "Howard boom" had receded in America, but all was not dark. Howard's works began to appear in translation throughout Europe and in Japan. Foreign publishers and readers found the breadth of Howard's work—not just the Conan stories—to be of interest. Nouvelles Editions Oswald in France released more than thirty Howard titles. The autobiographical novel *Post Oaks and Sand Roughs* was actually published in French in 1989, before it was published in English the following year. Today, Howard is read around the world. It was also in the mid-1980s that Howard's more obscure, marginal writings were made available in print for the benefit of the hardcore enthusiast, in the form of a series of small-press booklets published by Robert M. Price.

In 1984 Howard criticism came of age: Don Herron edited *The Dark Barbarian*, an anthology of insightful critical essays about Howard's work. The most eye-opening of these was written by Herron himself, under the pseudonym George Knight. Entitled "Robert E. Howard: Hard-Boiled Heroic Fantasist," Herron's essay revealed how Howard broke with the European fantasy tradition to create an edgier, more visceral school of American fantasy fiction. In this sense, his work resembled the "hard-boiled" school of detective fiction then being pioneered by Dashiell Hammett and Raymond Chandler in pulp magazines such as *Black Mask*. The classic drawing room mystery had given way to tough-minded tales of the streets. As Herron explained:

> Howard, in the pulp pages of *Weird Tales*, did much the same thing for the fantasy story—he broke away from the lush stylists like Hodgson, Dunsany, and Eddison and wrote in direct language. He eschewed the arty toying about with elves, enchanted princesses, and magical dragons

and cut loose with stories about thick-armed warriors, harem girls, and flesh-eating apes. He was not catering to the reader of James Branch Cabell, Dunsany, or Morris any more than Hammett was catering to the reader of the most popular American mystery writer of the day, S. S. van Dine . . . Howard and Hammett were each creating a distinct genre for their audience, the American pulp magazine reader. (118)

In other words, Howard's Conan has roughly the same relationship to J. R. R. Tolkien's *Lord of the Rings* that Chandler's Philip Marlowe has to Doyle's Sherlock Holmes. Herron's "Robert E. Howard: Hard-Boiled Heroic Fantasist" remains one of the best general essays about Howard's work, and *The Dark Barbarian* is a milestone in Howard studies.

Two years later, in 1986, a second biographical work about Howard appeared. *One Who Walked Alone* was a book-length memoir written by Novalyne Price Ellis, who vividly recalled her relationship with Howard fifty years earlier. In her youth, Novalyne Price had literary ambitions of her own and kept elaborate journals about interesting people she encountered, especially Bob Howard. She often recorded detailed accounts of her conversations with Howard just hours after they occurred. These journals formed the basis of *One Who Walked Alone*.

It is impossible to overestimate the value of this work in terms of the light it sheds on Howard. A key revelation concerning Howard's creative process occurred when Novalyne came to visit him and overheard him reciting his prose aloud as he composed it on the typewriter. This suggests a kinship on Howard's part to the skalds of ancient times who told stories as part of an oral tradition. Novalyne was also witness to Howard's most severe mood swings, owing to the fact that she was acquainted with him during his final years when he was undergoing considerable stress. She documents both his depression and his energetic, boisterous moods.

The picture she paints strongly indicates that Howard would today be diagnosed as bipolar or manic-depressive. The "manic" phase is evidenced by the episodes of odd, quirky behavior that she recounts. Early commentators on Howard frequently remarked that he was beset by "neurosis," but a clearer picture has emerged that identifies him as suffering from a chemical condition that would have been treatable with modern anti-depressant medications.

The following year, 1987, the first book-length critical study of Howard's work as a whole was issued. It was an earlier version of the present study. We the authors were deeply gratified that, for the most part, it was warmly received. We concluded our introductory chapter with the observation that Robert E. Howard was a visionary like William Blake or W. B. Yeats who wrote from inner necessity. We expressed the hope that our volume would lead to further Howard studies. It was a wish we were happy to see granted.

In 1990, Rusty Burke founded *The Dark Man: The Journal of Robert E. Howard Studies*, a scholarly journal that welcomed contributions from both academic and non-academic writers. Published sporadically at first, it has begun to appear with greater regularity. By virtue of his extensive biographical and bibliographical research, in addition to his insightful observations, Burke has emerged as the leading figure in Howard studies. However, his was by no means a lone voice. In addition to Don Herron and Rusty Burke, significant contributions to the study of Howard and his work have been made by Fred Blosser, David Gentzel, Morgan Holmes, Patrice Louinet, Frank Coffman, Mark Hall, Steven Tompkins, Steven R. Trout, Edward A. Waterman, Mark Finn, Leo Grin, Gary Romeo, Jeffrey Shanks and others.

Howard's Conan remained banished from the bookstores throughout the 1990s. However, in 1995 and 1996 Baen Books published a seven-volume "Robert E. Howard Library." The adventures of Bran Mak Morn, Solomon Kane, and Kull were all brought back into print after more than a decade's absence. The Baen series also offered a representative sampling of Howard's other fantasy and horror fiction.

Though these were mass-market paperbacks, they offered Howard's original texts free of editorial tampering. Although there was no second printing, copies of the various titles could be found in bookstores past the turn of the new century.

In 1996, *One Who Walked Alone* was adapted into a touching motion picture *The Whole Wide World*. Vincent D'Onofrio and Renée Zellweger gave moving performances as Robert E. Howard and Novalyne Price, respectively. Howard's creative genius and his mood disorder were both vividly dramatized. A small independent film, *The Whole Wide World* saw a limited theatrical release but garnered much critical praise. It subsequently became more widely available through home video and cable television. An impressive cinematic work, it easily overshadows the disappointing film adaptations based on Howard's characters.

Following the death of L. Sprague de Camp in 2000, Conan Properties changed ownership. Howard's original Conan stories became available once again in new editions. A specialty publisher, Wandering Star, offered expensive collectors' editions that scrupulously restored Howard's original texts and presented the stories in the order Howard wrote them, the result of painstaking research. These texts formed the basis of an affordable trade paperback edition from Del Rey Books. Wandering Star volumes of Solomon Kane, Kull, and Bran Mak Morn were also reissued in popular editions from Del Rey. In the meantime, Bison Books, an imprint of the University of Nebraska Press, and Wildside Press released new editions of Howard's westerns, historical fiction, boxing stories, and other lesser-known works. The Robert E. Howard Foundation Press was eventually established to offer splendid new editions of Howard's more obscure works for the discerning collector.

In 2004, Don Herron released *The Barbaric Triumph*, a second anthology of critical essays on Howard's writings. In sophistication, erudition, and depth, the essays in the new anthology easily surpassed those in *The Dark Barbarian*, issued twenty years earlier. It was also in 2004 that Leo Grin launched a second scholarly journal devoted to Howard and his work, *The Cimmerian*. The year 2006 saw the release of a new biography, *Blood and Thunder: The Life and Art of Robert E. Howard* by Mark Finn, as well as another collection of critical essays, *Two-Gun Bob: A Centennial Study of Robert E. Howard*, edited by Benjamin Szumskyj. Yet another collection of essays, *The Robert E. Howard Reader*, edited by Darrell Schweitzer, was issued in 2010. 2018 proved to be a banner year for Howard scholarship, with *The Robert E. Howard Guide* by Patrice Louinet and *Robert E. Howard: A Literary Biography* by David C. Smith, as well as *Ar-i-e'ch and the Spell of Cthulhu: An Informal Guide to Robert E. Howard's Lovecraftian Fiction* and *Western Weirdness and Voodoo Vengeance: An Informal Guide to Robert E. Howard's American Horrors*, both by Fred Blosser.

And now it is with great pleasure that we are once again able to offer our own critical introduction to Howard's works. The new version has been revised and updated. Such errors as appeared in the previous study, due to misinformation and expurgated texts of Howard's writings, have been corrected. We have also had the benefit of three additional decades' worth of new biographical information and critical insights concerning Howard.

It is hoped that the present volume will in some capacity help readers new and old to better enjoy and appreciate the dreams and visions of a modern mythmaker, Robert E. Howard.

II. Bran Mak Morn

Included in the very first batch of stories that Robert E. Howard sold to *Weird Tales* in 1924 was a short story entitled "The Lost Race." Though not a particularly memorable tale in itself, it is something of a milestone in Howard's career, perhaps as much so as the publication of his first story, "Spear and Fang." In "The Lost Race," Howard mentions for the first time in any of his published writings a strange aboriginal race that once inhabited the British Isles. He referred to them as "Picts."

"The Lost Race" is scarcely a story; it is virtually plotless and was in the main a device to introduce the Picts and Howard's personal theories concerning them. The title is appropriate, for most modern readers are only vaguely familiar with the term "Pict" and even anthropologists disagree to some extent about just who the Picts were. Howard himself admitted that his use of the term may have been incorrect:

> I am, of course, aware that my use of the term might be questioned. The people who are known in history as Picts are named variously as Celts, aborigines, and even Germans. Some authorities maintain they came into Britain after the Britons and just before the coming of the Gaels. The "wild Picts of Galloway" which figure largely in early Scottish history and legendry, were doubtless a very mixed race ... Probably the term "Pict" was properly applied only to the wandering Celtic tribe which settled in Galloway and presumably conquered and was absorbed by the aboriginal

---

All stories discussed in this chapter appear in *BMM*.

population. But to me "Pict" must always refer to the small dark Mediterranean aborigines of Britain. This is not strange, since when I first read of these aborigines, they were referred to as Picts . . . (REH to H. P. Lovecraft, 2 March 1932; CL 2.327)

Howard was at a loss to explain his obsession with this strange people about whom so little is known. However, this interest became a consuming one in his life and left its mark on much of his writing. As a child, Howard was curious about his roots. He read Scottish histories and therein encountered the term "Pict" for the first time. Though they were mentioned only in passing, they touched a responsive chord in Howard. His obsession, however, had its true beginnings a few years later:

. . . when I was about twelve I spent a short time in New Orleans and found in a Canal Street library a book detailing the pageant of British history . . . It was written for schoolboys and told in an interesting and romantic style, probably with many historical inaccuracies. But there I first learned of the small dark people which first settled Britain, and they were referred to as Picts. I had always felt a strange interest in the term and the people, and now I felt a driving absorption regarding them. The writer painted the aborigines in no more admirable light than had other historians whose works I had read. His Picts were made to be sly, furtive, unwarlike, and altogether inferior to the races which followed—which was doubtless true. And yet I felt a strong sympathy for this people, and then and there adopted them as a medium of connection with ancient times . . . (REH to H. P. Lovecraft, 2 March 1932; CL 2.328)

The vividness with which Howard recalls this episode and the subsequent importance he ascribes to it recall the curious psychological phenomenon explored in Peter Shaffer's play *Equus*, in which a disturbed adolescent comes to worship horses as deities due to a single childhood experience with one. Such incidents are examples of what Abraham Maslow termed a "peak experience." Peak experiences, like religious experiences, occur when an emotionally intense individual, through some physical or mental activity, is afforded a glimpse of wider vistas of meaning, often becoming open to a deeper intuitive consciousness. The religious variety may involve an acceptance of intuitive knowledge, faith, or belief, and the capacity for these experiences is the mark of a visionary personality.

One cannot attribute too much importance to this single incident in Howard's life. His discovery of the Picts stimulated his youthful imagination and at the same time satisfied an emotional craving of a lonely boy—a craving for identity. Unable to relate to the mundane children around him, he found a focal point for his imaginative energy and a symbol for his own alienation:

> I saw the name "Picts" first on maps, and always the name lay outside the far-flung bounds of the Roman empire. This fact aroused my intense interest: it was so significant of itself. The mere fact suggested terrific wars—savage attacks and ferocious resistance—valor and heroism and ferocity. I was an instinctive enemy of Rome; what more natural than that I should instinctively ally myself with her enemies, more especially as these enemies had resisted all attempts at subjugation. When in my dreams—not daydreams, but actual dreams—I fought the armored legions of Rome, and reeled back gashed and defeated, there sprang into my mind—like an invasion from another, unborn world of the future—the picture of a map, spanned by the wide empire of Rome, and ever beyond the frontier, outside the lines of subjugation, the cryptic legend, "Picts and Scots." And always the thought rose in my mind to lend me new strength: among the Picts I could find refuge, safe from my foes, where I could lick my wounds and renew my strength for the wars . . . (REH to H. P. Lovecraft, c. January 1932; CL 2.329)

The Picts as a symbol recur again and again throughout Howard's work, appearing in virtually all his major story cycles. In subsequent chapters, we shall meet them in tales of the Celts and Vikings as well as in stories set in Howard's fantasy worlds, from pre-Atlantean settings to the Hyborian Age of Conan. The characters Kull and Conan gain insights into themselves through comparisons with these aboriginal people.

It is only in the present story cycle, the tales of Bran Mak Morn, that the Picts are the protagonists. In other stories, the Picts appear as supporting characters or, notably, the antagonists. In the cycle of Bran Mak Morn, Howard gives them his full attention and sympathy; they are the central characters, heroes of their own epic saga. This saga begins with "The Lost Race."

In "The Lost Race" (*Weird Tales*, January 1927) Howard put the Picts on paper in a finished work for the first time, but his presentation of them was embryonic; in later stories he contradicts much of what he set forth in this first tale. Once Howard introduced his Picts to an audience of readers, the next step was to introduce an epic figure to represent them. A hero was needed to illustrate all the good qualities and aspects of the race, to be both the ideal pinnacle of the people and the ultimate representative Pict.

Bran Mak Morn, the king of the Picts, was one of the first characters that Howard created. Of all Howard's heroes, only Francis X. Gordon, a Mundyesque adventurer in the Middle East, had an earlier genesis, having been created by Howard when he was ten years old. Although several years passed before Howard put Bran on paper, he noted that "Bran Mak Morn has not changed in the years; he is exactly as he leaped full-grown into my mind—a pantherish man of medium height, with inscrutable black eyes, black hair, and dark skin." Howard named him after Brennus, the Gaul who sacked Rome, and an Irish hero, Gol Mac Morn. In Celtic mythology, Bran was the name given the sun god Lugh after he had transformed himself into a raven. However, Howard commented that "while Bran Mac Morn is Gaelic for 'The Raven, Son of Morn,' Bran Mak Morn has no Gaelic significance, but has a meaning of its own, purely Pictish and ancient, with roots in the dim mazes of antiquity" (REH to H. P. Lovecraft, c. January 1932; CL 2.329).

Bran Mak Morn appears in several of Howard's early writings: a long poem (nonextant) in which Howard put Bran on paper for the first time and never finished; a play entitled *Bran Mak Morn*, a mere five-hundred-word fragment; and a finished story written in the early phase of Howard's professional career titled "Men of the Shadows." It is in "Men of the Shadows" that Howard draws together the elements put forth in "The Lost Race" and the early fragments—the history of the Picts, their struggle for survival, Howard's racial theories, the hero Bran Mak Morn—and presents them all in the opening episode of an epic saga in miniature.

The plot of "Men of the Shadows" is virtually identical to that of "The Lost Race" in that each story is little more than a thinly disguised pseudo-history of the Pictish race. In both tales an outsider (in "The Lost Race" a wandering Celt, in "Men of the Shadows" a Viking mercenary employed by Rome) is captured by the Picts and taken to their tribal dwelling place, enabling readers to see something of their lifestyles and learn of their past. In "The Lost Race" Cororuc the Celt is shocked by the sub-human savagery of the Picts, as is the nameless Viking who narrates "Men of the Shadows." The Viking's knowledge of the Picts consists mainly of rumor and legend, and he regards them with mystery and awe.

In both stories, one fact is clearly evident: the Picts are a race on the wane. They are the last of the Stone Age Men, a living link with prehistory, whose life flame will soon be engulfed and extinguished in a rush of new races, new ideas, and new civilizations. The Picts are fighting for survival, but their existence is tenuous and the struggle has taken a ghastly toll. Their numbers have dwindled, they have been driven into the wastes, and, worst of all, their blood has become tainted with inferior strains. Once "'the highest type of men'" (16), the Pictish people have degenerated into a stunted, deformed race of ape-like freaks.

About midway through "Men of the Shadows," the Viking is captured following a fierce battle and taken before the Pictish king, Bran Mak Morn. Bran is an atavism who can boast of an untainted bloodline stretching back to the days when the Picts were a great people.

But he is also much more. In the ensuing tale, he is referred to as "The Wolf of the Heather" and "The Uplifter." It is made clear by the story's conclusion that Bran is the last hope of the Picts for survival. Although he does nothing in the way of physical action in the entire story, his personal and patriarchal presence is strongly felt.

The second half of "Men of the Shadows" consists solely of a pseudo-history of the Picts as envisioned by Howard—much more elaborate than that presented in "The Lost Race." Rusty Burke has duly noted that this narrative is Howard's earliest presentation of a vast imaginary prehistory of humanity detailing a cycle of nations and peoples rising, falling, and fading away. The narrative is presented by the tribal shaman and is accompanied by visions conjured from a fire. The story ends abruptly upon completion of this narrative.

"Men of the Shadows" is most interesting from a bibliographical and psychological standpoint. Though it is the first Bran Mak Morn story, it was not published until thirty-three years after Howard's death. It was written fairly early in his career and is therefore a prime example of the type of story Howard was inclined to write while still comparatively uninfluenced by commercial considerations. Samples of Howard's poetry are present in the tale in the form of chants, incantations, and a lengthy heading to the story proper.

The integration of verse into the narrative reveals youthful indulgence on Howard's part, as some ninety lines of poetry appear within the course of the story. This fact, coupled with the strong similarity of the plot to that of "The Lost Race," probably prompted Farnsworth Wright to reject "Men of the Shadows." Looking back at the work some years later from the standpoint of a professional writer, Howard was moved to write that it was "rightfully rejected" by *Weird Tales* (REH to H. P. Lovecraft, c. January 1932; CL 2.343).

The story does indeed contain serious flaws. The Viking narrator, a supposedly savage and uneducated man, is far too articulate, knowledgeable, and sensitive to be believable. Brilliant passages of great power are offset by awkward phrases and totally unnecessary authorial intrusions. Yet despite its deficiencies, "Men of the Shadows" has many good points. Signs of Howard's talent and potential are evident in this early effort. An intriguing element is the appearance of Bran's sister, who is not named and never seen again in the saga. It is she who requests that the Viking be set free to tell the tale. Finally, it is in "Men of the Shadows" that Howard sets the stage for the action to come and firmly establishes the somber atmosphere that prevails in the two remaining segments of Bran's saga.

"Kings of the Night" (*Weird Tales*, November 1930) was the first Bran Mak Morn story to be published. When it appeared, Howard's career was well underway and, unlike "Men of the Shadows," it is an ably crafted piece of fiction. The almost cinematic quality of Howard's vivid visual imagery can be seen in this story, as can his proficiency in describing conflict, be it between two individuals or armies of thousands.

In "Kings of the Night" the nebulous threat that promises extinction for Bran's race materializes into a tangible menace: the all-encompassing expansion of the iron legions of the Roman Empire. Howard expressed a strong antipathy for Rome, an antipathy he termed "instinct" and which manifested itself in his dreams (REH to H. P. Lovecraft, 2 March 1932; CL 2.344). In this matter he differed sharply with H. P. Lovecraft, an admirer of Roman civilization, and the two writers engaged in a heated debate over Rome's merits in their correspondence. Howard's knowledge of Roman civilization was perhaps influenced by the works of historians whose Christian leanings biased their judgments of the Empire's role in shaping the ancient world. The prevailing view during Howard's time and before was that the Romans murdered Christ, oppressed Judea, and were mere imperialist tyrants who copied their culture from the Greeks. The danger posed by the Roman Empire to the Picts is alluded to in

"Men of the Shadows." In "Kings of the Night," the Romans have arrived in force. From here on, Rome, in the person of her emissaries and as a pernicious entity in her own right, is the nemesis of Bran and the Picts.

The story begins on the eve of a crucial battle between the encamped Roman legions and an alliance of Picts, Celts, and Vikings. One of Bran's allies is Cormac of Connacht, and it is from his point of view that much of the story is told. As in "The Lost Race" and "Men of the Shadows," the actions of the Picts are seen through the eyes of an outsider observing them. Howard commented, "Only in my last Bran story, 'Worms of the Earth' did I look through Pictish eyes and speak with a Pictish tongue!" (REH to H. P. Lovecraft, 2 March 1932; *CL* 2.344). It seems a curious paradox that Howard, who fondly regarded the Picts as a sort of adopted people, apparently felt it necessary to resort to the use of an alien character to relate to them.

As for Bran himself, it is in "Kings of the Night" that we discover as much as we ever learn about his background. Cormac recalls how Bran, the son of a chief, has managed to unite all the other Pictish tribes and clans and claims kingship over them. The unity, however, is tenuous. Bran regards his kingship with bitter irony. He is painfully aware that both the Picts and their few allies lack solidarity and that the outcome of the imminent battle with the Roman legions will make or break the Pictish nation.

Bran's back is to the wall. From his vantage point he can see the far-distant campfires of his enemies. His own armies, a tenuous alliance, are disintegrating before his very eyes due to old tribal hatreds. Yet despite Bran's Cassandra-like warnings that Rome is a more malignant, inexorable menace to all who dwell on or near the British Isles, the allies and especially the Norsemen lack the vision to see beyond their own petty squabbles. They are too blind to see that the hand of Rome could end their ways of life forever.

Because of the death of the king who committed their forces to Bran, the Vikings, at the behest of their acting chief Wulfhere, now hint that they may desert and join the Romans. After some haggling, the Norsemen agree to fight for the Pictish cause on the condition that they be led into battle by a king "'neither Pict, Gael, nor Briton,'" a compromise that is meaningless as their condition is impossible to fulfill (43).

Things look bad for Bran; solidarity among the Picts depends on the outcome of the impending battle, which has already been lost due to the Vikings' betrayal. Bran fumes helplessly under the weight of the knowledge that he and the Picts are finished before they ever had a chance to begin.

A solution is provided by Bran's shaman, Gonar. The aged wizard reveals that time and space are illusions, and that yesterday, today and tomorrow are all "'like the dreams of ghosts'" (36). He tells Bran that, eons before the dawn of history, there were advanced civilizations and mighty empires compared to which "'Rome is as a village'" (44). The greatest of these vanished empires was Valusia, ruled by Kull, a barbarian usurper from legendary Atlantis. Bran Mak Morn possesses a gem once owned by a remote ancestor named Brule, who was the first of Bran's line. Brule was a friend and advisor to the fabled King Kull. The gem itself was a gift from Kull, and it is possible with the help of Gonar to employ the jewel as a link to the past by which they are able to dispel the mists of time and summon Kull to aid Brule's descendants in their hour of need.

Kull, another of Howard's heroes, was created long after Bran Mak Morn, but appeared in print first in two tales published over a year before "Kings of the Night." This tale is the only one in which two of Howard's major characters meet. In "Kings of the Night," Kull's character is less sharply defined than in other works in which he appears, but his characterization is nevertheless consistent with the other entries of the Kull cycle.

Kull, upon finding himself in a strange land and involved in a struggle with alien people, dismisses the episode as an exceptionally vivid dream, recalling that he went to sleep prior to finding himself in this strange place. Kull maintains throughout the story that the entire episode is but a dream. The confusion Kull experiences over the nature of reality is a major characteristic of the man and is prominent in other stories. Several of the Kull tales are devoted primarily to the king's metaphysical doubts. In Kull's continued insistence that his experience with the "modern" Picts is a dream, one detects a bit of wishful thinking on Howard's part—a half-wish/half-hope that his own vivid dreams of battle were somehow more than just that.

When Kull is taken before the Vikings, they do not accept him as their leader immediately. Initially, he must prove himself and battle to the death with Wulfhere. The struggle is short and savage; Kull is the victor. This matter decided, Bran and his allies, with Kull leading the Vikings, engage the legions of Rome. In writing of the carnage, Howard makes full use of the talent he possessed for writing about physical conflict. Few authors can rival Howard's action prose, and Howard also emphasizes military strategy and the skillful deployment of forces. His wide readings in history, especially about the Crusades, gave him a wealth of knowledge about ancient military tactics.

In the end Bran's army is victorious, but to ensure victory Bran finds it necessary to allow the three hundred Vikings to perish. Kull suffers great wounds during the battle, and when the Romans have been routed he vanishes back into the mists of time. In the aftermath, Cormac the Gael confronts Bran, intending to slay him for allowing the brave Norsemen to be slaughtered. Bran offers no resistance, expressing his sorrow for the death of these men and replying that "'a king belongs to his people'" (73) and cannot allow his personal feelings to sway his judgements. Cormac experiences an abrupt change of heart, realizing that Bran is "'a born king of men'" (73). Bran himself derives no satisfaction from his victory, and though he is but the ruler of a nation of savage aborigines, it is Cormac who realizes that Bran is the equal in spirit to the regal King Kull of the lost empire of Valusia. Bran's people are his whole life, and the sacrifice of the Vikings suggests the lengths in which he would go to save them. It is, however, in the next story examined that we learn the true extent of what Bran Mak Morn would risk to end the threat of Rome.

"Worms of the Earth" (*Weird Tales*, November 1932) is one of Robert E. Howard's finest stories. Written at the height of his career, just prior to the creation of Conan, it is the pinnacle of his Pictish saga. The tale has been reprinted and anthologized many times, and August Derleth regarded it as Howard's finest story. H. P. Lovecraft acclaimed it as a "masterpiece" ("In Memoriam: Robert Ervin Howard" 124). Praised by numerous other writers and readers throughout the years, "Worms of the Earth" is, like the best of Howard's fiction, more than just a mere fantasy adventure. It is a story of gut-wrenching horror and the chronicle of a man's spiritual descent to his own damnation.

The story begins with the crucifixion of a Pict accused of murdering a thieving Roman merchant. Here we are witness to the physical presence of Rome. In the two previous episodes, Rome is first alluded to in conversation and then encountered on the battlefield. Now, finally, we meet the Romans face to face. The grisly spectacle has been staged by the provisional governor Titus Sulla for the benefit of the Pictish ambassador to Rome, Partha Mac Othna, who is in reality Bran Mak Morn using a false identity to spy on the Romans. To maintain his cover, Bran must stand helplessly by and allow the Romans to butcher one of his subjects. Howard has blasphemously employed this crucifixion to mark, not the beginning of humanity's salvation, but the beginning of one man's damnation.

Returning to the quarters the Romans have provided for him, Bran rails about the many sins of Rome against the heather people and curses his own impotence, chastising himself as unfit to rule the Picts. He later recalls some of his experiences among the Romans, remembering "wild feasts where wine flowed in fountains," occasions replete with gambling and willing women (95). Howard adds a subtle nuance to the poisonous malignancy of Rome by showing how even Bran, molded by the wilderness and hating Rome, can be swayed by her charms.

As Bran broods bitterly about the injustices of Rome, his anger focuses on Titus Sulla, who in Bran's mind symbolizes Rome and therefore must suffer Bran's revenge. Bran's companion Grom, who acts as a sort of valet and bodyguard, reminds Bran that Sulla is always heavily guarded and therefore immune to any act of vengeance on the king's part. Bran, however, is not to be denied and has conceived a scheme of vengeance. He sends Grom to instruct the Picts to harry the Roman's wall, thus setting his plan into motion.

His resolve set, Bran sleeps and in a shadowy dream sequence speaks with his shaman, Gonar. The wizard suspects the nature of Bran's revenge and tries to dissuade him. Bran responds with an eloquent speech about racial unity and his kinship with the crucified Pict. Gonar, a sorcerer and mystic philosopher, advocates physical means of vengeance and calls for open warfare. Bran retorts that his tribesmen face the Roman legions and that he will use any and all means at his disposal—"'the thorn in the foot, the adder in the path, the venom in the cup, the dagger in the dark'" (94). Bran states that he would even use "'the worms of the earth'" (94). Gonar cries out in utter horror upon hearing the last cryptic phrase. Bran, a warrior and man of action, chooses to summon the forces of hell—and therein lies his damnation.

Bran awakens and sets forth to put his scheme into operation by seeking out these "worms." These creatures are Howard's most fully realized horrors. They are remnants of a race driven underground by the Picts centuries before who have lost all human semblance, devolving into hideous creatures shunned by all true human beings. They are, according to Howard, the source of the legends of the Little People that abound in Celtic mythology. Howard's "worms" have several precedents in supernatural literature, notably in stories by British fantasist Arthur Machen.

Bran's quest takes him far into the bleak fens and marshes of ancient Britain. Here the tone of the story is reflected by the stark, somber landscape that does credit to Howard's powers of description. Crossing the moors, he comes at length to the wattle hut of the witch-woman Atla. By her appearance, Bran deduces that she is only half-human, the repellent offspring of a mating between an unfortunate woman who strayed on the moors too late one night and one of the strange creatures for whom he searches. Bran announces, "'I have a song to sing to the worms of the earth!'" (102), and states that he wants the woman to take him to them. He offers both gold and physical violence as inducements, but neither gains him more than derisive laughter. The price of her cooperation is far higher than gold; she demands one night of love with the king of the Picts.

Bran submits to Atla's terms. The grotesque rite of passage is performed offstage, and Bran leaves her hut by dawn and continues on the next stage of his odyssey. He follows Atla's instructions and locates a mound of earth in which a stone door has been built. Bran descends into the deep, womb-like tunnel where the worms have secreted their most precious relic, the Black Stone. Bran finds the stone, steals it, and flees back the way he came. The close confines of the tunnels are suffocating, and Bran has no defense against the worms should he encounter them; but his hatred and lust for vengeance has deadened any fear he might feel. He emerges from the tunnel and hides the Stone.

That night Bran and Atla, who was amazed to see Bran alive and sane, go to a cavern and await the worms of the earth. Bran intends, through Atla, to strike a bargain; he will return the Stone only when the worms deliver Titus Sulla to him. Soon the creatures swarm about the Pict, but only their glowing eyes are visible in the dark. Bran can feel "waves of terrible menace emanating from them . . . the inhuman threat to body, mind, and soul," and he realizes that he confronts "the ultimate Horror of the dreams and legends of his race" (113). The worms are enraged at the theft of their relic but have no choice but to comply with Bran's wishes. The exchange of the Stone for Sulla will take place at the center of Dagon's Ring, a Stonehenge-like circle of stone monoliths at "the blackness that foreruns the dawn" (115).

At sunset the next day, Bran retrieves the Black Stone and rides to Dagon's Ring. His route brings him close to the Tower of Trajan, the fortress to which Titus Sulla had been summoned when the Picts began to harry the frontier at Bran's command. The king is startled to find the once-impregnable tower collapsed into a heap of rubble. Investigating, Bran discovers the mangled body of a dying legionary. He questions the man and learns how the tower caved in at the foundations. The dying man speaks of how he and his fellows had heard strange burrowing noises from underground throughout the day. As the tower fell, Titus Sulla was dragged into the bowels of the earth. The Roman then tells how he was crushed in the falling debris as he tried to escape. As he gasps out the story, Bran does what he can to comfort him in his final moments and gives him water from his flask. Howard tells us that "in that moment the dying Roman seemed to him almost like a brother" (120).

It is with this encounter that the full enormity of Bran's act is borne upon him. Bran's treating the dying Roman as he would a dying kinsman is as close as Howard ever comes to a statement of the universal brotherhood of all human beings. For Bran now realizes the truth his instincts screamed at him the moment he saw the worms, the truth that Gonar tried to reveal to him but that he was too blinded by hatred to see: that these malignant, inhuman, evil creatures are the true enemies of *all* human beings, and humanity's squabbles pale in the face of such a contagion. And when he arrives at Dagon's Ring, the sword-stroke that Bran Mak Morn delivers to the gibbering, insane Titus Sulla is given in mercy, not in hate or vengeance.

Bran hurls the Black Stone into the midst of the worms gathered about him and flees on horseback. But he can never flee far enough, for echoing behind him is the cry of Atla, "'Stay and let me show you the real fruits of the pits! . . . you are stained with the taint—you have called them forth and they will remember! And in their own time they will come to you again!'" (127).

"Worms of the Earth" is the last Bran Mak Morn story. Howard began another but never finished it. Certainly, any further installments would have contained an element of anticlimax. "Worms of the Earth" is arguably Howard's finest story, combining elements of both pre-Christian and post-Christian tragedy. One can easily imagine it unfolding on the Greek or Elizabethan stage. A hero of Homeric stature attempts to aid his people and through his actions brings about his own doom, no less than Oedipus Rex. He attempts to consort with evil forces for good ends, but finds himself not in control, but controlled. Like Faust, he sows the seeds of his own destruction.

The grim saga of Bran Mak Morn and the worms of the earth is equally striking as both a modern allegory and as a universal cautionary tale. From a modern perspective, it illustrates the evils of terrorism. Bran wishes to effect political change and avenge social injustice, but steps beyond all boundaries of acceptable human behavior in these pursuits. Even the loftiest goal does not justify any means. One should never call up the worms of the earth. And in a more universal sense, Howard's story starkly depicts the truly horrific toll that all-consuming hatred can demand.

At the conclusion of the story, Bran Mak Morn is a different man from what he was at the story's outset and regrets the bane his spell of vengeance has caused. But no amount of regret can erase the fact that Bran has failed himself by giving vent to all that was base and ignoble within him. In "Men of the Shadows," Bran is spoken of as having attained "the heights of self-conquest" (15), but apparently his self-mastery is less than fully realized. Another irony the reader notices is that in "The Lost Race" it is the Picts who are referred to as the source of the Little People legends. Perhaps the Picts abhor the worms as they do because they are aware of the similarity between them. And perhaps Bran's ruling urge to drive the Romans from Britain is due in part to the ancient tales of what happens to races that are driven into the wastes to degenerate and decay.

Unlike Howard's other heroes, the fate of Bran Mak Morn is almost certain. A doom such as the worms of the earth promise cannot be avoided. And though hints about Bran's ultimate fate are present in another story, "The Dark Man," it was written prior to "Worms of the Earth," and Howard may have had second thoughts when he wrote the latter tale. Thus, the hero Howard wanted to write about perhaps more than any other comes to an ignominious end. Of course, a man like Bran Mak Morn, a king, cannot die alone. As in the Arthurian sagas, the king and the land are one. Time and again, Bran is referred to as the last hope of his race, and in the end he failed them. The saga of Bran Mak Morn is a consummate tragedy both for an individual and an entire race.

These stories—gloomy in tone, bleak and brutal in imagery—take on an added dimension of fatalism when one realizes that the fate of the Picts was a foregone conclusion. "Who are these Picts?" one asks oneself before progressing very far in the first story. "Where are they now?" In some dim eon, long past, the last Pict died. Even to Robert E. Howard, the self-appointed scribe of the Picts, they are a lost race.

III. Solomon Kane

Solomon Kane was the first of Howard's heroes to appear in print, making his debut in the August 1928 issue of *Weird Tales*. Like Bran Mak Morn, Kane was created some years prior to being put on paper. Howard mentions that he was a sixteen-year-old high school student when he first conceived of the character and that Kane "was probably the result of an admiration for a certain kind of cold, steely-nerved duelist that existed in the sixteenth century" (REH, quoted by Perry 66).

In a number of ways, Solomon Kane is Howard's most distinctive character. He resembles Howard's other heroes in that he is an imposing and formidable figure, yet there are notable differences:

> A tall man... clad in black from head to foot, in plain, close-fitting garments that somehow suited the somber face. Long arms and broad shoulders betokened the swordsman, as plainly as the long rapier in his hand. The features of the man were saturnine and gloomy. A kind of dark pallor lent him a ghostly appearance in the uncertain light, an effect heightened by the satanic darkness of his lowering brows... Strangely, the Mephisthelean trend of the lower features was offset by a high, broad forehead, though this was partly hidden by a featherless hat.
>
> That forehead marked the dreamer, the idealist, the introvert, just as the eyes and the thin, straight nose betrayed the fanatic... (37–38)

While the adventures of Howard's other fantasy heroes take place in ancient or imaginary prehistoric epochs, Kane's exploits take place

---

All stories discussed in this chapter appear in *ST*.

in a comparatively modern period. The others are barbarians; Kane is a civilized man, a child of the Renaissance and part of an era of exploration and discovery. Solomon Kane is an English Puritan who takes his faith very seriously; he seeks to personally redress any wrongdoings and injustices that he encounters. Given his prowess as a swordsman, he is well able to do so, and because of his restless disposition and urge to wander, his adventures take him to distant corners of the earth. On several occasions he casually informs a companion that it has at times been his duty "'to ease various evil men of their lives'" (90, 189).

In writing of Solomon Kane, Howard demonstrates keen insight into the psychology of the fanatic. Kane's driving motivation is actually an irresistible wanderlust and desire for adventure. Yet Kane himself believes that he has become a righter of wrongs and nemesis of evildoers the better to serve God's will. Kane is moved by urges that his religion is unable to satisfy. He does what he must both to satisfy these urges and to sublimate them into a useful end compatible with his religious fervor:

> He was a man born out of his time—a strange blending of Puritan and Cavalier, with a touch of the ancient philosopher, and more than a touch of the pagan, though the last assertion would have shocked him unspeakably. An atavist of the days of blind chivalry he was, a knight errant in the somber clothes of a fanatic. A hunger in his soul drove him on and on, an urge to right all wrongs, protect all weaker things, avenge all crimes against right and justice. Wayward and restless as the wind, he was consistent in only one respect—he was true to his ideals of justice and right. Such was Solomon Kane. (127)

Although Kane resolves his inner conflict in this manner, he remains Howard's most emotionally unstable character. Howard calls him "fanatic" repeatedly (38, 127, 204) and refers to him as "paranoid" on more than one occasion (229, 264). In one instance, Kane even suffers a complete mental breakdown. The fact that Kane is Howard's most mentally unstable character and also his most civilized major character is no coincidence, but a typically Howardian statement.

Reading of Solomon Kane's religious zeal and his determination to work the will of God, one may wonder to what extent Kane's faith reflects Howard's own. Howard's mother was a Methodist and his father, while also a believing Christian, was nonetheless openminded enough to delve into Eastern mysticism. Dr. Howard was, in fact, an early researcher into alternative medical techniques such as hypnosis and yoga. Howard himself, however, was not a regular churchgoer. Around the time the Kane stories were appearing regularly in *Weird Tales*, Howard did attend Sunday School and meetings of the Epworth League, but this was due to an interest he had taken, not in religion, but in a woman active in these groups. He soon dropped out of both of these activities due to boredom, remarking, "It's nothing but a lot of infernal tripe, a lot of muck, a lot of nothingness" (REH to Harold Preece, c. March 1929; CL 1.402).

Howard was not overly impressed with the doctrines of Christianity. On the one hand, he was knowledgeable concerning anthropology and evolution, which undermined such metaphysical underpinnings of Christianity as a seven-day creation. On the other hand, his reading exposed him to various other creeds, giving him a more objective, cosmopolitan view of religion. Passages in some of his letters and stories reveal his acquaintance with such Eastern ideologies as Buddhism and Zen, an interest he shared with his father.

More significantly, such Christian precepts as peace, meekness, and humility did not suit Howard's temperament. In his poetry, he is more apt to identify with Lucifer, the rebel and fallen angel of Milton's *Paradise Lost*, than with Christ. Even Solomon Kane is occasionally described as having a satanic aspect, especially from the viewpoint of his foes. Howard, however, did not become a militant atheist, at least not a vocal one, out of respect for his religious parents. He seems to have preferred the more moderate stance of the deist or agnostic.

Even so, Howard was well read in the Bible, especially the Old Testament. However, his interest was more in the nature of academic study concerning history, literature, and legend. On occasion he shared this interest with the atheist Lovecraft:

> I have always felt a deep interest in Israel in connection with Saul. Poor devil! A pitiful and heroic figure, set up as a figurehead because of his height and the spread of his shoulders, and evincing a desire of be[ing] king in more than name—a plain, straight-forward man, unversed in guile and subtlety, flanked and harassed by scheming priests, beleagered by savage and powerful enemies, handicapped by a people too wary and backward in war—what wonder that he went mad toward the end? He was not fitted to cope with the mysteries of king-craft, and he had too much proud independence to dance a puppet on the string of a high-priest—there he sealed his own doom . . .
>
> David was wiser than Saul and not so wise, caring less for the general good, much more for his own. He was the adventurer, the soldier of fortune, to the very end, whereas Saul had at least some of the instincts of true kingship in his soul. David knew that he must follow the lines laid out for him by the priests and he was willing to do so. A poet, yes, but intensely practical . . . (REH to H. P. Lovecraft, c. February 1931; CL 2.205-6)

Given his wide knowledge concerning religious doctrines and practice, Howard was well able to understand the power of passions and obsessions to move human beings. The religious mania of Solomon Kane is convincingly rendered. Howard's Bible studies stood him in good stead when he bestowed the Puritan adventurer's name upon him, "Solomon Kane" being evocative of both the biblical wise man Solomon and Cain, the first killer.

"Red Shadows" (*Weird Tales,* August 1928) is the first Solomon Kane story. Originally titled "Solomon Kane," it was the first in the series to be written and also the first to see publication. In many respects, it is the quintessential Solomon Kane tale because it encompasses a number of themes and ideas that are dealt with individually in other stories. The most notable of these are the character of Kane himself and the use of the continent of Africa as a setting. "Red Shadows" is an excellent introduction to the character. It also recounts Kane's first voyage to Africa, an area of the world that becomes a recurring setting for many of his exploits, eventually taking on a deeper and deeper symbolic significance.

In this respect, "Red Shadows" can be considered the "keystone" of the series, and the other stories can be placed, not just chronologically but thematically, either before or after this crucial turning point. Profound differences in Kane's character and temperament, as well as in the stories themselves, can be noted following this "maiden voyage." The tales taking place prior to this crucial story are more or less simple horror stories in the standard *Weird Tales* mold. Those occurring afterwards take on much more profound connotations.

The brief opening chapter of "Red Shadows" is entitled "The Coming of Solomon." In a few short paragraphs, Howard sets in motion the events that will ultimately alter Kane's universe forever. The incident that initiates Kane's rite of passage is one of the most famous scenes in Howard's fiction, yet in itself it gives no hint of the momentous changes it initiates; like many such moments, it seems an isolated event with no far-reaching significance. The story begins with Kane, traveling alone through the darkly wooded French countryside by night, discovering a young woman raped and left to die by a vicious local bandit called Le Loup. Howard tells us that Kane swears no oath of vengeance but promises coldly, "'Men shall die for this'" (32).

In the second segment, Kane slays Le Loup's gang of outlaws one by one and finally corners the bandit chief in his mountain hideout. A brief dialogue ensues, and Le Loup is revealed to be an interesting character in his own right. In fighting prowess and physical presence he is Kane's equal, and Howard imbues him with several intriguing characteristics that help define his personality. For example, we are told that "His keen face, despite lines of wild living and dissipation, was the face of a thinker" (33).

As the story progresses, we come to know Le Loup better in the same manner we come to know Kane. If Le Loup is a thinker, he has come to different conclusions about life than Solomon Kane. The Puritan calls himself a "'friend to all in need'" (31-32) and obviously believes in high spiritual standards. His choice of a lifestyle of physical hardship and fanaticism has caused him to sacrifice much for very little tangible gain. Le Loup has opted for sacrificing intangible values, which may not even exist in any real sense, in exchange for wanton self-gratification with no regard for any life other than his own.

On the one hand, it can be argued that Le Loup has a more realistic outlook than Kane, as it is based on real conditions and tangible rewards rather than spiritual abstractions. After all, what is more natural than for the strong to prey upon the weak? On the other hand, it can be argued that Kane represents a higher form of man; the most important thing in his life is his set of values—something that cannot be seen or felt, and something that no animal can have. As it turns out, neither these ideological questions nor the matter of superior fighting prowess is to be resolved in the first confrontation. Rather than engaging him in combat, Le Loup outwits Kane and escapes.

The first two chapters feature a number of trappings of Gothic fiction: a tall, mysterious stranger in black, a beleaguered young maiden, a sinister ravager, bandits, a cavern hideaway, dark forests and desolate mountains. The third chapter, however, begins with a jarringly abrupt change of setting. The location is no longer the forests of Europe, but the jungles of Africa. The opening paragraph describes the monotonous throbbing of jungle drums. Howard has taken his tale of evil and revenge to a stage more befitting the primal drama about to be enacted. Kane disembarks a ship that has borne him to the coast of Africa, having trailed Le Loup to the area. After instructing the ship's crew to wait seven days before setting sail, he strikes out into the night-black jungle, heading for the native village where his prey has taken refuge.

As the jungle enfolds Kane, the atmosphere becomes increasingly oppressive and hostile. The setting could not seem more alien if Kane had been transported to another world. The jungle becomes a force, a living entity, with the incessant drumming emanating from some unseen source as its voice. Howard's personification of the jungle is very similar to Conrad's portrayal of it in his masterpiece, "Heart of Darkness," yet Howard once stated that he had never read Conrad (REH to H. P. Lovecraft, c. December 1932; CL 2.575).

Though Kane is steeped in hardship and self-discipline, he is a novice to the uncompromising laws of the jungle. The path he traverses is not an easy one; the jungle itself actively seems to bar his way because it has not yet accepted him. But as Kane presses deeper into the forest, he moves into deeper levels of perception. The jungle drums seem to speak to him of "the gods men knew when dawns were young" (43), and a responsive chord in Kane's soul is struck. There is much the jungle would teach Kane, but the first listless stirrings of atrophied awareness are not sufficient to see him safely to his destination. He is struck down by a silent figure. He has not had time to develop a "feel" for the jungle that might have enabled him to sense the unseen, unheard danger. (In *Jungle Lore*, Jim Corbett termed such a faculty "jungle sensitiveness" [Wilson, *The Occult* 42].)

Kane awakens to the throbbing of the drums to find himself a prisoner in the native village. Here he meets a person who is to become an important influence on his life, a native ju-ju man called N'Longa. Kane learns from N'Longa that Le Loup has become blood brother to the tribe's chief, Songa, and is now the chief's second-in-command. N'Longa has fallen out of favor and his life is in jeopardy. He offers to assist Kane if the Puritan will kill Le Loup. The shaman feels an affinity toward Kane that Kane does not as yet share.

Kane is soon taken forth and bound to a stake before the "hideous and obscene" icon referred to only as "the Black God" (46). The tribe is gathered, and Kane faces Le Loup for the second time. Le Loup mocks Kane, and in their second exchange we learn of Kane's pursuit of the Frenchman across Europe to Africa, a chase that has encompassed years. Le Loup asks why Kane has pursued him so doggedly. Kane replies simply, "Because you are a rogue whom it is my destiny to kill" (48). Howard, however, offers us a glimpse into Kane's psyche and reveals the driving force behind Kane's iron will. The Puritan regards himself as a "vessel of wrath" (48) to be unleashed upon the unrighteous, and there can be no rest for him while his vengeance is unfulfilled.

Kane, in his turn, asks Le Loup why he fled, since he knows the bandit called "The Wolf" does not fear him. Le Loup expresses the belief that he could kill Kane in a fair fight but admits a troublesome disinclination for facing the stern Puritan. Also, Kane's pursuit has given a new sensation to a man who had thought he had exhausted all life's thrills. Le Loup, a dissipated, amoral man, is not capable of experiencing such higher human feelings as generosity and love. He has the capacity only for such primal lusts as that of the hunt, and Kane has given him a better thrill than many he has experienced. But although he is closer in spirit to the animal for which he is named than his fellow man, he is still human enough to brag. Le Loup boasts that he came alone to a tribe of savages and rose to a position of power among them. Here the story parallels "Heart of Darkness" once more. However, unlike Kurtz, Le Loup truly belongs in the jungle. Kane belongs there too, but in a different capacity.

At this point another character is introduced, a jungle equivalent of Le Loup—Gulka the gorilla-slayer. He is a native of the jungle, born and bred in its dark environs, and embodying the primordial power and savagery of the land. He is in league with Songa and Le Loup; it was he who struck down Kane in the forest. Gulka has recently slain a female gorilla and brought the carcass back to the village. This grisly trophy adorns one of the huts, and Le Loup points this out to Kane as evidence of Gulka's prowess.

Despite this, a penetrating gaze from the bound and helpless Kane cows Gulka, whose power is solely physical. Kane's true power derives from his intellect and force of will, which together comprise something more elemental than Gulka's physical prowess. Le Loup at no time fears Kane because he too is a thinking man and able to confront him on his own level.

Gulka vents his wrath on a defenseless tribesman, hurling him on the altar of the Black God and running him through with a spear. He brandishes the bloody spear before Kane to signify that he, too, will glut the Black God's appetite. N'Longa appears suddenly, but Gulka subdues him before he can do anything to aid Kane. The unconscious witch doctor is bound next to Kane.

Kane, at the mercy of his enemies, has lost his one ally. Yet in what are possibly the last moments of his life, his mind is overwhelmed by the stirrings of ancient racial memories of the drums, the smell of freshly spilt blood, and the howling of the orgiastic worshippers of the grim Black God. Kane is beginning to regard what transpires around him as somehow familiar, for the jungle has begun to creep into his soul. A number of Howard's writings deal with reincarnation and racial memory. Kane, like several other Howard characters, is an uncommonly sensitive human and is in touch with his deep unconscious.

As Kane's racial memories subside, N'Longa revives and sends his spirit forth to animate the corpse of the tribesman killed by Gulka. He then compels the walking dead man to kill Songa. In the ensuing pandemonium, the tribesmen turn on Songa's cohorts and side with N'Longa. Kane is freed even as Le Loup flees into the jungle.

Kane sets out after Le Loup and finds him waiting in a moonlit glade. Le Loup has finally chosen to face the Puritan. Their third and final confrontation begins, and it is one of the fiercest man-to-man struggles in Howard's writings. They duel and, fittingly enough for a Howard story, we learn more about the two men by the way they fight:

> Rapier clashed on rapier as the two swordsmen fought. They were fire and ice opposed. Le Loup fought wildly but craftily, leaving no openings, taking advantage of every opportunity. He was a living flame, bounding back, leaping in, feinting, thrusting, warding, striking—laughing like a wild man, taunting and cursing.
>
> Kane's skill was cold, calculating, scintillant. He made no waste movement, no motion not absolutely necessary. He seemed to devote more time and effort toward defense than did Le Loup, yet there was no hesitancy in his attack, and when he thrust, his blade shot out with the speed of a striking snake.
>
> There was little to choose between the men as to height, strength and reach. Le Loup was the swifter by a scant, flashing margin, but Kane's skill reached a finer point of perfection. The Wolf's fencing was fiery, dynamic, like the blast from a furnace. Kane was more steady—less the instinctive, more the thinking fighter, though he, too, was a born slayer, with the co-ordination that only a natural fighter possessed. (64)

Though the opponents are evenly matched, Kane gets the worst of the battle. After minutes of furious combat, Kane is bleeding from a score of wounds while Le Loup is untouched. But as Le Loup begins to tire, he notices that Kane does not seem to have weakened from the exertion and loss of blood; his attack is unrelenting. Kane, a man of high moral values who has chosen a path of hardship and self-discipline, is able to tap inner reserves of strength unavailable to Le Loup, the man who has only lived for gratification and thrills. In due course, Kane kills Le Loup.

The death of the bandit brings to an end a chase that has taken years of Kane's life, and Kane feels only a sense of futility. This would be easier to understand had his victory been an easy one, but such was not the case. Kane's inability to know satisfaction is the result of the magnitude of the task he has set for himself, for his task is to fight evil, not merely one evil man or any number of evil men. Kane is a fanatic who can never know inner peace while evil exists.

III. Solomon Kane

Le Loup's death and Kane's musings regarding it would seem a logical place to bring down the curtain. Had the story continued in the same vein in which it began, it would have ended here. Originally, Kane's pursuit of Le Loup was the central concern of his life. But since coming to Africa, other, deeper matters have begun to emerge. Kane has had glimpses into previously unknown corners of his mind. He has had glimpses of truths previously undreamed. He has even seen the total certainty of death itself cast into doubt. His once single-minded vendetta against Le Loup is no longer of singular importance. He has seen the all-pervading cosmic evil personified by Africa and her "Black God." Kane's odyssey is not ending; it is just beginning. As in life, events do not fall neatly into episodes. There is no pause in the narrative, no space for Kane to stop and catch his breath. New events rush in trampling over the old, and Le Loup is quickly forgotten.

Kane drops his sword and crosses to a nearby stream to cleanse his wounds. Unexpectedly, a figure steps out of the jungle. It is Gulka the gorilla-slayer, come to reaffirm his prowess by killing the only man ever to make him feel fear. Kane realizes instantly that he is doomed. He is weaponless, weak from loss of blood, and physically outmatched in any event. But this time, Kane is fated to be not an actor, but a witness.

As Kane stands awaiting certain death, another figure emerges from the jungle, an entity more primitive and savage than even Gulka. It is a huge gorilla, the mate of the female Gulka had slain earlier. As Kane experiences another surge of racial memories, the monster ape breaks every bone in Gulka's body.

Like Kane, the gorilla has slain a mortal foe, and like Kane, it feels dissatisfied. The ape grabs the mangled corpse of Gulka and hurls it into the branches of a tree. It then melts noiselessly into the jungle. Kane retrieves his rapier. He glances once at the body of Le Loup and once at the body of Gulka dangling in the tree.

The final encounter is very meaningful. Howard draws a striking parallel between Kane, a product of the highest civilization yet seen on earth, and a subhuman denizen of the primeval jungle. There is a basic similarity: both kill to avenge the death of a female. The gorilla avenges his mate. Kane, a member of a higher species, avenges someone he never knew, but who was weak and human and therefore fell under his protection. Kane's higher ideals lead him to the same action as the gorilla. To the reader, Kane's action is logical; crime is followed by punishment. Justice has been done. But, as indicated by Kane's sense of futility after killing Le Loup, justice is an emotional necessity, not a high-sounding platitude of a logical system of civilized ethics. The ape, who knows no civilization and could never even dimly conceive of ethics, feels the same basic urge as Kane. It is a lesson that contradicts both the formal education of his European Renaissance culture and the precepts of his Puritan subculture. The result of this contradiction is Kane's feeling of emptiness when he finally kills Le Loup. The gorilla, however, is not frustrated by the conflicting urges of civilization and is able to obtain satisfaction through a primitive display of wrath that only a civilized human being would or could consider futile.

"Red Shadows" is marked by a curious dreamlike quality. The forest and jungle that Kane traverses are both eerie dreamscapes, representative of the subconscious mind. In the throes of a dream, a dreamer will sometimes experience an abrupt change in setting or narrative. So it is in "Red Shadows" when the story shifts unexpectedly from Europe to Africa. The story opens with Kane passing through a dark forest by night; pages later he is feeling his way through a night-dark jungle, indicating a descent into a deeper level of the unconscious. Both settings are haunted by menacing figures. Le Loup and his jungle counterpart Gulka behave in the inexplicable manner of dream figures, confident in their physical prowess yet cowed by Kane's emotional intensity. Both the jungle drums and a grotesque idol seem to speak directly to Kane's mind. "Was he dreaming? Kane wondered as he hurried on" (61).

When Kane first heard the jungle speak to him, the muttering of the drums said, "let us teach you" (44). But the jungle demands a great price for her lessons. At the story's end, Kane reflects that Songa, Le Loup, and Gulka, "the three who had stood in power before the Black God that night" (70), have all been obliterated in a few hours. As in "Heart of Darkness," the soul of the jungle is evil. More specifically, it is capricious and cruel. In the case of Gulka and Kane, the jungle has claimed the life of a son who has lived close to her and spared an intruder. The drums whisper a parting message to Kane: "Flee if you would live, but never will you forget our chant" (72). The story's final line simply states, "Kane turned to the trail which led to the beach and the ship waiting there" (72). The "ship waiting there" has been symbolically transformed into a spiritual vessel that will take Kane away from all this. But the jungle drums have stated their truth boldly and in no uncertain terms. Kane will never be the same again.

In addition to "Red Shadows," there are fifteen other Solomon Kane writings, including poems and fragments. Of the nine finished stories, five are set in Africa and the others take place in England and Europe. Only the stories set in Africa can be set in definite chronological sequence, due to internal evidence. Chronological placement of the others is arbitrary.

Three of the "European" adventures—"Skulls in the Stars," "The Right Hand of Doom," and "Rattle of Bones"—are short supernatural vignettes in which Kane is witness to some occult manifestation. Kane himself takes an active role in only one of the three tales. Howard may have been attempting to gain a wider audience by utilizing stock Gothic devices such as castles and warlocks that would be familiar to *Weird Tales* readers, and by using the character Kane to link otherwise unconnected stories together. If so, his inspiration might have been Seabury Quinn's stories of the occult investigator Jules de Grandin.

The only other finished Solomon Kane story not set in Africa is a tale of some length entitled "The Blue Flame of Vengeance." The title itself is an intriguing one. Natural-gas flames burn blue, and may have been seen by Howard on the Texas oil fields. Natural gas is also the cleanest-burning flame, and therefore an interesting metaphor for vengeance. And here is another perspective, one that serves as the story's heading: "'*Death is a blue flame dancing over corpses.*'—Solomon Kane" (179). Did Kane actually see this blue flame? Is it something that came to him in a vision, or as an epiphany? It is a possibility worth considering, given the intensity of his religious fervor.

The story itself was never published in Howard's lifetime, and reads like a rough draft. Flaws in pacing and narrative give the story a kind of raw edge; Howard's energy and vigor are present but without the narrative restraint of afterthought. Since the tale lacks a supernatural element, it would not have found a home in Howard's mainstay, *Weird Tales*, yet no records survive of submission to more suitable publications like *Adventure* or *Argosy*.

The plot concerns Kane's battle with a vicious crew of pirates and his attempt to aid two young lovers. In it, Kane is featured prominently in his capacity as redresser of wrongs and protector of the oppressed. The point-of-view character is a hot-headed young Englishman named Jack Hollinster. The story opens with Jack dueling the arrogant wealthy aristocrat Sir George Banway over an insult to Jack's sweetheart, Mary. Jack draws first blood and a magistrate stops the duel. Unsatisfied, Jack storms angrily off. On a stretch of the desolate English coastline, he meets Solomon Kane. Kane has come in search of the pirate captain Jonas Hardraker, known as The Fishhawk. His goal is to avenge another ravaged maiden.

Later, Mary is kidnapped by Banway and Jack is lured into a trap. They are held prisoner in the vast cellars beneath Banway's estate. It turns out that Banway is in league with Hardraker; a secret tunnel leading to the beach enables him to receive the Fishhawk's plundered and smuggled goods. Kane appears and frees the young couple. While Jack covers the henchmen with Kane's pistols, Kane kills Hardraker in a grueling knife fight. After Jack is bested by Banway in an unfair duel, Kane kills the scheming aristocrat as well. The story ends with the grateful lovers asking what will become of Kane:

> A strange intangible, almost mystic look flashed into his cold eyes. "I come out of the sunset and into the sunrise I go, wherever the Lord doth guide my feet. I seek—my soul's salvation, mayhap. I came, following the trail of vengeance. Now I must leave you. The dawn is not far away and I would not have it find me idle ... My work here is done; the long red trail is ended. The man of blood is dead. But there are other men of blood, and other trails of revenge and retribution. I work the will of God. While evil flourishes and wrongs grow rank, while men are persecuted and women wronged, while weak things, human or animal, are maltreated, there is no rest for me beneath the skies, nor peace at any board or bed. Farewell!" (220-21)

Kane returns to Africa in "The Moon of Skulls" (*Weird Tales*, June and July 1930). The longest story of the series, "The Moon of Skulls" was probably written not long after "Red Shadows" and represents one of Howard's earliest attempts at a longer piece of fiction. It is possible that it was conceived as a novel, but Howard may have felt he could not sell a novel-length serial at that point in his career. It is unfortunate that Howard restricted the length of this story, as its potential is not fully realized. The pacing is headlong, but suffers from too many coincidences to advance the plot. The setting is an ancient lost city, but it is not sufficiently explored. But "The Moon of Skulls" has intriguing concepts, adept description, well-defined characterization, and a highly charged atmosphere to recommend it.

"The Moon of Skulls" takes place in a lost city in an unexplored region of Africa, a setting familiar to readers of H. Rider Haggard and Edgar Rice Burroughs. Kane comes in search of a young English woman, kidnapped and sold into slavery years before, whom he believes is held captive in the legendary lost city of Negari. Kane finds the city and enters through its catacombs. From a hidden vantage point he observes the fearsome black warriors who now people the city. He takes special note of the alluring black queen, Nakari. Kane realizes that she and her subjects are not members of the race that erected the city.

Moving on, Kane locates the object of his quest. The woman, Marylin Taferal, has been a slave in the city for years and had long since given up hope of being rescued. Marylin, whom Kane knew as a child, tells of her captivity and relates her impressions of the horror and evil that seem to permeate Negari. As Kane is about to devise a plan to sneak Marylin out of the city, they hear the approach of Queen Nakari. Kane conceals himself and watches as Nakari caresses Marylin, speaking cryptically of some special fate in store for her.

Nakari, beautiful ruler of a lost city in Africa, is, of course, the literary descendant of H. Rider Haggard's "She." Howard describes Nakari as barbaric, haughty, tigerish, and sensual, taking care to note that she goes about nude except for a few ornaments (114–15). Kane feels his pulse quicken and later breaks out in a sweat while watching Nakari. He regards her with both attraction and repulsion, and he equates her with the mythical figure of Lilith. Nakari is one of Howard's most compelling female characters. A strong sexual image, she tempts even Kane. Howard's writings abound in provocative women, often in the standard pulp capacity of damsel-in-distress, but just as often as strong-willed, fully realized characters, occasionally warriors or leaders of men. Nakari is perhaps Howard's most beguiling evil woman. She is selfish, sadistic, and cruel, with the short temper of a spoiled child, yet she is intelligent and perceptive enough to be fully aware of her power over the male.

III. Solomon Kane

Nakari's uncanny intuition alerts her to Kane's presence. She confronts him, but before Kane can subdue her Nakari triggers a trapdoor that Kane just happens to step onto. This is one of numerous coincidences Howard employs in this story for the sake of expediency, and it mars the effectiveness of the scenes that precede and follow it. When Kane regains consciousness after his plunge through the trapdoor, he is bound hand and foot and at the mercy of the queen, who personally interrogates him. Kane shows no fear, which impresses her. Nakari offers Kane her kingdom, herself, and a chance to share in her dreams of conquest, for she feels it is possible for her warriors to take over Africa tribe by tribe.

Here we learn more about Nakari's character and are also afforded a glimpse of a previously unexplored aspect of Kane's personality as well. The presumably celibate religious fanatic's life is devoted to administering God's justice, but in "The Moon of Skulls" we see Kane's faith tested. Like Eve, Nakari leads Kane to the brink of original sin. She floods his imagination with power fantasies, but she herself is the most tempting inducement. Nakari, a sexual stimulus not easily ignored, possesses an uncommon degree of guile and skillfully churns the waters of Kane's unconscious. It is only Kane's deep-seated sense of purpose and a vision of purity (Marylin Taferal) that enable him to resist her temptation. Like Le Loup, Nakari is used to getting what she wants. Unlike him, she is a woman and does not have to depend on mere physical force. She instinctively knows she has shaken Kane's faith and vows to try again.

After Kane eats and sleeps, two guards come to escort him to Nakari's throne room. There Nakari plans to bend Kane to her will amid the voluptuous and decadent trappings of her power. She knows that the austere setting of the dungeon will only serve to reinforce the resolve of the ascetic Kane, but the sight of Nakari naked, sprawled amid gaudy finery, may yet sway him. This is a temptation Kane does not choose to face. He escapes the guards and retreats once more into the catacombs.

At length, Kane discovers the last of the city's former rulers, imprisoned by Nakari. The dying prisoner tells Kane the history of Negari and warns that madness and an inhuman bloodlust flicker in the brains of the present inhabitants. He also reveals the significance of the "Moon of Skulls." Each full moon a virgin is sacrificed before the skull of Nakura, a long-dead wizard now worshipped as a god. An acolyte hides behind the skull and speaks in a voice the people believe is Nakura's. Before dying from the tortures inflicted on him, the prisoner tells Kane that Marylin, his vision of purity, is to be sacrificed that very night.

Kane makes his way to the site of the sacrifice. Discovering his pistol in the possession of one of the city's warriors, Kane wrests it from the savage and uses it to blow the skull of Nakura to pieces. The dying prisoner had told Kane that the worshippers' "'brains hinge on the skull of Nakura'" (161), and when the center of their lives is destroyed before their eyes, their latent insanity leaps into full being. Kane batters his way through the throng and frees Marylin. Nakari, now totally insane like her subjects, is killed as the people turn on one another in an orgy of slaughter. Kane and Marylin make good their escape from the city, even as a well-timed earthquake destroys Negari and all her people.

Solomon Kane's faith was tested in a deeper manner than even he suspected. What appeared to be a battle of wills between Kane and Nakari was in reality a battle of religious ideologies, for the people of Negari are ruled by their religion as Kane is by his.

Howard has made no pro-Christian statement, however. Rather, he writes of the toll that religious fanaticism can exact from humanity. Howard tended to be skeptical of organized religion. This is a trait he shared with Edgar Rice Burroughs, as expressed in such novels as *Tarzan Triumphant* and *The Gods of Mars*. Howard is known to have owned a copy of the latter. Evil priests appear in such Howard stories as "Marchers of Valhalla," "The Tower of the Elephant," and "Rogues in the House." Howard viewed various religions as seats of dogmatic intolerance, tools of the powerful to control and oppress others. He remarked:

> Look at history: the pagans in Rome oppressed the early Christians. The Christians got control and began to maltreat the weaker sects. The Catholics in England oppressed the Church of England, then they got the upper hand and oppressed the Catholics, Presbyterians and Puritans, who fled to America and oppressed the Quakers who would have oppressed anyone who might have been weaker than they. (REH to Harold Preece, postmarked 4 January 1930; CL 2.3)

The religion of Nakura is blasphemous and loathsome, a pagan orgy of bloodlust. Yet it is from roots of superstition and witchery, not unlike those present in the cult of Nakura, that all religions spring, and even "enlightened" religions like Christianity bear this taint. Kane himself carries scars from both the Spanish Inquisition and "Moslem whips" (327). In "The Moon of Skulls," he reflects that Europe is torn by religious strife that may allow Nakari, as priestess-queen of a unified theocracy of savages, to forge a worldwide empire.

One might think that Kane, confronted with a fanaticism that exceeds his own, could not help but come away seeing his religion in a new perspective. However in a short epilogue to the story entitled "The Faith of Solomon," we see this is not so.

On the morning following the destruction of Negari, Marylin awakens in the jungle under the protection of Kane. As the memories of the evil city fall away from her like a bad dream, she expresses concern for their situation, as they are stranded and defenseless in the heart of the African jungle. Kane chides Marylin for her lack of faith in both Providence and himself. He speaks of "'a Power'" (168) that guided his footsteps and quotes passages from Chapters 24, 25, and 29 of Isaiah. These passages tell of a city wiped out in an instant and of a sinful people drunken, but not with wine. The "Power" Kane speaks of is not only the power of God, but also the power of Kane's faith. Strictly speaking, Kane is more a Puritan than a Christian. Nowhere does he speak of Jesus; Kane is a stern Old Testament man. As such, he believes that he became the vessel of God's wrath and that his hand brought about the fulfillment of the prophecies of Isaiah. What gave Kane the privilege of working God's will was his faith.

Faith is indeed a mighty power. Faith guided Kane across half a world directly to the object of his quest; it enabled him, in other words, to do the impossible. But what one has faith in is irrelevant; faith is a power unto itself, a palpable force in the universe. Just as Kane's faith in his God empowered him to perform a seeming miracle, the faith of the people of Negari gave them direction and a sense of purpose. Kane wondered by what method they preserved the skull of Nakura from decay. It was, one is led to assume, a thousand generations of faith that preserved the skull. The psychic emanations of countless worshippers over the centuries that were directed at it permeated it, just as they seeped into and saturated the material substance of the stones of the city itself. When the focal point was shattered, the very walls of Negari fell.

Kane, a single human being, carried within him a faith mightier than that of a whole people. And passing through this ordeal, Kane comes away with his faith stronger than ever. At the end of "The Moon of Skulls," Kane believes in his heart that he is now God's hand moving upon the earth. Filled with this energy and knowledge, he is ready to continue his spiritual journey.

"The Moon of Skulls," with its apocalyptic visions, is a provocative tale. It is especially so due to the juxtaposition of pious spirituality with outrageous sensuality. Particularly memorable is the image of a Bible-quoting English Puritan chained in helpless bondage in a dungeon where he is mocked and teased by a bare-breasted black temptress. Also memorable are scenes of the blonde English slave kneeling before her black mistress, or being subjected to her lascivious caresses, or the descriptions of the blonde being whipped by the black woman.

This mixture of ingredients makes "The Moon of Skulls" a heady witch's brew. Unfortunately, its effect was blunted for many readers when they first encountered the tale. The Solomon Kane stories were first collected for book publication in the late 1960s. Regrettably, the texts were carefully bowdlerized by the publisher to eliminate "offensive" racial references. Even the fact that Nakari was a black woman was deliberately obscured. Doubtless many readers simply assumed that Nakari was white like La of Opar, the queen of a lost African city in Edgar Rice Burroughs's Tarzan novels. The relationship of Kane and Nakari remained intriguing, but lacked the additional edge of racial tension the author had honed. To make matters worse, these corrupted texts formed the basis of subsequent hardcover and paperback editions. Only in recent editions have the stories been painstakingly restored to their original versions.

The next stage of Solomon Kane's spiritual odyssey begins in "The Hills of the Dead" (*Weird Tales*, August 1930). In the opening chapter, Kane and the conjure-man N'Longa hold "'blood-palaver'" (225) in N'Longa's hut, and Kane admits that the jungle has indeed crept into his soul. He intends to explore the unknown heart of Africa and confront whatever mysteries await him there. N'Longa presents Kane with a long black staff, one end pointed and the other carved in the shape of a cat's head, and tells him that it is a voodoo stave to be used against such supernatural menaces as Kane might encounter. Kane does not feel comfortable accepting a pagan artifact, especially one connected with voodoo and black magic, but does not wish to offend N'Longa. He justifies carrying it by noting that it would make a good weapon. It proves to be a more potent weapon than Kane realizes, and he uses it with telling effect when he and N'Longa battle a tribe of vampires.

The relationship of Kane and N'Longa is curious and complex. What began as a temporary alliance of convenience against common foes evolves into a bizarre friendship and something more. Kane, a Puritan who abhors witchcraft, seeks out this strange voodoo fetish-man who can animate corpses and commune with the spirits of the jungle. Kane senses that he needs a guide on the Dark Continent. As for N'Longa, perhaps he sees in Kane a kindred soul, a man of great spiritual power who has not yet learned to control it. N'Longa may be the only man in the world that Kane can truly call a friend. However, he does not reappear in the series, and Kane moves on into the heart of darkest Africa alone.

Solomon Kane encounters the Dark Continent's most obscene horror in "Wings in the Night" (*Weird Tales,* July 1932). Unlike "The Moon of Skulls," "Wings in the Night" is not flawed in any way; it is a meticulously crafted tale with superbly wrought narrative description, excellent characterization, and unrelenting emotional intensity. As with all the best of Howard's prose, the reader is mesmerized and ceases to be a mere spectator by the story's close. Few modern writers can elicit such a degree of reader participation. "Wings in the Night" is considered by many to be the finest Solomon Kane story, and indeed only "Red Shadows" can be said to equal it.

Though Kane confronts his most terrifying foe in "Wings in the Night," he does so without assistance. The voodoo staff of N'Longa is useless, for his enemy is not a supernatural one, and this time it seems that even Kane's God has turned his back on him. This conflict rests on the shoulders of man, with Kane the representative of all men. How he fares demonstrates how triumph can emerge from tragedy and suggests how, in the darkest reaches of prehistory, man, with his puny monkey-like hands, prevailed over a hostile world filled with monstrous beasts armed with fang and talon.

Kane has never been more ready for the test that awaits him. As

III. Solomon Kane

the story opens, we learn that he has been in Africa for some time and is no longer a novice. His extended travels across jungle and savanna have hardened him. Now deep in the bowels of Africa where no white man has previously set foot, Kane comes across a village whose inhabitants have all been massacred. He is mystified because, though the bleaching bones of the victims surround him, the village has not been looted. Kane notices that many of the roofs of the huts have been torn open. Pressing on, he finds a man bound to a stake as a human sacrifice. Mutilated almost beyond recognition, the native quickly expires. Kane swears vengeance against whomever is responsible for the atrocity.

Kane explores the region further and the following day is attacked by a flying monster. He shoots it with his flintlock and examines the corpse. The creature is a tall manlike being with talons on hands and feet, narrow yellow eyes, and large leathery wings. Howard describes it in considerable detail, noting that it is economically constructed of light bone and spare, stringy muscle. This description is not only vivid but also plausible. If such avian hominids existed, it would seem to most intelligent laymen that they would be formed in much the manner described by Howard. Howard took great pains to present these beings as natural creatures, a product of natural selection and evolution, albeit a strange and twisted branch.

As Kane examines the dead creature, another attacks and Kane is borne aloft by it. Kane struggles, stabbing the monster to death, and they plummet into the trees below. Kane survives but suffers great injury. He recovers consciousness days later to learn that he has been taken to another village by a group of natives who witnessed his struggle with the winged man. They have tended his wounds and brought back his weapons and ju-ju stave. He meets the chief and the priest of the tribe. The latter is the man who bound the sacrifice to the stake. However, he proves to be not the sadistic fiend Kane expected, but rather a conscience-stricken man who was forced into a compromising situation.

As Kane mends, he learns the history of his rescuers and the story of their present circumstances. The Bogondi were once a powerful tribe, but tribal wars broke their power and they were forced to flee. They traveled a thousand miles and built two villages, one being the village Kane found destroyed. For a while they lived in safety but soon learned of the horror that inhabited the region. The winged creatures, called "akaanas," soon overcame their fear of the settlers and began to steal children by night. Growing bolder, they appeared by day, eventually learning they could slay the humans.

Attempts by the Bogondi to invade and wipe out the akaanas resulted in the loss of many men, as did endeavors to flee the country through the tribes of cannibals in adjacent regions. The akaanas do not wish to wipe out the Bogondi. There is plenty of small game to sustain both the Bogondi and the akaanas, and the akaanas allow the humans to inhabit the region for their amusement, just as human beings stock lakes with fish and allow wild game to thrive. The priest, Goru, tells Kane that the akaanas have a sadistic sense of humor that delights in human suffering, and hideous laughter accompanies their appearances.

The Bogondi have endured this hellish existence for over a century, and in that time the numbers of akaanas have dwindled; no females have been seen for many years. The akaanas had been content with an occasional victim for their sport, but famine and drought have diminished the food supply. The akaanas began to feed on the people. When the lower village tried to resist, the akaanas wiped out the inhabitants. The remaining village staved off similar destruction by casting lots to choose a monthly sacrifice in the manner of the cannibals.

Kane is outraged and saddened to hear how man, the only animal to which God gave a soul, is reduced to the level of mere livestock. When Goru tells Kane that the akaanas have always inhabited the region, Kane recalls one of the many native legends he has heard in the course of his wanderings in Africa. According to the legend, a flock of "winged devils" who dwelt on a "great lake" far to the north was driven away by a great chief, N'Yasunna (303).

Kane is chilled by the sudden realization that this was a garbled version of the myth of Jason and the harpies. He wonders what grim realities might underlie the other bizarre legends of antiquity and reflects that Africa is truly the "land of shadows and horror . . . into which all evil things had been banished before the growing light of the western world!" (304). Goru pleads with Kane to save his people, but Kane replies that he is only one man and can do little to end the scourge of the akaanas. However, since both the akaanas and the cannibals fear Kane, he agrees to stay in Bogonda for the rest of his life.

Avian hominids appear in several of Howard's major works. In each case they are physically tailored along similar lines, but the similarity does not end there. Psychologically, they are portrayed in a nearly identical manner. Whenever Howard uses them, winged men are cast as cruel, vicious creatures lacking compassion and mercy. Howard's physical description of the akaana was thought out logically before he set it down. He realized that, like birds, they would need to be light, hence hollow bones, and that they would possess strong shoulder and breast muscles. However, such details would occur to even a competent pulp writer; it is in Howard's rendering of the psychological makeup of these creatures that his genius is apparent.

When the first humanlike creatures stopped scurrying on all fours and rose on their hind legs, they entered a new world. Apart from freeing their hands from the burden of locomotion, the ape-creatures gained another advantage in the struggle for survival: their field of vision was dramatically increased. Early human beings could see their enemies because their eyes were set higher than the tallest grass. Their sense of smell withered, their eyesight became sharper, they began to perceive colors, and the world took on new meaning.

Predators seemed less formidable because human beings could look down on them. If raising their level of perception by raising their eyes those few feet made such a difference in human beings' consciousness, how might this view be different if they had learned to fly?

Howard speculates, in this and other stories, on how such flying creatures would behave. The akaanas possess human or near-human intelligence, but have no tools or fire because they have no need for them. They need no weapons because they can simply fly away from any foe. Nor would they ever need fire for warmth, for they can migrate far faster and much more easily than any earth-bound thing. Avian hominids would have no need of developing even the simplest tools or the most rudimentary culture. How could they reach the point of developing civilization or higher spiritual values?

If Kane regards evil as the absence of good (the medieval viewpoint) rather than the other way around (that good is merely the absence of evil, our modern viewpoint), then he must regard the akaanas as an abominable evil, not only because of their deeds, but also because they are incapable of developing any sort of spiritual values despite their human intelligence. They are like human beings without souls. Moreover, their utter lack of concern for other living things seems inevitable given their point of view. When atop a tall building, people often casually remark that those below seem insignificant. Usually this insight soon fades, for only the wealthiest can afford to reside permanently in penthouses high above the masses. Humanity achieved flight in airplanes due to its cleverness as a toolmaker; it was not a natural birthright. For most of history, earth-bound humans regarded flight as something for superior beings, such as angels. However, to winged hominids like the akaanas, the pathetic creatures below would be fodder and nothing more.

That the akaanas do in fact possess human intelligence is not a conjecture, for Goru tells Kane that they speak a crude sort of language and acknowledge a leader among them. The single most telling piece of evidence for their intelligence, however, is that they laugh. A sense of humor denotes an ability to perceive irony and experience enjoyment. It has also been asserted that laughter is a survival mechanism, one of the methods human beings use to feel superior to their fellows. There is nothing inherently malicious in laughter of this sort, but a person who laughs at danger (as a psychological defense mechanism) differs from one who laughs while endangering others. In writing of the akaanas' cruel mirth, Howard may have been thinking more of the ridicule of childhood peers than the innocent laughter of childhood bliss. The concept of laughter as a cruel barb is a keynote of the chapter entitled "The Madness of Solomon."

This chapter begins as the ominous storm that has been gathering breaks. The Bogondi, confident that Kane's presence will protect them, have discontinued the monthly human sacrifice. One night Kane awakens in his hut to the sound of screams; the akaanas are attacking the village and destroying it. Kane races out into a scene of nightmarish horror. All about him the people under his protection are perishing in helpless agony. Men, women, and children are rent limb from limb under the talons of the akaanas. Kane is, as he knew he would be, powerless to stop the wholesale slaughter. Kane manages to slay several akaanas, as do some of the villagers before meeting their fate. But the odds are hopelessly against them. Avoiding Kane because of his ferocity and ability to deal death, the akaanas kill every last Bogondi.

The sequence is perhaps the bloodiest, most brutal Howard ever wrote. Howard is known for the violence of his stories, and sometimes the violence is romanticized. But in this story Howard did not intend for the reader to feel the bracing sting of battle or know the thrill of vanquishing a mortal foe in hand-to-hand combat. In marked contrast to the stories in which the reader is permitted to identify with a self-sufficient hero mastering a violent world, Howard now induces in the reader a gut-wrenching, sickening feeling of utter nakedness and helplessness before a malicious, pitiless oppressor.

Kane is unable to do anything to in any way alleviate the greatest moral outrage he has ever felt, an outrage compared to which Le Loup is a sadistic, bullying schoolboy. And in the face of such spirit-crushing futility, Kane goes mad. In all the stories, Kane is portrayed as a fanatic, an obsessive neurotic. Several times Howard refers to him as "paranoid," a man unable to accept the world on its own terms, ever seeking to impose his terms on the world.

In "Wings in the Night," Kane meets a reality that supersedes even his fanatical will to power, and he pays a heavy toll. Kane now experiences the foundations of his own belief crumbling like the walls of Negari, and he becomes a screaming madman. One of Howard's most important themes is humanity's struggle against that which is most horrible, evil, and destructive in the universe. Usually his heroes stand tall in a world in which evil forces surround them and seem to seek them out. Now, Kane's mind has been shattered by his inability to keep the forces of evil at bay, and Howard, never one to rely on subtlety to get his message across, likens his predicament to that of humanity:

> [Kane] threw back his head to shriek his hate at the fiends above him and he felt warm, thick drops fall into his face, while the shadowy skies were filled with screams of agony and the laughter of monsters. And Kane's last vestige of reason snapped as the sounds of that ghastly feast in the skies filled the night and the blood that rained from the stars fell into his face. He gibbered to and fro, screaming chaotic blasphemies.
> And was he not a symbol of Man, staggering among the tooth-marked bones and severed grinning heads of humans, brandishing a futile ax, and screaming incoherent hate at the grisly, winged shapes of Night that make him their prey, chuckling in demonic triumph above him and dripping into his mad eyes the pitiful blood of their human victims? (312)

This is a statement of almost Lovecraftian pessimism, but it is not Howard's last word on the matter. The final chapter of "Wings in the

Night" is titled "The White-Skinned Conqueror." The people Kane swore to devote his life to protecting are all dead; how, then, can Kane conquer? Clearly it will take potent medicine to restore Kane to his former self. For a man whose every breath was breathed for justice, only an act of cosmic—or divine—justice will redeem him.

In the days and weeks following the massacre, Kane works unceasingly, without heed of physical necessities such as food and sleep. Ignoring the needs of his body, he moves like an automaton, guided through the feverish haze of insanity by one clearly perceived mandate—revenge. When Bran Mak Morn failed his subject in "Worms of the Earth," he had to avenge him. Kane, having failed the Bogondi, must avenge them. Bran suffered damnation for seeking vengeance, but he consorted with monsters to avenge himself on his fellow man. Kane seeks to destroy monsters to avenge his fellow man.

Kane reinforces the walls and ceiling of the depopulated village's largest structure, once a meeting place. He transforms it into a trap for the akaanas, and when they become hungry and unable to find food, he baits it with the carcass of a buffalo and throws handfuls of blood into the air to summon the akaanas. They approach the trap warily, but driven by hunger they enter it. Kane seals his trap and sets fire to it, destroying the last remnants of an entire species and gaining his revenge.

What is the relationship between justice and vengeance? This is the question that Howard now ponders. Perhaps it is more important to punish the wrongdoer than to compensate the victim. The destruction of evil is a compensation, not only for the victim, but for all humanity. At the end of "Wings in the Night," the Bogondi are all dead, but they are just members of the human family. Humanity lives. The akaanas are extinct. In causing their extinction, Kane is flooded with the light of God as sanity returns. Indeed, he has functioned in the capacity of God in wiping out a form of life, chopping off a branch of the tree of evolution. This is the act of cosmic or divine justice through which Kane reconstructs his sense of rightness and order and regains his sanity.

"The Footfalls Within" (*Weird Tales*, September 1931) is the final Solomon Kane story. It is a brief tale, lacking the punch of "Wings in the Night." However, its metaphysical menace constitutes a fitting final foe for Kane, and the mystical revelations that come to Kane form an appropriate climax to his spiritual journey.

In "The Footfalls Within," Kane is once again in a part of Africa that is open to intrusion by invaders from other continents; he has either crossed the continent or made a gigantic circle through it in the course of his wanderings. The story begins with Kane's discovery of Arab slavers driving the native captives in chains before them. His moral outrage is increased by a personal vendetta, for Kane was once a prisoner in a Turkish galley and he bears the scars of Muslim whips.

Kane has undergone a change of character, due no doubt to the horror he was witness to in the previous story, and is no longer quite the steely-nerved duelist of old. Remaining hidden while awaiting the opportunity to free the slaves, Kane can hardly bear to watch as a woman is whipped. When one of the Arabs prepares to flay her alive, Kane draws a pistol and shoots him dead before he can stop himself. His presence revealed, Kane is taken prisoner after a fierce battle.

The Puritan is bound and interrogated by his captors. He is known to the Arabs, having gained a reputation in wars against the Turks. The slavers' leader, Hassim, appropriates Kane's weapons, except for the ju-ju stave given to him by N'Longa. Another Arab, a scholar named Yussef, takes an interest in the stave and questions Kane about it, but Kane admits he knows nothing of its origin. Yussef shows the stave to Hassim, and we are told its true history, heretofore an enigma. Yussef recognizes it as an ancient artifact, which was mentioned by the prophet Mohammed himself. Yussef makes the astounding revelation that Kane's staff is the very one that Moses set before Pharaoh. He adds that it was later carried by King Solomon and used by the biblical wise man to battle evil. Hassim is a narrow, materialistic, and mercenary man whose only interest in Kane is the price he will bring from his old Turkish foes, and he regards the staff with disdain. Yussef prophetically warns that Hassim will one day meet a power that will not fall before his sword or bullets.

Sometime later the slave train is still winding its way through the jungle, and Yussef and Hassim are still arguing about Kane, the staff, and matters of religious faith. As they bicker, Yussef mentions the fact that the trail they follow was once trod by Solomon, who drove the demons of Asia before him and pent them in strange prisons. Suddenly a shout interrupts them. One of the Arabs, sent to scout ahead, has discovered a bizarre mausoleum-like building, and the sight of it filled him with such horror that he bolted in fear. Hassim insists that they investigate the strange building before proceeding further. Moments later they come upon a clearing, devoid of vegetation as if blighted in some manner, in which sits an ancient crypt. All who behold it feel fear, but Kane, sensitive to such things, is aware of the presence of some unseen horror.

Hassim alone is unaffected by the sight. His perception is so distorted by his narrow-minded materialism and greed that he fails to notice the blasted earth and other unusual physical evidence around him, let alone the uncanny emanations from the area. Kane, in contrast, possesses the faculty to detect an unseen, immaterial presence. As Hassim orders the mausoleum broken into so that he might plunder the "'riches'" inside, Kane seems to hear the heavy sound of *"footfalls within"* (340).

The Arabs give no sign of hearing anything, and Kane is not sure of the origin of the sounds, unable to discern if he perceives them with his hearing or with some sixth sense. Kane's entreaties to leave the tomb alone fall on deaf ears. The doors are broken in and an amorphous horror billows forth. It engulfs Hassim and, true to

Yussef's warning, his physical weapons are useless against the "Thing." He dies horribly.

Hassim has paid the price for his pettiness. Howard's lesson is very clear. It is not enough to perceive the universe through the five physical senses, for one perceives only a fraction of the totality of being. It should be common sense that there is more to life than what one can see and touch. Nevertheless, most of humanity, like Hassim, choose to stumble through life in a narrow, robotic state of mind, avoiding physical pain and pursuing physical comforts and pleasures like an ass following a carrot on a stick. The artist, the scholar, the man of imagination, the visionary know instinctively that there is some higher goal for humanity than a Pavlovian reaction to external stimulus. They choose to pursue such will-o'-the-wisps as knowledge, wisdom, and meaning. Solomon Kane is a fictional counterpart of such men.

As Kane witnesses Hassim's gory death, he exerts seemingly superhuman strength and snaps his bonds. Snatching up his ju-ju stave from where it has fallen, he faces the Thing. His struggle is waged on several different levels simultaneously, for as Kane physically assails the Thing with his staff he feels his mind and spirit engaged in combat on another plane. The battle takes but an instant, and Kane is victorious. He realizes that King Solomon used the staff he now carries to imprison the Thing centuries earlier and wonders why his predecessor did not destroy the horror. That Kane is able to slay what King Solomon could only imprison is a testament to his true spiritual stature. He has indeed come a long way since we first met him.

Standing over the remains of the horror, other revelations are borne upon Kane. He is smitten with the awareness that the world teems with unguessed life, just as rot and decay spawns maggots, and that man is merely the "dominant maggot" (344) at present. These reflections are not those of the once-devout Puritan. They would be considered heresy by any believing Christian. Has Kane come all this way only to lose the faith that first set him on his path to awareness?

Kane contemplates the staff given to him by N'Longa, realizing finally that it is no mere voodoo artifact, but a weapon to be used by the good to combat evil. In "The Hills of the Dead," he looked upon N'Longa's gift with abhorrence and felt that he risked his immortal soul simply by carrying it. Then he almost threw it away, but now he realizes the truth about it. The reverence Kane feels toward the staff is evidence of faith unrestricted by dogma, a faith Kane has always carried within him, for he was always a protector and when need be an avenger. Whereas before he could only interpret good and evil through the precepts of Puritan rhetoric, Kane can now embrace a higher, universal form of religion.

Each evil that Kane has faced prepared him for the evil that he met in "The Footfalls Within." Kane confronted a corrupt man, a corrupt woman, a degenerate anti-life religious cult, a purely physical threat, and finally a purely spiritual one. In the concluding episode of his saga, Kane destroys an evil that the biblical Solomon could not. Kane, a red-handed slayer, fanatic, and landless wanderer, has attained greater spiritual power than the wisest man of the ancient world.

Although Kane has reached the conclusion of his spiritual journey, he remains the restless wanderer, pressing ever onwards. Howard has provided Kane's saga with a fitting epilogue; not a story, but a poem entitled "Solomon Kane's Homecoming" in which Kane, after many years away, returns to the English village where he was born. In a tavern in Devon, he tells of his days on the high seas and of his travels in Africa. He states that he intends to live out his remaining years in Devon, but when the ocean's roar reaches his ears, Solomon Kane sets forth again "and no man knew his road" (ST 383).

IV. King Kull

In August 1929, one year to the month after the publication of "Red Shadows," another Howard story with a similar title appeared in *Weird Tales*. This story, "The Shadow Kingdom," was Howard's eleventh story to be published in "The Unique Magazine," and it introduced another of his heroes, King Kull of Valusia.

With the publication of "The Shadow Kingdom," Robert E. Howard inaugurated a new subgenre of fantasy fiction. Today this now-common genre is referred to by several descriptive terms, the most common being that coined by Fritz Leiber: "sword and sorcery." Many "sword and sorcery" stories have been written since 1929, and most proceed along these lines: a brawny hero, living in some exotic imaginary era (the forgotten past, the distant future, or some other planet), finds himself pitted against powerful magics to gain a treasure, crown, and/or woman.

As with any genre, such stories are only as good as the author makes them. The entertainment potential of "sword and sorcery" is unparalleled due to the mingling of various elements of horror, fantasy, and adventure. While mediocre formula writers grind out lurid orgies of sex and violence, superior talents offer enthralling spectacles of unbridled imagination. In writing "The Shadow Kingdom," the other Kull and the later Conan stories, Howard laid the ground rules

---

All stories discussed in this chapter appear in *K*.

for this type of story.

There exists a controversy as to whether or not Howard deserves to be acknowledged as the creator of this genre. It has been pointed out that the various plot elements were present in the Eddas and Sagas of the Scandinavians, the epics of Homer, and far older works, such as *Gilgamesh*. Moreover, in modern times, fantasy literature had its beginnings in the nineteenth and early twentieth centuries with the works of William Morris and Lord Dunsany. Because Howard, in tales such as "The Shadow Kingdom," employs elements of both the epics and the works of these earlier fantasists, the term "epic fantasy" has also been applied to the writings of Howard and his imitators.

However, the epics were originally part of an oral tradition and, when finally set down, were recorded in verse, lengthy poems only distantly related to modern literary traditions. The term "heroic fantasy" has been used more frequently and emphasizes one of the key elements of such fiction lacking in its nineteenth-century forerunners; the central position of a protagonist of truly heroic stature.

Perhaps a more precise term would be "modern heroic fantasy." Howard did not invent the epic saga, but rather re-invented it. He took the oldest type of story—the tale of heroes, gods, and monsters—and reworked the essential elements to create jolting pulp fiction. Howard also eschewed the refined trappings of nineteenth-century British fantasy, which is actually a more direct predecessor to the popular works of J. R. R. Tolkien. Howard was writing for working class Americans of the early twentieth century. His prose has a sharper edge, and conveys an earthier, and at times bawdier, attitude.

Howard used modern narrative prose (as well as embodying modern ideas and attitudes in his tales) to tell of a heroic larger-than-life figure in a fantasy world. Modern heroic fantasy (or "sword and sorcery") may be derivative to some extent, but Howard's fusion of the various elements was unique. The Solomon Kane stories are regarded as "sword and sorcery," and in a sense they are. Still, "The Shadow

Kingdom" is the first story in which *all* the elements of modern heroic fantasy are present.

Moreover, "The Shadow Kingdom" was composed well before "Red Shadows." Howard began work on the first draft of the story in the fall of 1926. Its composition was a series of false starts by the then-inexperienced writer. Howard completed the story only by the following summer, then put it aside before revising it. He devoted considerable time, thought, and effort to this groundbreaking, genre-defining story. The final draft was submitted to *Weird Tales* in September 1927 and accepted for publication in October. "The Shadow Kingdom" then languished in the editorial offices of *Weird Tales* for almost two years before finally appearing in its pages.

In addition to being the first "sword and sorcery" tale, "The Shadow Kingdom" remains one of the finest ever written and is one of Howard's best stories. In it, we meet Kull—exile of Atlantis, warrior-king of Valusia, barbarian usurper to the throne of a mighty empire, feral child. A black-haired, gray-eyed, mighty-thewed hero in the Howard mold who rules a formidable empire that was old when Atlantis was young, Kull sits unsteadily on the throne. He is unsophisticated, at times confused, and lonely in his role as emperor of a hostile people.

Kull differs from the earlier characters Bran Mak Morn and Solomon Kane in the sense that he was put on paper the minute Howard conceived him. This was not in "The Shadow Kingdom" but, according to Howard, a brief tale that was never accepted for publication. Howard was undoubtedly referring to the story published posthumously as "Exile of Atlantis." In it, Kull's early life prior to kingship is detailed.

Kull began life as a feral child living in the forest with the wolves and tigers and possessing no knowledge of the language of men. Adopted by the Sea-mountain tribe of Atlantis, he grew to be a mighty warrior, though he frequently challenged the traditions of the tribe to its elders' dismay.

In this story, the only episode of the Kull cycle set in Atlantis and taking place prior to all the other tales, Howard presents us with his unique version of the fabled lost continent. In popular fiction, as well as the theories of pseudo-scientific cranks, Atlantis is invariably envisioned as the pinnacle of pre-industrial civilization and the fountainhead of all science and culture. Howard's Atlantis, on the other hand, is a barbaric aggregate of quarreling tribes of backward savages who hunt, fish, and make war, but do not build or cultivate. This picture of Atlantis is unfamiliar but, in view of the author's belief that barbarism is humanity's natural state, not surprising.

In "Exile of Atlantis," the young Kull discovers his tribe preparing to burn a woman alive at the stake for marrying a hereditary enemy of the Atlanteans. Kull is moved by her plight but unable to save her. Instead, he provides the comfort of a quick death by hurling his dagger into her heart. The brief tale ends with Kull fleeing the wrath of his fellow tribesmen; his act of mercy has cost him his home and adopted heritage. In other stories, we learn that shortly afterwards he was captured by pirates and languished as a galley slave for two years. Escaping to Valusia, Kull subsequently becomes outlaw, gladiator, mercenary, general, and finally king.

Each stage of Kull's life is a step toward civilization. From naked feral child wandering in the forest, he progresses to barbarism. Encountering civilization, Kull moves through its ranks until he occupies its highest seat. His physical prowess and force of will enable him to meet and overcome every new challenge until none remain. King Kull is a barbarian warrior who sits upon the throne of a kingdom whose people are ancient, decadent, and a mystery to him. This troubled ruler is the hero Howard presented to his readers in "The Shadow Kingdom."

"The Shadow Kingdom" begins with Kull reviewing a parade of the mighty army he now commands. More warrior than king, he finds more satisfaction in commanding the legions than in holding court. Riding with his commanders through the capital city, Kull evokes varied reactions from his subjects. Many love and respect him for liberating them from tyranny and bringing them peace and prosperity, but others cannot forget that he is a pagan barbarian and a foreign usurper.

Back in his council chambers, Kull routinely attends to his courtly duties, then dismisses his retinue. His boredom with the banalities of civil rule is soon to be shattered, for an attendant announces the arrival of an emissary from the Picts. In the Kull cycle, the Picts appear as a semi-barbaric race inhabiting islands on the fringes of the civilized world. Blood-enemies of the Atlanteans, the Picts are also longtime allies of Valusia. Both these facts are in the back of Kull's mind as the Pictish emissary enters. The Pict brings an invitation from Ka-nu, ambassador of the Pictish Isles, who wishes to meet with Kull away from the palace. The emissary instructs Kull to come alone, and Kull regards him with distrust. Kull is a man to whom the blood-feuds of his tribal heritage, now lost to him, are more real than the role of king he now plays.

In the second chapter, Kull accepts the invitation of Ka-nu and finds the aged Pict to be an extraordinary statesman. Long association with civilized men has wiped the old tribal hatreds from Ka-nu's heart. Once alone with Kull, Ka-nu gains his trust and reveals that he has learned of a plot against the king's life, the details of which he withholds. His parting instructions are for Kull to trust Brule the Spear-Slayer, who will come to Kull on the morrow.

A strange mood possesses Kull as he returns to the palace. Doubts and eerie forebodings wrack his brain. The all-pervading antiquity of Valusia oppresses him, making him feel small, insignificant, and unequal to the role of king. The meeting with Ka-nu is a pivotal one for Kull, for it will present him with a new challenge and a new foe to overcome, a foe far deadlier than any previously encountered.

The next night, Kull is visited secretly in his private chambers by Brule the Spear-Slayer, who turns out to be the Pictish emissary he met earlier. Before Kull can speak, Brule utters a strange phrase; "'Ka nama kaa lajerama!'" (27). Kull is puzzled, then shaken, for though he has never heard the phrase spoken, somehow the sound of it has touched a chord in his mind. Brule does not explain the meaning of the cryptic phrase but notes the king's reaction to it. Taking Kull through secret passages and panels in the palace of which the king is unaware, Brule shows him the bodies of a number of Red Slayers, the king's personal host. He reveals that Red Slayers identical to those slain now stand guard outside the king's chambers. When Kull demands an explanation, the Pict replies with another cryptic utterance, "'The—snake—that—speaks!'" (30).

Kull is shocked, for the phrase Brule has spoken is held in dread as a fearsome taboo, though few know why. Confused and bewildered, the king turns to Brule for enlightenment and thus initiates a bond of friendship that is to last throughout the series. Brule reveals that "the-snake-that-speaks" is an archetypal figure in the legends of the Picts, the Atlanteans, and the Valusians. It refers to the prehuman serpent men who were once masters of the earth. At the dawn of time, the infant man strove against these and other monstrous beings for dominion of the young planet. Humanity prevailed, and those races of monsters not totally extinct were driven into the wastes. Ages later, however, the serpent people adopted the illusion of human form, seeking to infiltrate and undermine human society by guile.

The mystic phrase "ka nama kaa lajerama" became integral to humanity's survival, for when spoken in the presence of a serpent man in human guise, the monster's true form was revealed. Man retained his mastery of the earth, and the phrase "ka nama kaa lajerama" and the image of the-snake-that-speaks were branded forever into the racial memory of all humanity.

IV. King Kull

The theme of Jungian racial memory once again figures prominently in Howard's work: as Brule speaks, Kull's mind is flooded by racial memories churned up from his unconscious, recalling Solomon Kane's similar experience in "Red Shadows." Writing before the works of Jung were widely known in America, Howard introduces an archetype prominent in the legends of all peoples, the dim memory of which, we realize, has come down to us in the garbled form of the Serpent of Eden myth.

Kull is now aware that the all-but-forgotten serpent men have come out of hiding and are preparing to threaten humanity anew. Soon after learning of their existence from Brule, Kull has bloodcurdling encounters with the breed in which a pair of serpent men attempt to assassinate him using the guise of the king's chief counselor, Tu, and Brule himself. Slaying the impostors, Kull witnesses an eerie transformation as their human faces fade away to reveal monstrous serpent's heads. He wonders which of his generals, councilors, and subjects are in reality inhuman monsters. Brule tells how past Valusian kings, slain in battle, have died as serpents. The true kings were secretly assassinated and replaced with members of the serpent breed. Deep within a secret passage of the palace, Kull and Brule encounter the ghost of one such victim, Eallal, a long-dead king whose spirit is in eternal bondage to the serpent men.

Realizing the consequences of death at the hands of the snake men, the pair strike a bargain: should either be mortally wounded by the fiends, the other shall slay him to liberate his spirit. A fate similar to that of Eallal was planned for Kull, but Ka-nu learned of the plot and set out to save him. Ka-nu, Brule, and the snake people themselves realize that Kull could unite all humanity against the common foe of the serpent men.

It is well documented that Howard suffered from ophidiophobia, an intense dread of snakes. He frankly admits:

> Snakes give me the creeps; it was only with the greatest repugnance that I could bring myself to handle even a dead snake. One of the most nauseating memories of my life is that of laying my hand on a live water moccasin as I climbed up a creek bank . . . Another time I almost put my foot on an eight-rattle diamondback in the darkness . . . It was fall weather and he was too sluggish to strike, but even so it was some minutes before my hair would lay down on my scalp again . . . I remember in one of Kipling's yarns somebody haunted somebody else with a "sending" of cats. A sending of snakes would be more disgusting. (REH to Clark Ashton Smith, c. March 1934; CL 3.197-98)

Howard's personal aversion to snakes undoubtedly contributed to his vivid realization of the serpent men, as well the numerous serpentine menaces that subsequently appear in his fiction.

Evil, inhuman, and alien, the serpent men are a particularly shuddersome menace. Deadlier than the akaana, more vile than the worms of the earth, the serpent men are the ultimate threat to humanity. Howard frequently warns of the price to be paid should humanity's civilizations become decadent, but few warnings are as potent as his suggestion that decadence could allow human beings to become the unwilling prey of such malevolent, inhuman forces. The snake people pose a threat to humanity that does not end with physical death, for they can imprison a person's very soul as well. The serpent men are the antithesis of humanity in all ways: physically, mentally, and spiritually. Like the race of shapeshifting witches in Jack Williamson's *Darker Than You Think*, these sinister beings are humanity's ancient enemy, the world's oldest conspiracy, and a cosmic evil that has existed at least as long as the human race.

In numerous instances, Howard dissects such human foibles as greed, pettiness, degeneracy, and cruelty with such precision that he frequently impresses the reader as a misanthrope. However, in fantasies such as "Worms of the Earth" and "The Shadow Kingdom," Howard is able to view the human family from a more detached perspective in which all men and women are seen as brothers and sisters—not bonded together by love but shackled together by fate—pitted against a seemingly hostile, certainly uncaring universe. He is able to convey this viewpoint by presenting us with an antagonist who is not the foe of any individual, tribe, or nation, but the enemy of humanity itself. In the present story especially, the nebulous sense of anxiety that modern man derives from his perception of an indifferent cosmos is given substance and shape by Howard. "The Shadow Kingdom" is a chilling evocation of paranoid dread, a masterpiece of dark fantasy.

The title of the last chapter of "The Shadow Kingdom" is "Masks." In this section, Kull realizes that the true face of the people he rules has always remained hidden from him. The preceding events have forever changed Kull's view of reality, and in subsequent stories he will be plagued by doubts concerning his perception of the universe. Kull has already seen ancient foes become trusted friends. He has also seen trusted councilors revealed as inhuman monsters, a situation many real-life leaders have come to know only too well. As he holds court, Kull doubts the nature of all he sees.

Kull has been ensnared in a web of metaphysical doubt. Although the doubts he feels in "The Shadow Kingdom" are justified and necessary for his survival, in the tales that follow it Kull's search for the true nature of reality becomes an obsession. He will attempt to pin down nebulous abstractions in a frustrating quest for absolute meaning. Just as Solomon Kane had to deal with questions of religious faith, Kull must confront another of the pitfalls awaiting the intelligent man as he grapples with oblique philosophical quandaries, which are ultimately insoluble. Already Kull's doubts and fears stemming from his discovery of the serpent men have become globalized, seeping into all aspects of his everyday existence. He wonders not only which of his subjects are in reality inhuman enemies, but also which human values are real. He wonders whether the somber king or the youthful barbarian tribesman is the real Kull.

Previously Kull progressed from feral child to king. Now he is undergoing a transformation from man of action to thinking man. This is not to say that Kull or any other Howard character is stupid or unthinking. Kull could not have reached the high position he occupies if he were a fool. But for Kull, thought has always been a prelude to action. The menace posed by the serpent men is not something that can be dealt with by mere physical strength, nor can it be dealt with swiftly. Kull, a man of action, must bide his time and wait as patiently as he can for the serpent men to make their next move. With waiting comes anxiety, and this type of warfare weighs heavily on Kull. Howard tells us that he "had aforetime gone for days without sleep, in his wild savage days, but now his mind was edged from constant thinking" (43).

The progression from man of action to thinker is a familiar theme in the works of Jack London. Like the protagonists of London's novels such as *The Sea Wolf* and *Martin Eden*, Kull has been reborn into a bigger, more complicated world.

Kull does not know when and how the serpent men will strike. As on the previous evening, they use the disguise of the chief councilor to spring their trap. Kull is lured to what he thinks is an assembly of the council. As he addresses the council, its members rise and approach him. Brule leaps forward and shouts the phrase *"ka nama kaa lajerama."* The faces of the trusted councilors melt in a fog to reveal the grinning serpent heads beneath. As Kull and Brule battle the would-be assassins, suffering many wounds but finally slaying all their unskilled opponents, the chamber itself shifts and fades, and Kull realizes that it was not the council chamber at all but the room where Eallal died a thousand years before. Kull and Brule race to the real council room, and as they near it they are shaken to hear Kull's voice emanating from the room.

Kull bursts into the room to confront a serpent man in his likeness. The guards and councilors are too stunned to intervene as Kull

IV. King Kull

and the creature battle to the death. The fight is swift and the true Kull triumphs. As the false Kull's face dissolves into its true form, Kanu, the Pictish ambassador, reappears and declares Kull's triumph over evil. The king, bloodied by his struggles, leads the councilors to the room containing the bodies of the serpent men and before all these men of power he seals it, vowing to hunt down and exterminate all the serpent men.

Having exposed the cosmic menace, Kull has taken on a crusade against evil. Like Bran Mak Morn, Kull forsakes old feuds to battle a common enemy. The war against the serpent men and their power over reality has forever altered Kull's outlook. As in the final conflict of the tale, when he battles a mask in his image, so will Kull be forever at war with himself.

Kull's inner struggle is explored in several other stories. Only one, "The Mirrors of Tuzun Thune," was published in Howard's lifetime. All the rest of Kull's adventures languished in manuscript until the 1960s. At the time he wrote the Kull series, Howard had yet to learn all the tricks of the pulp fiction trade. Encouraged by the sale of "The Shadow Kingdom" to *Weird Tales,* he then sent the editor a package containing all the other Kull stories, rather than submitting them one at a time. In such cases, a pulp magazine editor was likely to select the story he liked best and return the others. This was the fate of the Kull stories.

Of the unpublished stories, two deal directly with Kull's metaphysical dilemmas. They are "The Striking of the Gong" and "The Screaming Skull of Silence." Both concern the nature of reality or some aspect of it. "The Striking of the Gong" is an interesting piece of writing, unique among Howard's work. More a sketch than a story, it contains none of the action-oriented prose Howard is noted for, the author abandoning his usual straightforward style to experiment with an oblique stream-of-consciousness narrative. It has been suggested that Howard wrote this brief tale as an intellectual exercise not intended for publication. In it, Kull has an out-of-the-body experience in which he meets a shadowy figure with whom he discusses philosophical matters.

"The Screaming Skull of Silence" (originally published as "The Skull of Silence") also deals with abstract concepts, but in this case a concept becomes a physical presence. When Howard's heroes deal with abstractions, these ideas often have a way of manifesting themselves in a concrete manner. "The Screaming Skull of Silence" is the clearest, most obvious example of this device in all Howard's work. It begins with an intellectual discussion between Kull, Tu, Ka-nu, Brule and a scholar named Kathulos.

The latter expounds on the nature of reality, expressing a notion similar to Locke's concept of metaphysical dualism, that the true reality underlying all our illusory perceptions of it is beyond human experience. Ka-nu suggests that man's five senses may accurately perceive the world as it is. Kathulos counters by stating that none know the true nature of sight and sound. He goes on to assert that, although none have ever heard total silence, "'somewhere exists the essence of silence'" (120).

This assertion echoes Plato's concept of ideal essences and also reveals the story's premise. The ideal essence of silence and the truth underlying all other metaphysical mysteries are outside of human experience, but Howard, using fantasy fiction as few others have done, is able to intrigue us with an imaginary confrontation between a man and an idea described in a purely physical manner.

After Kathulos tells of "the soul of silence" (120), Ka-nu reveals that Raama, an ancient sage, imprisoned a specter of silence in a great castle called the Skull of Silence, which Brule mentions having seen. Kull expresses interest in seeing this castle, and the next day all present at the discussion and a number of soldiers set out in search of the site.

Days later they find it in a lonely region shunned by men where the countryside is strangely still. As they approach the edifice, Kathulos tries to dissuade Kull, telling the king he may unleash something no man can stay. On the sealed door is a warning inscribed by Raama himself. Kull ignores it and recklessly breaks open the door.

Howard once told Novalyne Price that "'in sound is reality. As long as you can hear sound, you're alive'" (Ellis 241). We can therefore surmise that he equated the absence of sound with unreality or oblivion. When Kull breaks the seal, the imprisoned soul of silence billows out in great invisible waves to engulf all present. They are ravaged by the silence, which is a physical presence that can slay them where they stand by entering their very souls and blasting them into nothingness.

Kull's sword is useless and he topples, falling against a great green gong that hangs outside the castle. As he does so, he feels a slight withdrawal of the force. The gong is Raama's safeguard, and Kull realizes that it is like the sea that crashes against the shore constantly from the beginning of the world to its end, the greatest enemy of Silence. Kull begins to beat the gong, and the Silence retreats back into the castle.

But rather than merely imprison Silence once more, Kull takes the gong from its frame and follows the essence, beating the gong again and again until all the sound in the universe rushes together and Silence "screams."

Unlike "The Striking of the Gong," which reads like a first draft, "The Screaming Skull of Silence" is more polished. It is believed that the final drafts of the Kull stories not published in *Weird Tales* are lost. Even so, the draft of "The Screaming Skull of Silence" that has come down to us is a well-written tale. The silence, something totally alien, was a challenge to Howard's powers of description. The challenge is met admirably, and this story stands as one of the finest in the Kull cycle.

In some respects "The Screaming Skull of Silence" is similar to "The Footfalls Within," in that both Kull and Kane meet a physical manifestation of an abstract concept and both heroes are able to destroy what the great wise men of their past were only able to imprison.

Because Howard seemed to advocate physical force as a means of settling complex problems of justice and government and even philosophical and metaphysical questions, critics have maligned him by saying he was not a thinker. Such statements hardly hold up when one considers some of the ideas put forth in "The Screaming Skull of Silence." Those expressed in the early part of the story paraphrase Locke and Plato. Howard may or may not have been familiar with Locke, although the works of Plato were most likely available to him. It could be that the Lockean ideas were reasoned out by Howard himself, hardly the pastime of a non-thinker.

Howard's formal education was not particularly elaborate. Even so, he is known to have had at least a nodding acquaintance with Kant, Spinoza, Schopenhauer, Nietzsche, William James, Herbert Spencer, and Ernst Haeckel. Howard's correspondence dating from the same period he was working on the Kull stories reveals some familiarity with both Eastern and Western philosophical and religious thought:

> Yet a man's mind must strive after *Greatness* and when he has progressed to the point where no commonplace thought is really great in scope consistently he must look beyond the human and if he finds nothing there— Jack London died because he could not untwine the human from the cosmic. Upton Sinclair has never looked beyond the human. Plato did and Christ and Confucius and Siddhartha. Some of the yogis do. Haeckel did and Spencer and Huxley and Darwin. Kant looked beyond and saw nothing. Nietzsche never untwined the human from the cosmic nor did Schopenhauer. (REH to Tevis Clyde Smith, week of 20 February 1928; CL 1.194)

In another letter from this period he mentions disagreeing with Haeckel concerning "material monism, as opposed to the dualist theory" (REH to Tevis Clyde Smith, c. March 1928; CL 1.206). At this time Howard was in his early twenties, an age when many a thoughtful youth is struck by a vast array of fascinating new ideas. His discussion of philosophical matters in his letters and his embodiment of philosophical abstractions in the Kull stories were no mere matters of coincidence.

It was not that Howard was not an intellectual, but more probably that his temperament was such that he preferred direct action as a means of getting things done. In this, Howard resembles Kull more than any of his other creations. When Howard wrestled with an abstraction, something unknown and unknowable, he probably wished it could be something he could confront directly and resolve once and for all. This is more than likely the reason for the personification of abstracts in "The Footfalls Within" and "The Screaming Skull of Silence."

It is only after Brule mentions the existence of the Skull that Kull takes any real interest in the philosophical conversation. His reckless action of opening the door suggests his belief that abstractions cannot hurt him. Yet Kull, the man of action, is better able to deal with "an abstract illusion that was a material reality" than any around him (125). Kathulos, who speculates endlessly about the nature of reality, is less prepared to face the truth about it when given a chance to do so. The scholar better understands what they face, but knowledge is not action and therefore of little use in the confrontation: "Here was a thing elemental and real. Silence was the absence of sound, Kathulos had said: Kathulos who now groveled and yammered empty nothingnesses" (125).

In "The Footfalls Within," Yussef, the Arab scholar, also understood the nature of the manifestation he witnessed, yet his reaction was to turn away and run rather than confront it. It is clearly stated in "The Screaming Skull of Silence" that if action without thought is mindless aberration, then it is equally true that thought without action is a futile exercise in rhetoric.

"The Mirrors of Tuzun Thune" (*Weird Tales*, September 1929), the only Kull story other than "The Shadow Kingdom" to appear in print in Howard's lifetime, is an atypical one for him, containing neither violent swordplay nor mighty sorceries. It is, rather, a quiet, eerie mood-piece reminiscent of Poe or Howard's colleague Clark Ashton Smith. The prose is delicately wrought and highly polished; undoubtedly Howard devoted considerable time and attention to this brief but memorable tale.

In lazy, languid prose, Howard recounts how the world-weary Kull sits brooding on his throne, unable to muster enough will power to throw off this lethargy. In this story, more so than in any other, Kull verifies the truth of Nietzsche's aphorism, "Under peaceful conditions, a warlike man sets upon himself" (81).

Kull, his conquests behind him, his war with the serpent men apparently won, can find no challenge to stimulate him. Brule tries to help, suggesting a sojourn at sea as a change of scenery, but Kull replies that he is "'weary beyond all these things'" (55).

A woman of the court comes to Kull and suggests that he seek the counsel of the wizard Tuzun Thune. Kull, impetuous as ever, departs instantly to the wizard's dwelling place, The House of a Thousand Mirrors. The king, an uneducated barbarian who usurped his crown, possesses the intelligent but ignorant man's awe of knowledge. Often in the Kull stories, Kull seeks the counsel of those he regards as wiser.

His meeting with the ancient wizard gives Kull no answers that meet with his satisfaction, for Tuzun Thune's philosophy is characterized by Howard as a kind of bastardized Zen, unfamiliar to the "Western" way of thinking. Sensing Kull's disappointment, Thune takes him before his mirrors, saying they will impart wisdom. The king selects a mirror at random, one set opposite another mirror. Therein he sees a long corridor with a tiny reflection of himself at the end, the image seeming to represent Kull's real proportions. Disturbed, Kull moves on to another mirror, one that Tuzun Thune informs him is the mirror of the past. In it, Kull sees the pageant of life before the dawn of man, the ceaseless struggle for existence in the primordial jungle.

Again, Kull turns away. Thune now shows him the mirror of the future. In it he sees a strange world in which his kingdom is destroyed and forgotten and even the face of the land is changed. Kull is dismayed, but the wizard replies that all things are destined to pass away, a recurring theme in much of Howard's work.

Kull chooses another mirror, one which Tuzun Thune tells him is "'the mirror of the deepest magic'" (59). In it Kull sees only a reflection of himself. Tuzun Thune prompts him to look more deeply, and Kull begins to wonder if the reflection is not part of some other world that regards Kull as a mere image. Here the story recalls how Chuang Tzu dreamed he was a butterfly and, upon awakening, wondered if he were not in truth a butterfly dreaming he was a man.

Kull does not turn away from this mirror, for this is the mirror of all knowledge to him. Hours pass and Kull seems to see "hard shallowness" at times and "gigantic depths" at other times (60). Kull, now a seeker of knowledge, here reveals his true nature, for he forsakes the knowledge of the historian (the mirror of the past) and the knowledge of the scientist (the mirror of the future) and turns to the knowledge of the artist—that is, the knowledge of oneself. Kull has mastered an empire, but he is not the master of himself.

In the days that follow, Kull comes before the mirror again and again to gaze at himself, neglecting his kingly duties. And the longer Kull looks upon himself, the more that self seems to take on the aspect of an alien entity. Kull has taken up the artist's path to self-knowledge, and here Howard warns us that even art can have dangerous pitfalls. For the self-searching of the artist all too often turns into an incessant, morbid self-attention that can be unhealthy. Too much of this self-attention can produce not a better understanding of self, but confusion or a sense of self-alienation that can lead to neurosis or worse.

Eventually, Kull's image seems to possess an individuality apart from him. As the days pass, Kull comes to doubt everyday reality more and more. He wonders if he might enter the world beyond the mirror. He expresses his doubts to Tuzun Thune, and the wizard replies that form and substance are an illusion. In "The Screaming Skull of Silence," Howard paraphrased Locke, a realist who believed that human perceptions reflect an underlying reality that exists apart from any perception of it. Now Tuzun Thune takes the idealist view that no such underlying reality exists.

More time passes and Kull's grip on reality continues to slip. Finally, he feels he understands all the wizard has told him and can by an act of will alter his form and substance, entering the world beyond the mirror. He begins to feel himself change and merge. Suddenly Kull's concentration is broken as Brule shouts his name. He finds himself back in the wizard's chamber. Tuzun Thune has been slain by the Pict, and the mirror before Kull is shattered.

Brule now tells Kull of a conspiracy against him, plotted by a treasonous baron, the woman who sent the king to the wizard, and Thune himself. Brule tells Kull how he actually saw the king begin to fade away and rescued him in the nick of time. The Pict claims that Tuzun Thune had bewitched Kull, but the king is not so sure and wonders if he might have been on the verge of uncovering some great secret after all. There are clues to the conspiracy throughout the story, and Kull, while gazing at the mirror, wonders if he is in complete control of his own thoughts. However, the existence of the conspiracy does not diminish the impact of the dilemma that Kull has faced, and we are told that "Kull is less sure of reality since he gazed into the mirrors of Tuzun Thune" (63).

In both "The Mirrors of Tuzun Thune" and "The Shadow

Kingdom," Brule, Kull's constant companion, is instrumental in helping Kull overcome his antagonists. In "The Shadow Kingdom," Brule is Kull's guide and mentor in his initial confrontation with the serpent men; in "The Mirrors of Tuzun Thune," it is he who saves Kull's life.

Brule is without question the most important supporting character in Howard's writings. His role in the tales is at times equal to that of Kull himself, and there exists a fragment of a story in which Brule is the main protagonist. It is fitting that we pause to examine this character and his relationship with Kull more closely.

It is, of course, ironic that Brule's race is a blood-enemy of Kull's people. In "The Shadow Kingdom" as in "Worms of the Earth," Howard shows us that even enemies can be drawn together against foes that are the enemy of all humanity. However, Howard goes several steps beyond this concept in the relationship between Kull and Brule. Both men are what Howard regarded as a superior type; i.e., barbarians reared in natural surroundings as opposed to individuals produced by the artificial environments of civilized society.

When Kull and Brule first confront each other, Kull regards Brule as a younger, freer version of himself. What Kull fails to recognize, but what Howard does not let us fail to see, is that Brule, being psychologically closer to his natural state than Kull, is able to trust his simpler intuitive insights, which are unconfused by the conflicting demands and responsibilities of civilization. At the climax of "The Mirrors of Tuzun Thune," there is an important exchange of dialogue between the two men.

After slaying the wizard, Brule reveals Thune's role in the conspiracy against Kull. Though Kull accepts this, he cannot help but ask, "'But being a wizard, having knowledge of all the ages, and despising gold, glory and position, what could Kaanuub [the rebellious baron] offer Tuzun Thune that would make of him a foul traitor?'"

The Pict replies, "'Gold, power and position ... The sooner you learn that men are men whether wizard, king, or thrall, the better you will rule, Kull" (62).

The civilized notion that Kull expresses, that one who knows more than you should somehow be better, is an assumption that Brule would never make. Just as might does not necessarily make right, superior intellect or education does not necessarily make for superior moral character. Brule is more like Conan than Kull, although, as we shall see, Conan possesses attributes of both characters.

While Kull longs for concrete solutions to abstract dilemmas, he realizes that, "The Screaming Skull of Silence" to the contrary, seldom can this be. Brule, on the other hand, is perfectly satisfied with his notion of reality and does not seek beyond the realm of his five senses. Which of these two ways of looking at the world displays greater maturity, wisdom, and common sense? It is unlikely that Howard himself ever drew any definite conclusions.

Still, we can see Kull as a step forward both in terms of Howard's personal development and his writing, for we detect in the latter a departure from the religious concerns of the Solomon Kane series. Why, after all, is it Kull—not Brule—who is the hero of these tales? Brule is more pragmatic, a superior judge of character, better adjusted, and, for what it is worth, happier than Kull. But Kull's main concern is not with happiness or well-being, but with truth—truth about the universe and man's place in it.

Though his involvement with the serpent men was thrust upon him, Kull's encounters with the Skull of Silence and Tuzun Thune's mirrors were due to a desire on his part to confront these things, and these confrontations bear witness to the strength of his desire to know the unknowable. Kull's yearning for truth and Kane's passion for justice both ultimately spring from the depths of each man's soul. Kane possesses a deeper sense of purpose than Kull, but Kane satisfies his spiritual needs through dogmatic faith. Kull attempts to do so through an objective search for the truth.

Most of Howard's protagonists, like Solomon Kane, are loners. Kull is not. Brule is his companion in his adventures in search of truth. Though generally open-minded and objective, Kull is still prone to errors in judgment. Brule is the first to criticize Kull for his misjudgments. Brule is unconcerned with the true nature of reality, but he nevertheless respects Kull's quest for it. Kull and Brule each possess attributes that compensate for the other's deficiencies. Both characters are better for knowing each other.

Howard did not have much success with the Kull series, having sold only "The Shadow Kingdom" and "The Mirrors of Tuzun Thune" to Farnsworth Wright. He was soon to abandon the character. One outstanding story rejected by *Weird Tales* because it lacked a supernatural element may be considered a conclusion to the Kull cycle. It is a brief tale of powerful emotional impact called "'By This Axe I Rule!'"

The writing is extremely tight, as this is so short a tale. It is well plotted and realized, using elements seen in other episodes of the series: court intrigue, conspiracy, the plight of two young lovers, and the uneasy burden of kingship. Howard now employs these elements to maximum effect, weaving them together with concise, economical prose that keeps the story moving to its stirring climax.

The story revolves around a conspiracy to assassinate Kull. The five conspirators are the wealthy Baron Kaanuub; Enaros, a commander of the legions; Count Ducalon, a dwarf with many powerful connections; Ridondo, a mad poet and minstrel; and finally Ascalante, a once-powerful scion of the old regime, recently an exile and outlaw, now the leader of the assassins. These plotters have been at work bribing officials to ease their transition to power and sowing sedition among the populace.

Everything is in readiness for the murder itself. A foreign king has been persuaded to summon Ka-nu, Brule, and a number of Red Slayers away on a state visit. An officer of Kull's bodyguard has been subverted and will remove the guard while the king sleeps. The conspirators, backed by sixteen disreputable mercenaries, will murder the king in his sleep.

Kull, though unaware of the plot against him, has noticed the discord that has spread throughout his realm. He complains to Brule that his subjects revile his name and eulogize the tyrant Borna, whom Kull deposed. Brule remarks that the songs of the minstrel Ridondo have swayed the people and stirred them to discontent. The Pict suggests that Kull resolve the matter by putting Ridondo to death. Kull, however, is reluctant to do so, for he feels that "'a great poet is greater than any king'" (162).

This is a very civilized notion coming from a barbarian. Ridondo is a dangerous political enemy, yet Kull spares his life and does not censor him because he is an artist. Art is a byproduct of civilization. When human beings mastered their environment enough to allow themselves leisure time, they had to fill that time with something. Kull, who constantly complains of ennui induced by inactivity, has learned to appreciate art.

By his own admission, Kull was prepared to "'seize the throne; not to hold it'" (K 162). He attained his ultimate ambition when he became king and had no dreams or goals or direction beyond that. The ennui that led Kull into many of his misadventures is due to a lack of direction. In a candid moment he admits that he did not look beyond the kingship and "'From there it has been a maze of illusion and mistakes'" (162).

Ironically, Ascalante remarks, "'A few months ago I had lost all ambition save to waste the villages and caravans as long as I lived. Now, well—now we shall see!'" (160). He has agreed to lead the conspirators in their bid to depose Kull because he has been galvanized by a sense of destiny and purpose.

Brule departs on his diplomatic mission, leaving Kull alone with his private thoughts. His musings are soon interrupted by the entrance of Seno val Dor, a young nobleman who petitions the king for the right to marry a female slave. The woman, Ala, is owned by one of the conspirators who is willing to sell her. Seno val Dor, however, wishes not merely to own her, but lawfully wed her. He is forbidden by Valusian law from doing so, and the king is his last hope.

Subplots concerning the plight of young lovers occur in several of Kull's adventures not covered here, such as "The Cat and the Skull," "Swords of the Purple Kingdom," and "The Altar and the Scorpion." It is difficult to say exactly why Howard became obsessed with this particular subplot. Perhaps a closer look at Kull's feelings concerning love may provide a clue.

When Seno val Dor enters the throne room, he is the very picture of the Elizabethan concept of love so prevalent in the works of Shakespeare; love as a sort of all-consuming divine madness. He pours out his soul to the barbarian king, and Howard tells us that "Kull moved restlessly. He had never been a lover" (164). This fact is mentioned elsewhere, in "The Shadow Kingdom," in which Howard refers to the love of women as something "which Kull had never known" (42).

Kull's whole life has been a bitter struggle, first to stay alive, second to gain power, and third and finally to confront the inhuman evil of the serpent men and grapple with his own doubts about the nature of reality. Though Kull is not unsympathetic to the young noble, he has never allowed himself to succumb to the emotion of love.

It seems that, like Kull, Howard was never a lover, at least not at the time of writing the Kull cycle. This was in the late 1920s, when Howard was about twenty-two. It was not until his late twenties that he regularly enjoyed the company of a young woman. This was most likely due simply to the difficulty of meeting somebody compatible while living a fairly isolated existence in a small town located in the vastness of West Texas. However, his desire for a romantic relationship is evidenced by his endeavors to relate to Seno val Dor, Ala, and the other young lovers he writes of in the Kull tales.

Kull wishes to help the lovestruck young noble and summons Tu to bring the ancient stone tablets containing the law of the land. The laws are explicit in forbidding such a marriage as desired by val Dor. When Kull asks if he, as king, can change the law, Tu replies that the law has stood for thousands of years and no king may alter it. His inability to change such a little thing in Valusian law presses heavily on Kull, and he wearily dismisses Seno val Dor.

Sometime later, while walking through a forest glade, Kull happens upon a young woman weeping pathetically. She is, of course, val Dor's lover, the slave Ala, who does not recognize the king. Kull asks her what is wrong and, because of his sympathetic demeanor, she tells him of her troubles. When Kull asks Ala if the king refused to permit the lovers to wed, he is moved by her reply that, although the king wanted to help, the laws of Valusia are "'greater than the king'" (166). As their conversation continues, Kull begins to confide in the woman, telling her that "'the king is only a slave like yourself, locked with heavier chains'" (169).

Since Brule is not around and Ala is unaware of his identity, Kull takes this opportunity to unburden himself to a sympathetic ear. However, although Kull speaks of "the king" in the third person, it is not long before Ala realizes that the kind stranger to whom she has bared her soul is the king himself. Overcome with confusion and embarrassment, she flees, leaving Kull alone once more.

Before departing the woman remarks, "'I thought you were a human tiger, from what men had said'" (171). This is part of a recurring motif that runs through the Kull cycle. From time to time in the tales, Kull is likened to a tiger. The reader will recall that Kull is, in fact, a feral child. In "Exile of Atlantis," Kull talks of his early life among the animals, stating, "'I have run with the tigers'" (4).

IV. King Kull

Howard was an admirer of Kipling and, to a lesser extent, Edgar Rice Burroughs, and on occasion (as with feral children) made use of their concepts. In another story Kull tells how, as a youth, he could almost understand the roaring of the tigers and remarks that the tiger is his totem. Howard made more subtle and credible use of the concept of the "speech" of animals than Burroughs, who had Tarzan matter-of-factly converse with various denizens of the jungle.

The Howard approach is more reminiscent of Jack London's novel *The Sea Wolf*, than the work of Burroughs or even Kipling. London's protagonist Wolf Larsen, a savage brutal man, is a spiritual brother to the archetypal wolf, the savage predator of medieval folklore. Mention that the tiger is Kull's "totem" is an aside, but it is for the better that Howard did not explore this facet of Kull's personality too extensively. The relationship between the tiger and Kull remains primarily a symbolic one.

The story's final segment begins as the conspirators and their henchmen steal through the palace by night to assassinate Kull. The guards have been removed by the bribed officer. Fired by their separate ambitions, the assassins strike but find to their dismay not a sleeping victim but a wide-awake and wrathful warrior. Kull, unable to sleep, noticed the absence of his bodyguard and became suspicious. The assassins burst into the king's bedchamber to find Kull ready, sword in hand and partially clad in armor.

L. Sprague de Camp has pointed out this sequence was probably inspired by the death of Francisco Pizarro as recounted in volume four of William H. Prescott's *The Conquest of Peru*. Pizarro, of course, was murdered despite being forewarned. As for Kull, even though he has time to prepare himself to some degree, the odds are twenty to one against him. Despite this advantage, the assassins are wary. Only a few wear armor, their numbers hinder them in such close quarters, and the enraged Kull is a formidable figure.

The desperate battle that follows is one of the most memorable in

Howard's fiction. Howard himself liked it so much he used it twice, incorporating it into the first published Conan story, "The Phoenix on the Sword," after failing to sell the present tale. The suspense is riveting and the combat action furious. Kull dispatches several of his opponents before his sword is shattered. In a desperate bid, Kull pulls an ancient battle-axe from the wall and wades into his foes, holding his own against them. He suffers many wounds, but thanks to his armor, none are mortal. However, a moment's hesitation on Kull's part is almost fatal.

The mad poet Ridondo springs forward, dagger in hand. Yet he is not instantly felled by the great axe, for Kull is reluctant to slay the minstrel due to the firmness of his belief that "a great poet is greater than any king." Kull utters an urgent warning, almost a plea, but to no avail. Ridondo presses the attack, and "Kull delayed the blow he was loath to deliver until it was too late. Only when he felt the bite of steel in his unprotected side did he strike, in a frenzy of blind desperation" (174).

Throughout the series, Kull has endeavored to submerge the savage side of himself in an effort to conform to the values of the society he rules. Now his attempt to spare the life of Valusia's favorite poet has left him with a gaping wound in his side.

The remaining assassins are moments from doing Kull in, but he is saved by the arrival of reinforcements in the persons of Seno val Dor and a number of his family retainers. The remaining assassins flee at the sound of their approach, all except for Ascalante. He leaps to strike Kull down as the king wipes blood from his eyes but is struck dead by a knife hurled by Seno val Dor. It is revealed that Ala overheard her master and one of his fellow conspirators going over their plot and, at her earliest opportunity, fled and informed her lover, who hurried to the king's rescue.

In "Exile of Atlantis," Kull the savage ends the misery of a young lover with a hurled dagger. Now King Kull has been saved from assassination thanks to a dagger hurled by a young lover. Howard himself is known to have practiced the art of knife throwing. Like boxing, it is a skill the author shared with several of his characters.

The battle over, the lovers render first aid to their king. The entire palace has been roused by now, and the ladies and gentlemen of the court are now present. Kull orders Tu to bring the stone tablet containing the marriage laws. When Tu returns, Kull announces that Seno val Dor and Ala are free to marry as they please. The lovers embrace happily, but Tu is foolish enough to protest the king's flouting of "'the law'" (179).

The story reaches its climax with Kull's explosive outburst to those present:

> "I am the law!" roared Kull, swinging up his axe; it flashed downward and the stone tablet flew into a hundred pieces. The people clenched their hands in horror, waiting dumbly for the sky to fall.
>
> Kull reeled back, eyes blazing. The room whirled before his dizzy gaze.
>
> "I am king, state, and law!" he roared, and seizing the wand-like sceptre which lay near, he broke it in two and flung it from him. "This shall be my sceptre!" The red axe was brandished aloft, splashing the pallid nobles with drops of blood. Kull grasped the slender crown with his left hand and placed his back against the wall; only that support kept him from falling, but in his arms was the strength of lions.
>
> "I am either king or corpse!" he roared, his corded muscles bulging, his terrible eyes blazing, "If you like not my kingship—come and take this crown!"
>
> The corded left arm held out the crown, the right gripping the menacing axe above it.
>
> "By this axe I rule! This is my sceptre! I have struggled and sweated to be the puppet king you wished me to be—to rule your way. Now I use mine own way. If you will not fight, you shall obey. Laws that are just shall stand, laws that have outlived their time I shall shatter as I shattered that one. *I am king!*"
>
> Slowly the pale-faced noblemen and frightened women knelt, bowing in fear and reverence to the blood-stained giant who towered above them with his eyes ablaze.
>
> "I am king!" (179-80)

Kull's final statement, in which he declares himself the absolute power in the realm, may cause some readers to leap to the conclusion that Howard was a fascist. Such was not the case, however. Indeed, Howard would be best described today as a libertarian. His rebellious, anti-authoritarian personality, which manifested itself so strongly at school and on the job, would never allow him to be supportive of a repressive, authoritarian regime. He condemned Mussolini and Hitler while contemporaries like Lovecraft were sympathetic toward these fascist leaders.

An assumption that Howard advocated totalitarian leadership in a modern industrial society would not be valid. Howard was obsessed with freedom, and having finished with Kull would move on to a character free of self-doubt, free of the burden of religion, and aware of his total freedom as an individual.

The reader might also wonder if Kull would now become a despot. This is unlikely. If Kull were to rule as a despot, he would have done so after seizing the throne. The extreme measure he adopts at the conclusion of "'By This Axe I Rule!'" is one that he has been driven to throughout the series. The conspirator Ascalante, had his coup been successful, would have been a despot due to a world-weary cynicism that would have led him to exercise power in perverse ways.

Kull, on the other hand, has always sought a creative, positive outlet for his energies and will continue to do so. In the past, Kull's restless energy led him on a fruitless quest for metaphysical truth and esoteric knowledge. But now he has taken absolute authority unto himself and must truly rule. Kull's saga would seem to support Blake's belief that "the tigers of wrath are wiser than the horses of instruction" (Blake xix).

It is doubtful ennui will ever plague Kull again.

V. Conan

Virtually any mass market paperback edition of Howard's works features a caption somewhere on the cover that reads "by the creator of Conan." For better or worse, Howard and Conan are as inseparable as Burroughs and Tarzan.

By far Howard's most famous creation, Conan is known to millions who have never read a word of Howard's prose. Known at first only to a comparatively small but enthusiastic audience of *Weird Tales* readers, the Conan character suffered several decades of obscurity before exploding on the paperback scene in the 1960s. With little help from those who create a bestseller through hype, he became a prominent cult figure on the order of Tarzan and James Bond.

Why Conan? Who is Conan, and what is it about this character that has captured the imagination of so many?

A "fantasy hero" in more ways than one, Conan is a character whose appeal to the male reader is as basic as it is universal. He is bigger, stronger, and tougher than any single foe he may encounter in an environment teeming with tough, dangerous men. The most desirable women are his by right of natural superiority. Rather than being shackled like most men to a drab, routine existence, he is free to wander and seek adventure in a fascinating world brimming with excitement and exotic wonders. In short, Conan is what many men want to be.

Adolescents are unabashed in embracing the fantasy. Some

adults, however, are reluctant to admit that the fantasy is attractive, in deference to liberal notions contemptuous of even a modicum of male audacity or aggression. Still, many men, be they office drones, convenience store clerks, or Ivy League professors, are apt to feel a stirring beneath the layers of such cultural conditioning when they read of Conan.

As described in Howard's sparse prose, Conan is truly an awesome figure. The mighty barbarian warrior is "almost a giant in stature"—"an image of primal strength cut out of bronze" (CSC 213, 273). He is described as "mightily shouldered and deep of chest, with a massive corded neck and heavily muscled limbs . . . His brow was low and broad, his eyes a volcanic blue that smoldered as if with some inner fire. His dark, scarred, almost sinister face was that of a fighting man" and is framed by a "square-cut black mane" (*BCC* 89-90). His powerful frame combines "the strength of a grizzly with the quickness of a panther" (CCC 280). "His slightest movement spoke of steel-spring muscles knit to a keen brain with the coordination of a born fighting man" and he is possessed of "a catlike speed that blurred the sight which tried to follow him" (CCC 11). Lastly, Howard tells us that "A fierce vitality that was evident in each feature and motion set him apart from common men" (CCC 329).

Howard's giant barbarian was a remarkable and original achievement. In a pulp magazine jungle where dozens of characters were vying for space on the newsstands by flaunting such characteristics as golden eyes or an icy laugh, Conan dominated the reader's imagination by the sheer force of his presence. He also dominates all other characters he encounters in the course of his adventures. Gordian knots of characters, plots, dooms, and menaces are inevitably cut by Conan's sword.

Howard's writings abound in fighting men of various types: barbarians, raiders, mercenary soldiers, pirates, desert chieftains, rogues, and adventurers. At one time or another in his long and bloody career, Conan is all these things. Reared in a harsh wilderness environment, Conan learns the arts of war in the armies of many nations, among the people of different cultures, and in every climate. Equally at home in the saddle or on the deck of a ship, a juggernaut in battle, strong, swift, and cunning, Conan is the greatest fighting man in an age of fighting men.

Howard's vision of the ultimate warrior, Conan came to dominate his writing in the last four years of his life. Howard wrote twenty-one completed Conan tales between 1932 and 1935. All but four of these were published during his lifetime, appearing regularly in *Weird Tales* up to the time of his death and beyond. The readers were enthusiastic, but several of Howard's colleagues such as Lovecraft and E. Hoffmann Price expressed a preference for his earlier tales of Kull and Solomon Kane. One reason for this, no doubt, is that Howard wrote twice as many stories about Conan than any other fantasy character and, while some Conan stories are as good as anything Howard ever wrote, others are more or less standard pulp adventure yarns written in accordance with a formula. Howard admitted this to Price, at the same time making the startling confession that some of his stories, such as "The Mirrors of Tuzun Thune" and "The Shadow Kingdom," originated in his dreams.

With Conan, however, Howard's visionary faculty expressed itself in a different way, usually focusing on the character rather than some specific exploit. Howard said that "Conan simply grew up in my mind a few years ago when I was stopping in a little border town on the lower Rio Grande. I did not create him by any conscious process. He simply stalked full grown out of oblivion and set me at work recording the saga of his adventures" (REH, quoted in Perry 66).

Howard elaborates on the genesis of Conan in a letter to Clark Ashton Smith:

> While I don't go so far as to believe that stories are inspired by actually existing spirits or powers (though I am rather opposed to flatly denying

anything) I have sometimes wondered if it were possible that unrecognized forces of the past or present—or even the future—work through the thought and actions of living men. This occurred to me when I was writing the first stories of the Conan series especially. I know that for months I had been absolutely barren of ideas, completely unable to work up anything sellable. Then the man Conan seemed suddenly to grow up in my mind without much labor on my part and immediately a stream of stories flowed off my pen—or rather off my typewriter—almost without effort on my part. I did not seem to be creating, but rather relating events that had occurred. Episode crowded on episode so fast I could scarcely keep up with them. For weeks I did nothing but write of the adventures of Conan. The character took complete possession of my mind and crowded out everything else in the way of storywriting. When I deliberately tried to write something else, I couldn't do it. I do not attempt to explain this by esoteric or occult means, but the facts remain. I still write of Conan more powerfully and with more understanding than any of my other characters . . . (REH to Clark Ashton Smith, 14 December 1933; CL 3.150-51)

Howard's experience is certainly not without precedent. William Blake composed prophetic works such as *Jerusalem* in precisely the same manner. Despite the compelling intensity of his vision of Conan, Howard was nonetheless able, in a later letter to Smith, to analyze somewhat objectively the subconscious process by which he created Conan:

It may sound fantastic to link the term "realism" with Conan; but as a matter of fact—his supernatural adventures aside—he is the most realistic character I have ever evolved. He is simply a combination of a number of men I have known, and I think that's why he stepped full-grown into my consciousness when I wrote the first yarn of the series. Some mechanism in my subconsciousness took the dominant characteristics of various prizefighters, gunmen, bootleggers, oil field bullies, gamblers, and honest workmen I had come in contact with, and combining them all, produced the amalgamation I call Conan the Cimmerian. (REH to Clark Ashton Smith, 23 July 1935; CL 3.367-68)

Conan and most of Howard's other heroes are presented far more realistically than the characters of Howard's fellow pulp writers

Edgar Rice Burroughs and Lester Dent. One of the ways in which Howard tempered the fabulous vision of his fantasies with a stiff dose of reality was to stress the humanity of his protagonists.

Howard's heroes are always formidable, but never invincible. They can and do get hurt as a result of their dangerous exploits. Solomon Kane gets the worst of his duel with Le Loup in "Red Shadows." Kull is nearly cut to ribbons in both "The Shadow Kingdom" and "'By This Axe I Rule!'" Conan is no exception; he suffers great wounds in many of his adventures, which in reality is the price a hero usually pays for an action-filled life.

Another way in which Howard's protagonists differ from the general run of popular culture heroes is that they are motivated by impulses more complex than the simplistic good guy/bad guy morality to which most genre writers adhere. The Shadow and Solomon Kane both fight for good against evil. However, while The Shadow's motivations are never made clear, Solomon Kane is driven by impulses that Howard renders recognizable and plausible to the reader.

Howard's ability to fully realize subtle aspects of characterization was especially evident with Conan. Indeed, each of the characters we have examined displays characterizations far more sophisticated than that usually found in popular fiction. Bran Mak Morn's obsession with preserving his race and culture, Solomon Kane's religious fanaticism, and Kull's philosophical brooding are all clearly and concisely presented by Howard in the body of each short work. Because he worked within the limits of the short story, Howard was compelled to be spare. Nevertheless, his characterization is convincing, and Conan is another step forward in Howard's crafting of believable characters.

That Howard considered Conan to be his "most realistic" character was undoubtedly because Conan possesses a more "normal" personality than his previous characters; that is, Conan's personality is more readily understandable to the average reader. Like most men,

Conan is motivated by personal gratification, a healthy sex drive, a desire for wealth, and a hunger for experience. Conan is spoken of as having "'a keen relish for women and strong drink.'" (CCC 325).

Howard also mentions Conan's "gigantic melancholies and gigantic mirth" (CCC 7). If the latter statement suggests a manic-depressive nature, Conan nonetheless possesses a greater capacity for pleasure than Bran Mak Morn, Solomon Kane, and Kull put together. Though Conan is referred to as being frequently sullen and moody, he is usually only *spoken of* in this manner. The aspect of Conan we are most often shown, however, is one of vitality, humor, and charisma. Conan is an extrovert, a magnetic figure who inspires loyalty. No religious fanatic he. Nor is he a slave to obsession or morbid introspection. Devoid of neuroses and inhibitions, Conan is free of what William Blake called "the mind-forg'd manacles" ("London," stanza 2). Howard would consider these "manacles" to be the trappings and conventions of civilization.

At the core of Conan's personality is an unmistakable purity, and he has frequently been likened to what John Dryden called "the noble savage." The cult of the noble savage, at least in modern times, began with the Swiss philosopher Jean-Jacques Rousseau. Rousseau considered humanity in its natural state to be free of vice. Contrary to hasty critical assumptions, Howard did not espouse such a naïve view. He sought to clarify his position in a letter to H. P. Lovecraft:

> I have no idylic view of barbarism—as near as I can learn it's a grim, bloody, ferocious and loveless condition. I have no patience with the depiction of the barbarian of any race as a stately, god-like child of Nature, endowed with strange wisdom and speaking in measured and sonorous phrases. Bah! My conception of a barbarian is very different. He had neither stability nor undue dignity. He was ferocious, vengeful, brutal and frequently squalid. He was haunted by dim and shadowy fears; he committed horrible crimes for strange monstrous reasons . . . His religion was generally one of dooms and shadows, his gods were awful and abominable. They bade him mutilate himself or slaughter his children, and he

obeyed because of fears too primordial for any civilized man to comprehend ... But he was lithe and strong as a panther, and the full joy of strenuous physical exertion was his. The day and night were his book, wherein he read of all things that run or walk or crawl or fly. Trees and grass and moss-covered rocks and birds and beasts and clouds were alive to him, and pertook [sic] of his kinship. The wind blew his hair and he looked with naked eyes into the sun. Often he starved, but when he feasted, it was with a mighty gusto, and the juices of food and strong drink were stinging wine to his palate ... (REH to H. P. Lovecraft, 2 November 1932; CL 2.514-15)

Though not necessarily noble, Howard's savages are possessed of many qualities lacking in civilized people. Attributes of actual barbarians are present in Conan. He is stronger and fleeter than someone raised in a civilized environment. Having been bred in the wilderness, he is inured to discomfort and hardship, even pain. His senses are keener than those of civilized people, and his reflexes are set on a hair trigger. All these qualities, says Howard, give Conan an edge in any situation or conflict.

In addition to traits possessed by actual barbarians, such as strength, speed, stealth, hardiness, and so on, Howard bestows upon Conan other, subtler attributes stemming from his barbarian origins. These consist of attitudes and modes of thinking that are always shown by Howard to be radically different from those of civilized people. In "Beyond the Black River," Howard stresses just how different Conan really is:

> The Cimmerian might have spent years among the great cities of the world; he might have walked with the rulers of civilization ... But he was no less a barbarian. He was concerned only with the naked fundamentals of life. The warm intimacies of small, kindly things, the sentiments and delicious trivialities that make up so much of civilized men's lives were meaningless to him. A wolf was no less a wolf because a whim of chance caused him to run with the watch-dogs. Bloodshed and violence and savagery were the natural elements of the life Conan knew; he could not, and would never, understand the little things that are so dear to civilized men and women ... (CSC 79)

The significance of all this can be expressed in terms of survival. Conan is perfectly suited, mentally as well as physically, not only to survive, but to thrive in and dominate the most hostile of milieux. "Jungle sensitiveness" is but a modicum of Conan's mental equipment. Conan's mind, heart, soul, and will are an almost mystical fusion producing a state of consciousness ideal for ascendancy in the natural order.

Howard was obsessed with the undiluted superiority in many respects that the barbarian enjoyed over his civilized counterpart. Many of his protagonists are barbarians of one breed or another. Whether Pict, Celt, Comanche, or Kurd, Howard almost always portrayed the barbarian, if not as a "noble savage," at least with some measure of empathy and respect. Nowhere is this more evident than with the character Conan. Just as he is Howard's vision of the ultimate warrior, Conan is also Howard's ultimate barbarian.

The twenty-one Conan stories range in quality from competent but uninspired pulp fiction to the pinnacle of Howard's literary craftsmanship. In them, Conan matures from a callow youth aimlessly wandering the fringes of civilization to the enlightened monarch of the mightiest realm of his epoch. This milieu, which Howard called the Hyborian Age, is said to have existed approximately twelve thousand years ago, between the sinking of Atlantis and the beginnings of extant history. At this time, according to Howard, the continents of Europe, Asia, and Africa formed a single large landmass.

Spread across this supercontinent were such fabulous realms as "Nemedia, Ophir, Brythunia, Hyperborea, Zamora with its dark-haired women and towers of spider-haunted mystery; Zingara with its chivalry, Koth that bordered on the pastoral lands of Shem, Stygia with its shadow-guarded tombs, Hyrkania whose riders wore steel and silk and gold" (CCC 7).

The Hyborian world was an ingenious device of Howard's that enabled him to concoct any sort of pseudo-historical adventure he fancied, for the Hyborian Age was a conglomeration of ages and cultures lifted from the volumes of history that Howard pored over as a youth. Thus, Aquilonia resembles the late Roman Empire, while Stygia evokes the mystery of ancient Egypt, Hyrkania replicates the grandeur of the Ottoman Empire, and Zingara recalls the color of pre-Renaissance Spain. All told, the Hyborian Age is an impressive creation, a fitting stage for Howard's mightiest hero to stride.

The Conan series was not carefully thought out or presented as a unified concept. Rather, it is an episodic account of Conan's exploits as a wandering adventurer. The stories were not originally presented in any sort of chronological order. The first two stories to appear in *Weird Tales*, "The Phoenix on the Sword" (December 1932) and "The Scarlet Citadel" (January 1933), feature Conan as a middle-aged king. This is because Howard used segments of the unsold Kull story "'By This Axe I Rule!'" in writing the former tale. The third Conan story was called "The Tower of the Elephant" (*Weird Tales*, March 1933) and featured Conan as a young man in his late teens, green to the ways of civilization. This was followed by "Black Colossus" (*Weird Tales*, June 1933), the first "formula" Conan story, which introduced such now familiar elements as the scantily clad heroine and Conan himself in his best-remembered guise, that of the wandering soldier-of-fortune.

After this, the stories were set at various stages of Conan's career, with no design other than that of Howard's muse. Howard commented:

> In writing these yarns I've always felt less as creating them than as if I were simply chronicling his adventures as he told them to me. That's why they skip about so much, without following a regular order. The average adventurer, telling tales of a wild life at random, seldom follows any ordered plan, but narrates episodes widely separated by space and years, as they occur to him... (REH to P. Schuyler Miller, 10 March 1936; CL 3.428)

The stories were set in chronological order, not by Howard, but by various fans and editors years after they were written. Yet despite the seeming haphazardness with which Howard penned the Conan saga, there is a growing complexity to the character of Conan and indeed to the stories themselves as Conan ages. The stories set in Conan's youth, such as "The Frost-Giant's Daughter" and "The Tower of the Elephant," are short, dealing only with one event and with no subplots and few secondary characters. The later stories in the chronology are novella-length tales with more complex plotting and more advanced characters and themes. The final tale in the saga, *The Hour of the Dragon*, is Howard's only fully realized novel.

The earliest Conan tales occur when the young barbarian is just on the verge of adulthood. We are told little of his earlier life, save that he was reared in the bleak northern wilderness called Cimmeria, a land "all of hills, darkly wooded, under skies nearly always gray, with winds moaning drearily down the valleys" (CCC 13). Howard wisely decided against actually setting any of the Conan stories in Cimmeria; it is occasionally mentioned, but never presented to us. Nor do we ever encounter any other Cimmerian in the course of the stories. Thus, Conan's homeland remains forever shrouded in mystery.

Regarding Conan's earliest sojourns beyond the boundaries of Cimmeria, Howard wrote to a fan that "This, strange to say, was north instead of south. Why or how, I am not certain, but he spent some months among a tribe of the Æsir, fighting with the Vanir and the Hyperboreans" (REH to Miller; *CL* 3.429).

This is the background of a story that Howard was unable to sell to *Weird Tales* entitled "The Frost-Giant's Daughter" (CSC). In addition to being Conan's earliest exploit, this was also the second Conan story to be written, probably composed in late February or early March 1932. Howard embodied many contrasts in this short but unforgettable tale. Set in a land of ice, snow, and bitter cold, it deals with the heat of primal lust and savagery laid bare. It is at once an eerie, haunting mood piece and an intense account of physical strife and passion.

Howard begins the story on an icy battlefield littered with frozen corpses, the aftermath of a battle between the Æsir and Vanir, the two breeds of the Hyborian Age's pseudo-Vikings. Conan kills the last of his foes and, the sole survivor, he is overcome by battle fatigue and snow-blindness. He sinks to the ground, dazed, and when his vision clears he notices a strangeness about the land. Before him is a strange golden-haired young woman, naked except for a gossamer veil. Howard's description of her is not precise; eschewing detail, he opts for the poetic statement that "Her ivory body was as perfect as the dream of a god" (32). Howard does not describe a woman's body; he conjures an image of feminine perfection, one that allows the reader to readily accept the fact that "Conan's pulse hammered in his temples" (32).

Though aroused by this naked beauty, Conan asks only to be given refuge in her village. In answer he is given cruel taunting, the woman mocking him and daring him to rise up and follow her. Goaded in this manner, Conan rears up and chases the woman out across the snows. Her supernatural nature is evident, for while Conan's progress is impeded by deep snowdrifts, she dances across them as though weightless. The strange woman leads him far into the northern wastes, where the auroras flash in the sky above.

Suddenly two giant warriors, glistening with frost and bearing huge ice-covered battle-axes, appear to bar Conan's path. The woman commands her "brothers" to take Conan's heart as an offering to their father. Such is the intensity of Conan's wrath and the single-mindedness of his determination to possess the beautiful but cruel vision that has tormented him that he dispatches both giants in astonishingly short order. As they topple to the ground, the woman flees from Conan in fear, "all the mockery gone from her face" (35). The woman runs from Conan again, this time fleeing in earnest. Pressing himself to the limits of his physical endurance, Conan finally catches her and "In his untamed soul leaped up the fires of hell she had fanned so well" (35).

Conan seizes the woman in a fierce embrace, but she slips free, leaving him clutching her gossamer veil. The woman spreads her arms in naked supplication to the auroras flashing above and cries out for her father, Ymir. The heavens erupt in a fiery display, and she vanishes in a blinding crackle of icy blue flame. Dazed by these pyrotechnics, Conan reels and loses consciousness.

When Conan comes to, he is in the grip of his Æsir companions who are laboring to revive him. Arriving at the battle late, the Æsir warriors followed Conan's tracks in the snow and brought him back to safety. When Conan tells his story, his comrades regard it with skepticism, having found no other tracks or the bodies of the giants, and assert he was delirious. One old tribesman, however, disagrees, having seen the snow-woman when he was a boy, and tells them that Conan has seen "'Atali, the frost-giant's daughter'" (38). The Æsir remain unconvinced until Conan reveals what he still clutches in his clenched fist—"a wisp of gossamer that was never spun by human distaff" (CCC 38).

In rejecting "The Frost-Giant's Daughter," Farnsworth Wright tersely commented that he didn't care for it. This was not typical of Wright, who usually wrote lengthier criticism to a regular contributor like Howard. Often Wright would suggest approaches for a rewrite and offer other editorial comments. It is safe to assume that Wright, a conservative gentleman, was taken aback by the frank sexuality at the heart of this story.

Eroticism abounds in Howard's later works, most notably the Conan stories. However, in most cases the sensuality is merely an element of the story, one that adds spice to the narrative. In only a few of Howard's stories is sex presented as the main theme. The most notable are the horror story "Black Canaan" and "The Frost-Giant's Daughter."

In both tales the menace is not a monster or demon, but the grip of dark sexual forces that cloud reason and destroy judgment. In describing Conan's sexual torment, Howard speaks of "Passion fierce as physical agony" (33). He was a physically vigorous twenty-six-year-old when he wrote "The Frost-Giant's Daughter." Like most men that age, he was no stranger to sexual longing and frustration.

As much as Howard may have identified with Conan's violent sexual passion in this story, it must be remembered that the awesome intensity of Conan's desire is not natural, but supernatural, owing to the goddess Atali's magical allure. In telling of his adventure, Conan says, "'The land lay like a dream before me. Only now do all things seem natural and familiar. The woman came and taunted me . . . A strange madness fell upon me when I looked at her, so I forgot all else in the world'" (36-38). The irresistible attraction of the frost-giant's daughter is similar to that of the legendary lorelei and siren, both of whom reflect the Jungian Nixie. Like Odysseus, Conan escapes the trap set by an inhuman female, but he does more than merely escape.

At the climax of the story, Howard touches upon one of the darkest aspects of human sexual relations, for when Conan catches Atali, his sexual frustration is almost extinguished in a violent act of rape. Furthermore, Howard describes this near-rape in an erotic manner: "the feel of her slender body twisting in his mailed arms drove him to a blinder madness" (35). The rape of an uncooperative object of sexual desire is a fairly common male power fantasy. Also a staple of popular fiction, this fantasy has been with us since the earliest folk myths. This male tradition of romanticizing rape, at least in fiction, as the exploit of a macho he-man or colorful rake is what feminist Susan Brownmiller has termed "the myth of the heroic rapist"

(283-308). In her study of rape, *Against Our Will*, Brownmiller states that "no theme grips the masculine imagination with greater constancy and less honor than the myth of the heroic rapist" (289).

Lest we judge Howard too harshly, we must remember that, first of all, rape or abuse of women, even by villains, is not a prominent fixture in his stories. Second of all, Howard takes pains to make it clear that Atali not only provoked Conan, but also cast a spell upon him. Third, Conan is a barbarian, and barbarians throughout history have traditionally regarded women as spoils. In another story we will examine, "The Vale of Lost Women," Conan expresses pride that he has never taken a woman against her will. This bears witness to an exceptional innate nobility on Conan's part, since his peers would have scarcely given a second thought to rape. Finally, there is the fact that Howard, who is after all the final arbiter of the fates of his characters, allows no rape to take place.

The significance of this story lies in Howard's modern interpretation of the myth of the heroic rapist. In *Against Our Will*, Brownmiller cites the classic Greek myths as the earliest examples of the myth of the heroic rapist, specifying Zeus's rape of Leda and other rapes committed by Apollo and Poseidon. In these myths rapes between gods and mortals abound, but interestingly, it is the gods who rape the hapless mortals. In "The Frost-Giant's Daughter," a mortal man humbles a goddess through rape or, more precisely, the threat of rape. This is an extremely modern attitude, and one of many aspects of the Conan series that mark Howard as a writer of modern fiction.

"The Tower of the Elephant" (*Weird Tales*, March 1933; CCC) is one of the most popular and widely read Conan stories. In it, we now find Conan in a civilized setting, an unnamed city in the eastern kingdom of Zamora.

New to civilization, uneducated and unfamiliar with civilized ways, Conan pursues the only livelihood open to him during peacetime, that of a common thief. A fixture in stories and folklore since earliest antiquity, thieves have always evoked a romantic image due, perhaps, to their flouting of convention and defiance of authority. In Howard's Zamora, thievery is esteemed a profession and an art. Thus we find that Conan enters civilization at its lowest level, the underworld.

In a robber's den, Conan learns of the fabled Elephant Tower, the dwelling place of the high priest Yara and a repository for his vast wealth, the most valuable item of which is the mysterious jewel known as the Elephant's Heart. None have ever attempted to steal this prize, for the tower is surrounded by walls and a peril-filled garden, and all are fearful of Yara's magic.

After slaying a kidnapper in a bar fight, Conan takes leave of the thieves' den and heads impulsively for the Tower of the Elephant. He has no plans formulated for entering the tower or even a reason for doing so other than a vague notion of looting it in spite of, or perhaps because of, the fact that others had said it could not be done. This reckless action is typical of the young Conan, who will grow more wary in later years.

En route to the tower, Conan muses not on a possible course of action, but upon what he has heretofore observed in civilization. Of special interest to him are the teachings of civilized scholars. This belies the popular image of Conan as a violent lout interested in little else besides drinking, fornication, and mayhem. Howard tells us that "He had squatted for hours in the courtyards of the philosophers, listening to the arguments of theologians and teachers" (64). Like Kull, Conan possesses a lively intellect and evidences intellectual curiosity. Unlike Kull, however, Conan is "sure of only one thing, and that, that they were all touched in the head" (64).

Arriving at the tower, Conan joins forces with a famous thief named Taurus, whom he meets there. The pair overcome perils and successfully scale the tower. However, when they enter it from the roof,

Taurus is killed by a hideous giant spider, which Conan destroys in a desperate struggle. Ignoring the treasure that surrounds him, he descends deeper into the tower in search of the Elephant's Heart. At length he comes to an ornately furnished chamber. On a marble couch sits a strange green idol with the body of a man and the head of an elephant. This, Conan realizes, is the reason for the tower's name.

Believing the Elephant's Heart to be concealed within the idol, Conan approaches it. Suddenly the eyes of the "idol" open, and Conan realizes that it is no statue, but a living being. When the strange being speaks, it is soon apparent that he is Yara's maimed and blinded prisoner and that he offers Conan no danger.

Gazing upon the scars left by the tortures the monstrous creature has undergone, Conan is overcome by a "strange aching sadness" (76). Howard tells us that Conan "felt that he was looking upon a cosmic tragedy, and he shrank with shame, as if the guilt of a whole race were laid upon him" (76).

Conan's reaction, one of deep sympathy for the deformed elephant-man and abhorrence for the human hand that has reduced him to his present pitiful state, once again contradicts the brutish image of Conan commonly held by those with a superficial familiarity with Howard's work. Although in these first two stories we have seen Conan as a thief, a killer, and nearly a rapist, we are also shown that he is neither stupid, cruel, nor insensitive.

Having overcome his fear and revulsion, Conan speaks with the bizarre creature, who is called Yag-kosha, and learns of his origins.

Thousands of years old, Yag-kosha flew through space to Earth under his own power many eons before and witnessed the rise and fall of Kull's kingdom of Valusia and the sinking of Atlantis. The ultra-telluric alien came to be worshipped as a god in a far land. The sorcerer Yara at first learned wisdom at Yag-kosha's feet but eventually used treachery to use Yag-kosha's own power to enslave him. Finally, Yag-kosha tells Conan of the sorcery of the Blood and the Jewel.

This is his most closely guarded secret, the key to both his liberation and his revenge on Yara. The thief Conan is to be the tool of this final enchantment because, for it to work, Conan must kill Yag-kosha and cut out his heart.

Euthanasia is touched upon by Howard from time to time in his writings: Bran Mak Morn's mercy killing of Titus Sulla, Kull's killing of the girl about to be burned at the stake, and the pact between Kull and Brule to save their souls from the serpent men. Howard was able to conceive of a number of fates worse than death. Thus, Conan does not flinch from his grisly task and does as he is bidden.

Following Yag-kosha's instructions, Conan takes the alien's still-beating heart to the nearby altar on which rests the jewel known as the Elephant's Heart and squeezes blood from the heart onto the jewel, which absorbs it and turns blood-red. Conan takes the jewel to the chamber below where Yara sits in a drug-induced trance and sets it before the sorcerer.

Yara awakens and is drawn hypnotically to the jewel. He begins to shrink and, when no larger than an insect, is sucked into the center of the gem. Within the jewel, Yara is pursued by the avenging figure of Yag-kosha, no longer blind or crippled. The jewel vanishes in a blinding burst of color. Conan flees in a panic, but, as Yag-kosha promised, his way has been made clear. Emerging into the garden at dawn, Conan turns back to see the Tower of the Elephant come crashing down.

By the end of the story, Conan has been reduced to the status of a mere spectator, a witness to cosmic forces beyond his ken. Still, Yag-kosha tells him, "'You are the hand of Fate'" (79), and Conan is indeed the catalyst in bringing about cosmic justice. Conan is often at the center of great events and always on the side of "good." Although he is uninfluenced by societal mores and is motivated mainly by self-interest, Conan possesses an innate sense of honor and a knack for doing the right thing.

In "The Tower of the Elephant," the young Conan encounters civilization, getting a taste of wonders and terrors to come. The prevailing mood of the story is not one of headlong action and carnage, but one of mystery and awe. Howard goes to great lengths to create a lush, colorful texture, embellishing the narrative with all manner of exotic details. The story's language is well wrought, and this is especially evident in Yag-kosha's account of his adventures and downfall, which reads like prose poetry. Undoubtedly the richness of this particular story contributed greatly to its popularity.

The next story we shall examine is "Rogues in the House" (*Weird Tales*, January 1934; CCC). Where "The Tower of the Elephant" is embellished with exotic detail, "Rogues in the House" is a straightforward, sparely written narrative with little in the way of detailed description. Howard completed a single draft of this tale and was evidently sufficiently satisfied with it to submit it to *Weird Tales* without a rewrite. Though the events described are less portentous than those in the previous two stories, "Rogues in the House" provides important clues to the understanding of both the character of Conan and his enduring popularity today.

As in "The Tower of the Elephant," Conan's role in the events that transpire is, at first glance, a minor one. Murilo, an unscrupulous young courtier of an unnamed city-state, runs afoul of the Richelieu-like Nabonidus, the city's Red Priest and the real power behind the throne. Realizing he is a marked man, Murilo decides to strike first by hiring an assassin to go to Nabonidus' house and liquidate the Red Priest. In the city's dungeon, he finds a barbarian thief, Conan, and offers him freedom in exchange for the murder of the Red Priest. The barbarian readily agrees.

Murilo has Conan's chains removed and food brought to him. He tells Conan that after he departs a guard, suitably bribed, will release him. Later, back in his chambers, Murilo is alarmed to learn that the guard has been replaced and that Conan has not escaped. Fearing the hand of the Red Priest in this new turn of events, Murilo sets out to kill Nabonidus on his own. Stealing into the Red Priest's house, his suspicions are aroused by the ease with which he gains entry, encountering none of the traps the house is rumored to contain. At length, he confronts a red-robed figure.

Meanwhile, in the dungeon, Conan, having finished his meal, wonders when his corrupt jailer will appear to turn him loose. When the new jailer arrives in his stead, Conan, unchained, brains him with a beef bone, escaping by his own devices. Though he escapes on his own, it was Murilo who removed his chains and brought him the joint of beef he used as a weapon. Considering himself still somewhat in Murilo's debt, Conan decides to fulfill his part of the bargain and enters the Red Priest's house through a sewer.

In the house's cellar, Conan finds Murilo regaining consciousness. Murilo tells of his own attempt to assassinate Nabonidus, and how he discovered a hairy beast-like horror wearing the garb of the Red Priest, which caused him to pass out in shock.

Believing the Red Priest to be some sort of were-creature, the pair decide to flee but cannot leave the way Conan entered, for an iron grille had dropped in place behind him. Wandering through the labyrinthine chambers under the house, they come across the inert form of Nabonidus himself. Conan and Murilo revive Nabonidus, who reveals that the strange apelike creature that Murilo encountered is a "pet" of his called Thak.

The Red Priest explains that he found Thak as a cub in a distant land and raised him to be a servant and bodyguard. Neither wholly animal nor wholly human, Thak nonetheless developed a "'bestial ambition'" (292) of his own. He finally struck Nabonidus down, making his former master his captive and ruling the house in his stead. Nabonidus takes Murilo and Conan to a spy device consisting of an elaborate network of mirrors and allows them to observe Thak. Murilo recognizes that Thak is indeed "budding awfully into something vaguely human" (292) and is "nauseated by a fleeting realization of the abysses of bellowing bestiality up through which humanity had painfully toiled" (292).

The trio—"'rogues together'" (290)—know that Thak is alerted to their presence and waiting for them. They plan to create a diversion that will enable Conan to take Thak by surprise and slay him quickly, before the monster's superhuman strength can prevail. Before they can do this, they observe the arrival of other enemies of Nabonidus through the mirror device.

Thak's semi-human intelligence is sufficient to trigger one of the house's many booby-traps and effortlessly dispatch the conspirators. It is then that the three rogues set their desperate plan into action. Murilo catches Thak's attention, allowing Conan, poniard in hand, to leap upon the creature's back. What follows is Conan's first, but not last, struggle with an apelike monster. Stabbing Thak repeatedly, Conan finally manages to slay him, suffering painful wounds in the process.

As Murilo tends to his wounds, Conan gasps, "'I have slain a man tonight, not a beast'" (299). However, when Nabonidus attempts one final treachery, Conan smashes him like an insect. The long night over, Conan and Murilo depart the house of the Red Priest.

It is surprising that no critic has yet mentioned the number of similarities between "Rogues in the House" and the stories of Edgar Allan Poe. The story takes place in a bizarre house like those in "The Fall of the House of Usher" and "The Masque of the Red Death"; often in Poe stories powerful men reside in such imposing edifices. The Red Priest himself is a Poe-esque figure, garbed in a single hue and exerting Machiavellian influence over a small kingdom. The apelike Thak recalls the murderous orang-outang in "The Murders in the Rue Morgue."

The image of Thak moving through the great house clothed in

his master's robes is a reversal of Poe's "Hop-Frog," in which the king masquerades as an ape—a purely Howardian turnabout. Murilo's recognition of a "faint and hideous kinship between his kind and that squatting monstrosity" (292) was a vision Howard never lost sight of. Beneath the veneer of civilization—the mantle of emperors and the robes of priests—lurks always the slavering visage of the ape.

Thak, the "man" Conan slays at the story's climax, is a character as complex and fully realized as any of the others. No mere supernatural menace, he is actually the fourth "rogue." Nabonidus speaks of Thak as being motivated by "'hate, resentment, and some sort of bestial ambition'" (292). Jungle predators kill to survive. That Thak is indeed "budding awfully into something vaguely human" (292) is evidenced by his use of his primordial strength to take what is not rightfully his, typically human behavior.

Nabonidus and Murilo, two "civilized" men, possess more finesse but less scruples than either Thak or Conan. They take by guile what they cannot take by force, using the gift of intelligence for base ends. The irony that such rogues should be trapped together does not escape the characters themselves. When Nabonidus accuses Murilo of treason, Murilo points out that Nabonidus exploits the kingdom for his own ends, and concludes, "'This Cimmerian is the most honest man of the three of us, because he steals and murders openly'" (290).

Conan, the only one of these characters to be imprisoned by society for wrongdoing, is thus deemed the most admirable. He has already proven himself the most ethical by keeping his word to Murilo. In these first three stories, we have seen Conan as thief, near-rapist, and assassin. Nevertheless, Conan possesses a set of ethics. He helped Yag-kosha because the alien needed and deserved his aid; he helped Murilo because Murilo helped him. Conan is a man of his word and therefore a man of honor. However, Conan's ethics are his ethics, not those society would impose upon him.

As we shall see in the next story, religion is not a factor in his moral convictions. Neither are the laws and customs of the civilized society to which he is a stranger. Conan's behavior is not subject to "the laws of man and God." Conan is an existentialist. He and he alone decides what he is and what he will become. In determining his own ethics, Conan himself determines who he is.

Though a character of heroic stature, Conan is also one of that new breed of modern protagonist, the antihero. The concerns of the antihero are not those of the traditional hero. Odysseus battles to save Ithaca; Conan left Cimmeria out of boredom and battles for the joy of combat. Robin Hood steals to help the poor; Conan steals for personal gain. True to his own code, the values of the status quo mean nothing to him. Antiheroes have been present in literature for some time.

Dostoevsky's Ivan Karamazov is one example of an antihero, and Jack London's Wolf Larsen is another. However, the proliferation of antiheroes in popular culture is a much more recent phenomenon. The postwar generation strongly identified with James Dean and Marlon Brando in such films as *Rebel without a Cause* and *The Wild One*, and later with the protagonists of the cult film *Easy Rider*. In these films the main character is usually a restless loner who regards authority with indifference, disrespect, or downright contempt. In "Rogues in the House" we are told that Conan "had none of the fear or reverence for authority that civilization instills in men" (280).

In the 1960s, around the same time the Conan paperback boom was getting underway, movie audiences eschewed John Wayne in favor of an existential antihero of the Old West called the Man with No Name. In the James Bond spy films, a pop culture sensation of the '60s equaled only by the Beatles, 007's main interests are gambling, high living, and womanizing; saving the world is a secondary concern. It is no coincidence that the Conan character first began to garner enormous popularity during the same period.

But Conan was first introduced to the reading public in the pulp magazines of the '30s, during an era when popular heroes such as The Shadow and Doc Savage held sway and fought doggedly to preserve the status quo rather than challenge it. It may well be that Robert E. Howard, in addition to creating modern heroic fantasy, gave popular culture its first existential antihero.

"Rogues in the House" completes the first phase of Conan's career in which, as a thief, he discovered the pleasures and pitfalls of civilization. He does not remain a thief long and moves on to the more agreeable role of hired swordsman. As a mercenary for the Hyrkanian armies of the east, whom Howard modeled after the Ottoman Turks, Conan expands and refines his knowledge of warfare, adding archery and horsemanship to his repertoire of martial arts skills. Howard wrote no stories set in this period, but made mention of it elsewhere.

The Cimmerian next appeared in one of the most memorable tales of the saga, "Queen of the Black Coast" (*Weird Tales*, May 1934; CCC). This tale marks a new level of maturity for the Conan character, for it is here that he forms his first enduring relationship with a woman. He is also seen for the first time as a professional soldier and leader of men.

Though "Rogues in the House" and "Queen of the Black Coast" are separated by a few years in Conan's life, thematically the latter takes up where the former left off. Once again Conan is in trouble for challenging authority because his personal code of ethics is at odds with society's.

The story opens with Conan pursued by soldiers to the waterfront of a large port city, where he leaps aboard an outbound trading ship. The captain of the vessel aids Conan because he at first fears the warrior and because he feels a certain amount of contempt for the law himself.

Safely underway, Conan tells the captain that he had been taken before the magistrate and questioned about the location of a friend who was being sought for murder. When Conan explained that he could not betray his comrade, the judge lectured him on civic duty and then threatened to throw him in the dungeon. Conan split the judge's skull and fled.

The captain of the ship *Argus* is glad to have a fighting man aboard, for they are bound for waters teeming with pirates. The most dreaded of all is "'the wildest she-devil unhanged'" (125)—Bêlit, a Shemite woman who commands a crew of black raiders from the pseudo-African countries far to the south of the Hyborians.

Days later, as they near the southern Black Coast, Bêlit's pirate ship, the *Tigress*, attacks. Taking up a bow, Conan picks off the pirates of the approaching ship as the crew of the *Argus* attempt to sell their lives as dearly as possible. Some strange whim prevents Conan from doing the logical thing and killing Bêlit.

Presently the pirates are boarding the ship, and Conan draws his sword. One of the most violent battles in the series takes place. Conan is armored; his foes are not. The "fighting madness of his race" (126) upon him, he wades into the pirates, and we are told how he "cleft skulls, smashed breasts, severed limbs, ripped out entrails, and littered the deck like a shambles with a ghastly harvest of brains and blood" (126).

Conan, however, is outnumbered, the merchant crew dies quickly and he is alone, his back to the mast. Death is inevitable, but abruptly the tone changes from one of violent carnage to unbridled sexuality as Bêlit leaps before her crew, ordering them back.

Nearly naked and "formed like a goddess; at once lithe and voluptuous" (127), Bêlit approaches Conan, who realizes the danger has passed, for "he had held too many women, civilized and barbarian . . . not to recognize the light that burned in the eyes of this one" (127). Nor is Conan wrong, for "With the unerring instinct of the elemental feminine, she knew she had found her lover" (127).

Jack London, Howard's favorite writer, espoused the concept of the "mate-woman"—a woman who, though embracing most feminine qualities, is nonetheless her man's equal in physical and intellectual capabilities and, in all ways, his perfect companion. A "mate-woman" is to be sought after and prized for, according to London, no human relationship is greater than that of a man and his "mate-woman." Bêlit—strong-willed, leader of men, warrior in her own right, acting with the same impulses and instincts which drive Conan—is his perfect mate. They both realize this instinctively and immediately. Conan agrees to roam the seas with the "white-skinned young tiger-cat" (128).

The intense passion of this story is remarkable to say the least. From Conan's slaughter of Bêlit's warriors through the initial confrontation between Bêlit, "her bosom heaving," and Conan, his "dripping blade" (127) extended, to the ardor of Bêlit's declaration of her love for Conan and his reaction, the writing can only be described as feverish. Nor is Howard quite finished, for the opening chapter climaxes in a frenzy as Bêlit strips off her scanty garments, does an incredibly erotic "'mating-dance'" during which "dying men forgot death" (128), and hurls herself at Conan's feet.

The second chapter begins with a brief account of how Bêlit and Conan roam the ocean as pirates. Elsewhere Howard alludes to this period in Conan's life when he becomes known and feared along the Black Coast as Amra the Lion. However, the only adventure of Conan and Bêlit to be related by Howard is their last. It begins as they embark on a new search for treasure.

A lost city is said to lie far up a poison river inhabited by venomous reptiles and shunned by all other creatures. The *Tigress* ventures up this river. Howard describes how the surrounding jungle grows darker and more oppressive as they travel upriver, recalling "Heart of Darkness."

It is during this passage that the fundamental differences between

Conan and Howard's earlier characters Kull and Kane are reinforced. Sensing that they are entering a region rife with danger, Conan and Bêlit uncharacteristically ponder philosophical matters. When Bêlit asks him what he believes about life after death and what is ultimately real, Conan replies:

> "I have known many gods. He who denies them is as blind as he who trusts them too deeply. I seek not beyond death. It may be the blackness averred by the Nemedian skeptics, or Crom's realm of ice and cloud, or the snowy plains and vaulted halls of the Nordheimer's Valhalla. I know not, nor do I care. Let me live deep while I live, let me know the rich juices of red meat and stinging wine on my palate, the hot embrace of white arms, and the mad exultation of battle when the blue blades flame and crimson, and I am content. Let teachers and priests and philosophers brood over questions of reality and illusion. I know this: if life is an illusion, then I am no less an illusion, and being thus, the illusion is real to me. I live, I burn with life, I love, I slay, and am content." (133)

Where Kull gazed for hours into the mirrors of Tuzun Thune, Conan is content to leave philosophy to the philosophers. Nor does Conan feel any pressing need to affirm or deny the existence of gods; in this respect he resembles his creator, who was an agnostic rather than an atheist.

Conan's Nietzschean declaration of life-affirmation would, of course, not have impressed Solomon Kane. For the better part of the Christian era, life was regarded primarily as a preparation for the afterlife. The salvation of the immortal soul was considered humanity's most important concern; physical comfort and earthly experience were deemed unimportant. The above quotation reveals Conan's worldview to be a very modern one.

Bêlit's response is both passionate and revealing of her character, showing what she considers all-important:

> "There is life beyond death, I know, and I know this too, Conan of Cimmeria ... my love is stronger than any death! I have lain in your

arms, panting with the violence of our love; you have held and crushed and conquered me, drawing my soul to your lips with the fierceness of your bruising kisses. My heart is welded to your heart, my soul is part of your soul! Were I still in death and you fighting for life, I would come back from the abyss to aid you—aye, whether my spirit floated from the purple sails on the crystal sea of paradise, or writhed in the molten flames of Hell! I am yours, and all the gods and all their eternities shall not sever us!" (133-34)

Bêlit and Conan share a sort of "primal passion" that is neither wholly love nor wholly lust as we understand these concepts but something entirely more primitive and basic. Both spiritual love and physical lust are merely different aspects of this "primal passion," which has become fragmented through countless centuries of customs, mores, and social taboos. Conan and Bêlit, the elemental man and woman, seem to know this passion in its pristine, unadulterated form.

The passion of Conan and Bêlit is matched by the passion of Howard's writing. This is most obvious in such scenes as the "mating dance" and is evident in the dialogue as well. The above passage may be judged bombastic by some, but it bears witness to the fact that Howard employed virtually no restraint when composing these and other passages of dialogue and description.

Raymond Chandler said that a writer who is afraid to overreach himself is as useless as a general who is afraid to be wrong. A less "virile" wordsmith than Howard would have undoubtedly elected to tone down these passages in the final draft. It seems more than likely that Howard wrote key scenes of "Queen of the Black Coast" feverishly, like a man possessed. Reading over them later, he instinctively realized the appropriateness of his dialogue between his ultimate man and ultimate woman and let it stand.

The *Tigress* arrives at length at her destination, the ancient ruins of a once-great city. Disembarking, the crew notices a monstrous winged ape (reminiscent of the akaana in "Wings of the Night") lurking in the jungle nearby. With unerring instinct, Bêlit leads the pirates to the treasure's hiding place. Her intuition again proves sound when she calls Conan away from a booby-trap that kills several crewmen. At the sight of the treasure now revealed, however, Bêlit's wits leave her, for "The Shemite soul finds a bright drunkenness in riches and material splendor" (136).

The most fascinating item is a necklace of crimson stones. Returning to the ship, the pirates learn that the winged ape has caved in their water casks. Unable to drink form the poison river, Conan takes some men into the jungle in search of fresh water. Bêlit, the necklace now adorning her "naked white bosom" (136), is so blinded by avarice that she scarcely notices their departure.

In the jungle, Conan is separated from his men and inadvertently wanders into a cluster of the black lotus, a potent narcotic plant "whose scent brought dream-haunted slumber" (137). Conan is rendered unconscious, and in some mysterious manner the lotus causes him to see visions that reveal the truth about the city and its bizarre inhabitants. Many eons before, the city was inhabited by a noble race of winged, godlike people—"they resembled man only as man in his highest form resembles the great apes" (138).

As the ages passed, the climate gradually changed, causing the race to devolve. Eventually their water became tainted with a terrible poison that altered them more drastically. We are told that "They who had been winged gods became pinioned demons, with all that remained of their ancestors' vast knowledge distorted and perverted and twisted into ghastly paths. As they had risen higher than humanity might dream, so they sank lower than man's maddest nightmare's reach" (139). Preying on one another, they all died out but one.

A greater cosmic tragedy can scarcely be conceived, but the horror awaiting Conan is no less tragic. The black pirates have all been slain by the monstrous winged ape and a pack of were-hyenas under its command. When he returns to the ship, Conan finds Bêlit hanging from the yardarm, the jeweled necklace knotted around her neck like a hangman's noose.

The next chapter finds Conan grimly awaiting the return of the winged horror, having placed Bêlit's body on a pyre aboard ship. Conan knows the vision he saw was true, just as he knows he must kill the beast. He realizes that the winged demon is possessed of superior intelligence by the way it divided the forces and its "grim jest" (143) of the jeweled noose. He is aware that the fiend spared him so far to inflict psychological torture. Knowing it must now finish him off, Conan awaits his tormentor's return atop a pyramid in the midst of the ruins.

When the moon rises, the pack of bewitched hyenas bursts from the jungle. Conan kills most of them with arrows before they reach him; he battles the rest with sword and sinew. As he kills the last of the hyenas, the monster ape attacks, attempting to crush Conan beneath a massive pillar. Conan leaps aside, tumbling down the pyramid's steps. His legs are pinned under the rubble, his sword out of reach. The monster closes in for the kill, but suddenly an apparition bursts between it and Conan, driving the creature back. It is Bêlit's ghost, "vibrant with love as fierce as a she-panther's." In her eyes Conan sees "her love flaming, a naked elemental thing of raw fire and molten lava" (147).

Bêlit, true to her words, has pierced the veil of death itself to be at her lover's side in his hour of greatest need. What we earlier referred to as "primal passion" is shown by Howard to be the very essence of life; life springs from it, and in this one instance, death is denied by it. One wonders if Howard felt the love of a Dante for a Beatrice could engender a similar miracle.

Bêlit's intervention enables Conan to free himself. He retrieves his sword, and "the oldest race in the world was extinct" (147). Howard's choice of words here recalls Solomon Kane's extermination of the race of winged devils in "Wings in the Night."

In the story's epilogue, Conan sets fire to the ship bearing Bêlit's body as it drifts out to sea. Thus, one of the only two love stories Howard wrote comes to an end.

By the time "Queen of the Black Coast" appeared in *Weird Tales* in 1934, Howard was involved in his first and ultimately only love affair. This was with Novalyne Price, a strong-willed, independent-minded young woman. High-spirited and intellectually keen, Novalyne was a fit companion for Howard, perhaps even a potential "mate-woman." They argued frequently, however, and ultimately the relationship succumbed to the couple's incompatibility.

"Queen of the Black Coast" is not a typical love story. As in "The Tower of the Elephant," a note of cosmic tragedy creeps in, only here the tragedy is of apocalyptic proportions and is related in a passage evocative of Milton.

The vision imparted to Conan by the black lotus is a Howardian version of the Fall. Howard conceived of Earth's oldest race as "winged and of heroic proportions" (138), which is, of course, the classic image of the angels. They are not supernatural beings, however, for although they were "not a branch on the mysterious stalk of evolution that culminated in men," they were "the ripe blossom on an alien tree" (138). Still, "In spiritual, esthetic and intellectual development they were superior to man as man is superior to the gorilla" (138). Their downfall is brought about, not through any spiritual shortcoming on their part, but by an accident of nature. The world changed and these beings were not immune to this change. It is as though, as with the dinosaurs, the Earth would no longer tolerate their presence, and so they were toppled from the pinnacle of evolution. Like his colleague H. P. Lovecraft, Howard possessed the capacity for recognizing the true scope of space and time and the insignificance of earthly life when measured against it.

The ignominious fall of the once-noble winged race is perhaps the greatest cosmic tragedy imaginable, and yet what does it ultimately lead to? The death spasm of this race is the murder of Bêlit, the Queen of the Black Coast and the love of Conan's life.

"Queen of the Black Coast" is a love story, but a tragic one. For Howard, it could not have been otherwise. Throughout his life, he was acutely aware of the transience of all things. He knew that, no less than the stars themselves, all love affairs reach their ends. In 1935, Howard broke off his relationship with Novalyne Price. It ended over a silly quarrel. But for Conan's love affair to end, a race of angels had to fall.

Following the loss of Bêlit, Conan reverts once more to his original state—that of a savage denizen of the wilderness. After the burning of the *Tigress*, Conan has no recourse but to turn inland into the primordial jungle that surrounds him. When we see him next, he is living among a tribe of jungle blacks called the Bamulas. There is a difference, however, for the authority he shared with Bêlit has given him a taste for leadership. Though a white man, his cunning, ferocity, and prowess have elevated him to the position of war-chief of the tribe. This brief period of Conan's life is depicted in a short tale called "The Vale of Lost Women" (CCC).

Like "The Frost-Giant's Daughter," this story never saw print in Howard's lifetime. Perhaps because of its length and deceptively simple plot, many readers have dismissed it as one of the lesser tales of the canon, some even going so far as to designate it the worst Conan story. In fact, the opposite is true and it is necessary to correct this oversight by examining one of Howard's most underrated works.

Others have noted that Conan is most impressive when seen through the eyes of another character. In "The Vale of Lost Women," the witness is a helpless, terrified, captive white woman. The story begins with Livia cowering in the hut where she is kept prisoner, reliving the horrors of her capture by the howling black savages who feast and hold parley without. Her hatred and loathing center on the grossly obese chief, Bajujh, who had her brother hideously tortured to death before her eyes.

As she watches through a crack in the wall, another arrives to hold council. This tribe, she is astonished to observe, is led by a white man. "Whoever he was, Livia knew the man must indeed be powerful in that wild land, if Bajujh of Bakalah rose to greet him" (305). It is, of course, Conan.

Seeing this indomitable war-chief, a member of her race, as her last hope of salvation, Livia steals from her hut after the natives have passed out from their debauch and sneaks into Conan's quarters. There she pleads with him to rescue her and avenge her brother. She offers her virgin body in exchange for Bajujh's head. Conan pragmatically points out that as a captive, her sexual favors are no longer hers to bestow or withhold as she pleases and that she is his for the taking. Livia's spirit is crushed, but for his own reasons Conan relents, saying, "'I'll play this game your way . . . tomorrow night it will be Conan's bed you'll warm, not Bajujh's'" (309).

The next night, Conan keeps his vow. At a prearranged signal, Conan's men unexpectedly slaughter their half-drunk hosts and massacre the village. This one-sided slaughter is rendered in a grim, brutal manner by Howard, rather than portrayed as an exciting action sequence. Livia derives little satisfaction from her revenge. When she sees Conan stalking toward her carrying the grisly trophy of Bajujh's head, terror overwhelms her and she bolts through the chaos and confusion, fleeing naked on horseback into the jungle.

After riding at a headlong pace for many hours, Livia comes to a strange valley where, according to native legend, a race of brown-skinned women fled long ago to escape their ravishers. She is glad because "There was none to threaten her, or seize her with rude violent hands" (312).

Livia wanders through the vale in an enchanted state of idyllic bliss, adorning her hair with blossoms. In the center of the valley, she finds a stone altar bedecked with blossoms. Suddenly she is surrounded by silent, brown-skinned women. Looking into their eyes, she can tell that their souls have undergone a terrible change. The loveliest of the women embraces Livia and kisses her upon the lips. Paralyzed by this kiss, Livia is laid upon the altar while the silent naked women perform a ritual around it. From the sky descends an indescribable horror, "cosmic foulness born in night-black gulfs beyond the reach of a madman's wildest dreams" (314).

But before this horror can claim Livia's soul, Conan appears and gives battle to the thing, driving it away and rescuing Livia. The spell is broken, and all the women have disappeared mysteriously. Conan takes Livia away, telling how he tracked her through the jungle to the vale.

In the final paragraphs, Conan reveals his true intentions regarding Livia: "'It was a foul bargain I made ... After I thought awhile, I saw that to hold you to your bargain would be the same as if I had forced you'" (316). Conan will take Livia to the borders of civilized lands, where she can be sent safely home.

When Livia flees from Conan to the vale of lost women, she is fleeing not only her captors, but all males. As she enters the vale, Howard tells us that "One thought reiterated itself continually; there she was safe from the brutality of men" (313). She nearly surrenders herself to the vale, as did those who came before, seeking comfort in the embrace of other women. However, this refuge proves to be a deadly trap, and Livia's soul is almost lost to her.

What Howard seems to be saying is that, although men and women constantly brutalize each other physically and mentally, they belong together nonetheless. To seek refuge from the battle of the sexes in homosexuality is to deny one of the most important constants of the human condition. In Howard's day, homosexuality was not well understood, and he may not have been fully aware that sexual orientation involves little in the way of choice. In the case of some males and females, it appears to be a form of innate behavior.

On the other hand, women have been known to experiment with lesbian experiences due to curiosity, or as part of a man-hating phase. The present story suggests that this is playing with fire. At best it can bring about spiritual emptiness; at worst it can cause spiritual degradation. When Conan rescues Livia, he saves her not from physical harm, but from a shadowy existence without a soul.

"The Vale of Lost Women" is an interesting counterpoint to "The Frost-Giant's Daughter." Neither story was published in Howard's lifetime, almost certainly owing to their explicit sexual themes. But, though sexuality lies at the heart of each short tale, in execution they are polar opposites.

Most readily noticeable is the startling contrast in setting: "The Frost-Giant's Daughter" occurs in a frigid, sub-arctic clime while "The Vale of Lost Women" takes place in a steaming jungle. In "The Frost-Giant's Daughter," the malefactor is an unearthly female; in "The Vale of Lost Women," Howard unflinchingly shows his own sex at its absolute worst, wallowing in rapine, murder, and wanton cruelty.

Driven to attempt rape in "The Frost-Giant's Daughter," Conan opposes it in word and deed in "The Vale of Lost Women." He turns against sworn allies to keep Livia's body unsullied by her rapist-captor, he battles a monster to prevent her spirit from being violated, and finally he forsakes any ulterior motives of his own concerning her.

The story's denouement is that Livia will be returned home. Conan has re-established normalcy in her life. By keeping her body and spirit inviolate, and by restraining his own passions, Conan also symbolically restores Livia's normal sexuality.

The stories telling of Conan's adventures from the middle period of his career, from his mid-twenties to mid-thirties, take him from one end of the Hyborian world to the other. He garners a formidable reputation as pirate, bandit, and soldier-of-fortune. These exploits are recounted in such tales as "Black Colossus" (*Weird Tales*, June 1933),

"Jewels of Gwahlur" (*Weird Tales*, March 1935) and "The Devil in Iron" (*Weird Tales*, August 1934).

There is no need to examine these particular stories in detail, for they lack the depth of those previously studied. However, all the hallmarks of top-notch adventure fiction are present. The pacing is headlong, the settings exotic, and the narrative gripping. Although the quality varies from story to story, even the least successful contains some redeeming element—a memorable passage, an interesting characterization, or a clever exchange of dialogue. And, of course, Conan himself is never less than impressive. Brimming with gusto, these stories have gained Howard his worldwide following.

For years, Howard criticism consisted primarily of praise for Howard's superlative talents as a master of high adventure. Many who examined Howard's writing did not attempt deep literary or philosophical scrutiny, preferring instead to extol its virtues as entertainment. The aforementioned stories are among those in which Howard fulfills this reputation as the adventure writer extraordinaire. In this capacity, Howard takes his place alongside H. Rider Haggard, Talbot Mundy, and Edgar Rice Burroughs. If not particularly thought-provoking, these tales have been relished by armchair adventurers for over half a century.

Some years later, Conan is a widely traveled adventurer and leader of men with years of broad experience behind him. From this point in his fictional chronology, Conan is seen taking the reins of history in his own hands as a leader of armies or even peoples, becoming a force in the shaping of the world around him. The first of these tales is "A Witch Shall Be Born" (*Weird Tales*, December 1934; BCC).

The story begins as Taramis, noble young queen of the small kingdom of Khauran, is visited in her bedchamber by her identical twin sister, Salome. Salome was left in the desert to die as a baby, for an ancient curse prophesied that "a witch shall be born" every century to the royal family, and Taramis's twin bore the telltale birthmark.

Found in the desert by an eastern sorcerer who recognized the mark, Salome was raised steeped in the black arts. Now she has returned to claim the throne of her virtuous sister. She is aided by Constantius, "The Falcon," the red-handed leader of Shemite renegades.

Salome has Taramis secretly imprisoned and in her guise admits the Shemites to the city. "Taramis" orders her own army to stand down, but one officer does not comply. He is Conan, and his unerring barbarian instincts alert him to the sham. He boldly denounces the witch in public by shouting, "'This isn't Taramis! It's some devil in masquerade!'" (266). A short battle ensues and the rebellion is crushed by the Shemites. Conan is laid low by sheer weight of numbers and crucified by Constantius.

Conan's ordeal on the cross is one of the most brutal and best-remembered scenes in the series. Constantius leaves Conan unguarded to invite the vultures to gnaw at his living flesh. When one attempts to do so, Conan breaks the bird's neck with his teeth. This display of will and defiance impresses a passerby, Olgerd Vladislav, chief of the Zuagirs, nomadic desert tribesmen who harry the caravans. He orders Conan cut down.

Months pass during which Salome conducts a reign of terror. In the desert Conan recovers and, in a bold move, deposes Olgerd as chief of the Zuagirs. With this desert army under his command, he seeks to liberate the city and revenge himself on Constantius. Conan employs bogus siege engines to lure Constantius's army into the field. The Falcon is duped by this deception, and Conan's forces win the day. In the meantime, patriots in the city rescue the real Queen Tamaris.

Her power broken, Salome attempts to unleash a demonic monstrosity she had summoned, only to be slain by one of the patriots. Conan's desert army rides into the city just in time to destroy the monster before it can claim its human sacrifices. Constantius, whom Conan ordered taken alive, is nailed to the cross and Conan wryly comments, "'You are more fit to inflict torture than to endure it'" (300).

"A Witch Shall Be Born" is an excellent Conan story, brimming with terror and excitement, but the most striking aspect is its reworking of the New Testament gospels in purely Howardian terms.

The name of the witch, Salome, is not merely another example of Howard's oft-noted penchant for using historical or mythological appellations familiar to the reader. The biblical Salome was, of course, the daughter of Herodias whose dance pleased Herod so much that he fulfilled her desire of having John the Baptist's head presented to her on a platter (Matthew 14:1-2; Mark 6:14-29). Unnamed in the Bible, her identity comes down to us from a contemporary chronicler, Josephus, and Howard clearly intended his Salome to be identified with her biblical counterpart. The witch boasts to Taramis that:

> ". . . even when the mountains of ice have roared down from the pole and ground the civilizations to ruin, and a new world has risen from the ashes and dust—even then shall there be Salomes to walk the earth, to trap men's hearts by their sorcery, to dance before the kings of the world, and see the heads of the wise men fall at their pleasure!" (259)

To make her point, Salome torments Taramis with the severed head of her faithful councilor, Krallides.

Howard also stresses that Salome is not a sorceress, a celibate mystic devoted to occult studies, but a witch. Salome tells Taramis how the sorcerer who raised her finally cast her out as unfit to be her student:

> "'He drove me from him at last, saying that I was but a common witch in spite of his teachings . . . He said I was but an earthly sprite, knowing naught of the deeper gulfs of cosmic sorcery. Well, this world contains all I desire—power and pomp, and glittering pageantry, handsome men and soft women for my paramours and my slaves . . .'" (260)

When witches appear in Howard's writings, they are most often presented as strong sexual images. Atla, the witch who demanded one night of Bran Mak Morn's love in "Worms of the Earth," or the witch in "Black Canaan" are examples.

Constantius, Salome's paramour, is a mercenary adventurer like Conan. As with Solomon Kane and Le Loup, there are superficial similarities between them, and one vital difference: Conan is a barbarian while Constantius is a renegade outcast, embodying only the negative aspects of civilization. His degeneracy and casual but studied cruelty are worthy of a Caligula. Ironically, the name "Constantius" derives from the name of the emperor who made Christianity the state religion of Rome.

The armies commanded by Constantius are composed of outcast Shemites, Howard's Hyborian counterparts to the biblical Hebrews, described as "thick-bodied . . . with curled blue-black beards and hooked noses" (266). Conan's love, Bêlit, was also Shemite, and perhaps Howard wished to endow her with an additional larger-than-life quality by likening her to the biblical heroines Esther and Ruth. The Zuagirs, mercenaries commanded by Conan, are Arab-like nomads.

Nowhere, however, is Howard's biblical allegory more fascinating than in regard to the contrast between the crucifixion of Conan and Christ's sacrifice on the cross. Howard previously used a crucifixion to mark the beginning of Bran Mak Morn's spiritual descent. Now he has his greatest hero undergo an ordeal identical to that of the western world's greatest archetypal figure, a parallel that invites comparison.

Christ was crucified by Jews under Roman rule. Conan is crucified by Shemites led by the Roman-like Constantius. Christ accepted his fate and meekly submitted to his own humiliation, torture, and death. Conan strives with every iota of his being against this fate, breaking the neck of a vulture that sought to eat his still-living flesh. After this grisly victory, Howard tells us that "Ferocious triumph surged through Conan's numbed brain. Life beat strongly and savagely through his veins. He could still deal death; he still lived. Every twinge of sensation, even of agony, was a negation of death" (270).

Christ's death, in Christian myth, led to a rebirth that initiated the redemption of all humanity. Conan is not concerned with redeeming anyone: "The city had betrayed him—trapped him into circumstances that left him hanging to a wooden cross like a hare nailed to a tree. If he could but descend from this tree of torment and lose himself in that empty waste—turn his back forever on the crooked streets and walled lairs where men plotted to betray humanity" (268). It is misanthropic rage rather than philanthropic benevolence that ultimately frames his future actions: "A red lust for vengeance swept away the thought" (268). Conan survives his crucifixion to become the leader of barbarian tribesmen. His liberation of the city is a means to his reckoning with Constantius.

In essence Howard's message is clear. Christ died on the cross and Conan did not because one is a lamb and the other a lion. Conan embodies a kind of Nietzschean life-affirmation that is not concerned with a spiritual afterlife.

Conan is the most pragmatic of Howard's heroes, a man who would never devote his life to religion, mysticism, or spiritual abstractions. An existentialist, Conan's ethical code and lifestyle are of his own choosing. Civilized people bear many crosses: obligations to family, to church, to community standards. Conan, unencumbered by physical or spiritual restraints, is truly free.

Written to satisfy *Weird Tales* readers' requests for a longer Conan story, "The People of the Black Circle" (*Weird Tales*, September, October, and November 1934; *BCC*) is perhaps the most famous Conan adventure. Only *The Hour of the Dragon* is longer, and the novella's length allows for a richer narrative, along with a plot that encompasses an exotic far-off kingdom, the clash of armies, the intrigue of court espionage, breathless chases, passions unleashed, dazzling swordplay, a mountain stronghold of black-hearted sorcerers, and a headstrong and beautiful queen. Events are piled on events, and the reader is swept up by the sheer power of Howard's vision.

"The People of the Black Circle" is cited by many readers as their favorite Conan story. Fritz Leiber considered it "the best of the Conan stories and perhaps the pinnacle of Howard's writing" and noted that, "Tightly plotted, pithily poetic, gorgeously ornamented, manned by grand heroes and villains and also by characters torn between good and evil, and above all brimming with glamour and glory, it can be compared without over-praise to the plays of Christopher Marlowe and John Webster" (8). The editors at Lancer Books wisely chose "The People of the Black Circle" as the first story in the first volume of the original Conan paperback series in the 1960s, where a new generation of admirers discovered the awesome barbarian adventurer.

"The People of the Black Circle" is set in Vendhya, modeled after the India of Kipling and Talbot Mundy. The Himalayas become the Himelians; the Khyber Pass becomes the Zhaibar Pass, and so on. In the capital, the king Bhunda Chand lies dying from a spell laid on him by the Black Seers of Mount Yimsha. His sister, the Devi Yasmina, watches helplessly until her brother begs her to end his life before his soul can be sucked away by the wizards. Once again euthanasia recurs in Howard's writing as an act of salvation when the anguished Yasmina plunges a jeweled dagger into Bhunda Chand's heart.

Other characters are revealed. Kerim Shah, a Turanian spy seeking to undermine Bhunda Chand's kingdom, meets with Khemsa, an acolyte of the Black Seers ordered by them to assist the Turanians for unfathomable reasons of their own. Gitara, the Devi's treacherous handmaiden, loves Khemsa with unquenchable passion and urges him to defy his masters and use his magical powers for their own ends.

V. Conan

The scene shifts to a frontier outpost where Governor Chunder Shan has received orders to delay the execution of seven chieftains of the Afghuli bandits who dwell in the impenetrable mountain regions beyond the Zhaibar Pass. The order was issued by Yasmina herself, who wishes to use these hostages to coerce the chief of the Afghulis, Conan, into using his forces against the stronghold of the Seers. Yasmina, accompanied by Gitara, arrives at the outpost to implement her scheme of revenge, but plans go awry when Conan, having come to parley with the Governor, abducts her.

Conan flees into the mountains and hides out in the village of an ally. Khemsa and Kerim Shah learn from Gitara what has happened, and each decides to secure the Devi for his own purposes. Kerim Shah wants to deliver her to the king of Turan. Khemsa, at the passionate urging of Gitara, finally rebels against his masters, and together they plot to ransom the Devi. Khemsa uses his magic to slay the seven Afghuli headmen to prevent the Governor from surrendering them to obtain the Devi's release. Meanwhile, Kerim Shah sends an urgent message calling for Turanian troops to meet him in the Himelians.

Yasmina is Conan's prisoner in the village of Yar Afzal, chief of the Wazulis. Khemsa appears and slays Yar Afzal by sorcery. The Wazulis turn on Conan and drive him and Yasmina from their village.

Later Khemsa confronts Conan, but before they clash the Black Seers intervene. Khemsa loses a battle of wills with the more powerful wizards, and he and Gitara are obliterated in an avalanche caused by the Seers. The sorcerers vanish in a mystical cloud, taking the Devi with them. Conan resolves to rescue Yasmina somehow, even though he has learned that she is now useless as a hostage. The Afghulis have also learned of the seven chieftains' deaths and believe Conan is responsible; five hundred of them now pursue him.

Deeper in the mountains, Conan meets Kerim Shah and several

of his henchmen, and they form an uneasy alliance to rescue Yasmina. Together they boldly invade Mount Yimsha. Avoiding physical and supernatural traps, they gain entry into the sorcerers' castle. At length they confront the Master of Yimsha, a human being who summoned the Black Seers from another dimension to serve him and who, having fancied Yasmina for a slave, has been subjecting her to terrifying visions to break her will. The confrontation ends with most of the participants meeting hideous fates. Conan severely wounds the Master and escapes with Yasmina.

Yasmina has grown to admire Conan but protests when he insists that she become his woman, citing her responsibilities to her people. The argument is rendered futile when Conan spots his Afghulis trapped by the Turanians summoned earlier by Kerim Shah. Conan determines to help them while Yasmina departs on horseback. She returns with her armies, which have been combing the hills searching for their Devi.

The Turanians are routed, Conan's men are saved, and he is in their good graces once more. Conan foils one last supernatural attempt on the Devi's life, and destroys the Master of Yimsha. Conan and Yasmina part with mutual respect and admiration.

Howard used the length of "The People of the Black Circle" to good advantage. Especially notable is a larger-than-usual cast of characters and its wide array of motives and emotions. Howard was far abler to craft believable characters than his two *Weird Tales* colleagues, H. P. Lovecraft and Clark Ashton Smith, though many critics have never given him credit for this skill. The colorful and diversified cast of "The People of the Black Circle" attests to his abilities in this regard.

Kerim Shah, the conniving Turanian spy, possesses a vaulting ambition that ultimately leads to his grisly demise. Khemsa, the sorcerer's apprentice, has as his last link to humanity his love for the willful and passionate Gitara. The inhuman and unfathomable Master of Yimsha is yet human enough to be moved by the Devi's beauty. Each of these characters are skillfully and convincingly rendered, as are a host of lesser characters: Chunder Shan, the wary, experienced governor of the frontier outpost; Yar Afzal, the battle-hardened chief of a bandit tribe; Bhunda Chand, the beloved king whose death initiates the events.

Conan and the Devi Yasmina are a fine match. Strong, determined and intelligent, Yasmina will stop at nothing to avenge her brother's death. Conan the adventurer is a hardy, indomitable man-of-action and a capable, sharp-witted leader of men. His knowledge, experience, and insight concerning the characters of both civilized and barbaric men and women stand him in good stead.

Howard's potential for assembling a rich cast of diversified characters and skillfully weaving their interactions together was not fully realized at the time of his death. In time he might have achieved a mastery comparable to that of the best-selling novelist James Clavell. In "The People of the Black Circle," no fewer than six different factions are involved. The Devi Yasmina seeks vengeance for her brother; all other parties seek the Devi for various reasons. Conan and Yasmina initially attempt to use each other for their own ends, but by the novella's close each aids the other unselfishly and in the process gains a measure of mutual respect.

Yasmina is one of Howard's most fully realized female characters. While not a warrior like Bêlit, she nevertheless functions to the utmost of her ability within the constraints of her society. Howard was aware of the constraints society imposes on women. Though not always considerate to the women in his life, intellectually he was sympathetic to their second-class status in society and defended their rights and abilities.

One of the most interesting sequences of the novella, perhaps because it is unexpected, is the chapter perceptively entitled "Yasmina Knows Stark Terror." In this segment the Master of Yimsha, wishing to break Yasmina's will to his own, causes her to relive all her past incarnations, a variation on Howard's familiar racial memory theme that we might awkwardly term "gender memory":

> Back beyond the dimmest dawns of Time she crouched shuddering in primordial jungles, hunted by slavering beasts of prey. Skin-clad, she waded thigh-deep in rice-swamps, battling with the squawking water-fowl for the precious grains. She labored with the oxen to drag the pointed stick through the stubborn soil, and she crouched endlessly over looms in peasant huts.
>
> She saw walled cities burst into flame, and fled screaming before the slayers. She reeled naked and bleeding over the burning sands, dragged at the slaver's stirrup, and she knew the grip of hot, fierce hands on her writhing flesh, the shame and agony of brutal lust. She screamed under the bite of the lash, and moaned on the rack: mad with terror she fought against the hands that forced her head inexorably down on the bloody block.
>
> She knew the agonies of childbirth, and the bitterness of love betrayed. She suffered all the woes and wrongs and brutalities that man has inflicted on woman throughout the eons, and she endured all the spite and malice of woman for woman . . . (57)

Compelling as this scene is, it is but a single thread in the colorful tapestry that is "The People of the Black Circle."

A longer length also served Howard well in two other Conan novellas. They are "Beyond the Black River" and "Red Nails," controversial tales that take place at about the same period in Conan's life and serve to illustrate Howard's most consistent literary themes. Both stories deal with a juxtaposition between barbarism and civilization, but the approaches and viewpoints differ.

"Beyond the Black River" concerns the encroachment of civilization on a pristine wilderness and its native inhabitants. "Red Nails" takes place in a completely enclosed, self-contained city, cut off from the natural order and representing a microcosm of modern urban society. Each story is outstanding in its own right; but viewed together they offer a staggering array of insights into man's place in the natural world and civilization.

"Beyond the Black River" (*Weird Tales*, May and June 1935; CSC) is one of Howard's most memorable stories. Many vividly recall, years after their first reading, the powerful impression the story made on them. Seldom is Howard's philosophy more grim or his mood and imagery more somber. Few of Howard's other fantasies are so sparing in exotic details, and seldom is sudden, violent death so close at hand. And nowhere else in his writings is the core of Howard's philosophy so bluntly stated as at the close of "Beyond the Black River."

The setting of the story is the "Pictish wilderness," an arboreal vastness to the west of the most powerful Hyborian kingdom, Aquilonia. The plot concerns an attempt by the Aquilonians to extend their boundaries into this howling wilderness, one teeming with savage denizens both animal and human. The disaster that ensues is the toll exacted by the natural order for its harsh lesson to the arrogant forces of civilization.

Most of the story is seen through the eyes of a young pioneer, Balthus. George H. Scithers, in his short essay "Balthus of Cross Plains," pointed out many similarities between this character and Howard himself. Balthus resembles Howard physically, and their backgrounds are similar. Balthus was born in a settled frontier region and inherited many of its pioneer traditions. The beginning of the story finds Balthus having left his home to take part in the settlement of Aquilonia's newest frontier, an area acquired by political boldness and military might. However, most of the soldiery had been withdrawn and only a few outposts remain to protect the settlers from the savages whose land has been usurped.

These savages are the Picts. Once again Howard uses the Picts as a symbol for the most primordial state of human existence, living as one with nature. The Picts are a constant in Howard's writing, appearing in each epoch with their name unchanged. They adamantly resist any intrusion into their way of life. In the Hyborian Age, they are painted savages living in huts, striking suddenly and melting back into the forest they inhabit. These Picts lack unity, however, for as yet they have no Bran Mak Morn to unite their quarreling tribes into a nation.

Conan appears in this story as a wilderness scout and military advisor employed by the Aquilonians. His advice is sound but seldom heeded, for he warns that their attempt at expansion is doomed to failure. Once established, this sense of impending doom is never lifted. Conan rescues Balthus from a Pictish ambush, and in the forest they converse, speaking of their backgrounds. Conan is more open with Balthus than most of the other characters he encounters. Balthus is quick to realize the difference between himself and his companion, mentally likening him to the Picts. Conan asks Balthus if he had ever heard the story of the fort-town, Venarium. Balthus immediately recalls it, for it represented a black blot on the military annals of Aquilonia.

Many years earlier, Aquilonia attempted a campaign of territorial expansion similar to their present undertaking. Only then they attempted to push their borders northward into Conan's homeland of Cimmeria. The bloody massacre of Venarium by a number of Cimmerian clans was recounted to Balthus by a relative who was present and survived. Conan, in his early teens, took part in that massacre. Now he has come full circle to another confrontation between civilization and barbarism. He grimly warns that history will soon repeat itself.

As a youth at Venarium, Conan was among the enemies of encroaching civilization. Now he assumes the role of a protector of wayward children of civilization. He seeks not to further their ends, but to protect them from their own folly.

Some of the Aquilonians have earned the enmity of a Pictish shaman named Zogar Sag. In the forest, Conan and Balthus discover

V. Conan

the headless body of one of Zogar Sag's victims, slain by a swamp demon under the shaman's command. The pair return to the frontier outpost of Fort Tuscelan. Here the officers and soldiers are alarmed by an ominous increase of Pictish activity along the Black River. Rumor has it that Zogar Sag is attempting to unite a number of the Pictish tribes. The fort's commander asks Conan to lead a suicide mission into the unplumbed Pictish territory beyond Black River to kill Zogar Sag. Balthus volunteers to accompany them.

That night, Conan, Balthus, and a small party of seasoned woodsmen slip silently across the river in a canoe. Balthus and another guard the boat while the others go ashore. Almost immediately, Balthus and the woodsman are set upon. Balthus is knocked unconscious and comes to bound to a stake in the center of the Pictish village. Balthus soon becomes aware that Picts from many tribes have gathered here in conclave. He learns from another survivor who has been taken prisoner that Conan's party has been ambushed, though Conan himself may have escaped. Soon Zogar Sag appears to impress the gathered tribes by working his evil magic on the captives.

The supernatural element in this story differs from that usually found in the other Conan stories. Here the magician is a simple feathered shaman controlling the beasts of the forest. With his magic, Zogar Sag summons from the forest a saber-tooth tiger, a creature thought long extinct by the Hyborians.

Balthus wonders what other horrors are hidden from civilized eyes by the vast Pictish wilderness. He is soon to find out, for after the saber-tooth kills his companion, Zogar Sag calls a monstrous python from the woods. The enormous serpent is about to crush Balthus when Conan hurls a spear from a hidden vantage point and transfixes the snake. In the ensuing confusion, Conan frees Balthus and they flee.

Conan and Balthus plunge deep into the nighted forest, pursued by the blood-mad Picts. Thanks to Conan, they elude them. As day breaks, they realize that an attack on the fort and settlement is imminent. Somehow they must cross the river and warn the fort. Going to great lengths to avoid the Picts, they reach the fort by evening, arriving too late. The fort is already doomed. They run ahead of the Picts to warn the settlements beyond.

On the road, Conan and Balthus find a large savage-looking dog named Slasher, whose master was slain by the Picts. In his essay, George Scithers remarked that Slasher might have been inspired by Howard's memory of his own dog, Patch. Accompanied by the dog, who can alert them to the Picts before they can be seen or heard, Conan and Balthus reach the first settlements. Their urgent news that "'The Picts are over the river!'" is greeted with horror and alarm (91). The problem is compounded when they learn that the men have gone into the swamp for salt. Conan sets out after them while Balthus sees the women and children to safety.

In the swamp, Conan meets Zogar Sag's swamp demon. From this strange creature Conan learns the origin of Zogar Sag and of a mystical bond between the shaman and his demon-brother. Conan's experience with the supernatural has taught him that "any being clothed in material flesh can be slain by material weapons, however grisly its form may be" (97). He kills the swamp demon with his sword. Meanwhile, Balthus tries desperately to buy time for the settlers, making his last stand on the road with Slasher at his side.

The story's epilogue takes place a few days later. The frontier has been pushed back to Thunder River. Fort Tuscelan has been wiped out almost to a man, but most of the settlers managed to escape. Conan is drinking in a tavern when a forester enters and gives an eyewitness account of the carnage at the fort. The Picts broke off their attack when Zogar Sag died, mysteriously stricken at the moment Conan slayed the demon in the swamp. The forester also tells of the discovery of the bodies of Balthus and Slasher, found atop a heap of dead Picts. Conan drinks a toast to Balthus and swears to avenge him.

The forester gazes at Conan intently, mentally comparing him with the savages they had just battled. The story ends as he observes grimly, "'Barbarism is the natural state of mankind . . . Civilization is unnatural. It is a whim of circumstance. And barbarism must always ultimately triumph'" (100).

"Beyond the Black River" has been consistently referred to as a "transplanted western." It has been pointed out that Howard used the setting of Robert W. Chambers's novel *The Little Red Foot* (1921) as a model for his Pictish wilderness. Some of the story's place names derive from actual regions in the Mohawk River Valley during colonial days.

However, if Howard had merely wished to write a western, he could have done so quite easily, for he produced numerous westerns for better-paying markets. Moreover, having been born and bred in what had a few generations before been Comanche territory, he would have little need for so distant a source of historical lore. Though elements of settlers-vs.-Indians sagas are present, the brooding forest, the dark river running through it, the beasts that haunt it, and the Picts that inhabit it are all archetypes too ancient for a young genre like the western.

The lyrical title "Beyond the Black River" is itself a fitting metaphor for that region of the human soul where the Primordial Self howls in savage glee. It is also an apt metaphor for death. In Greek Mythology, the River Styx is the boundary between the lands of the living and the dead. In Howard's tale, death is ever-present beyond the Black River.

In this tale, the power of Howard's prose combines with the passion of his deepest convictions. The oppressive brooding of the forest primeval is beautifully rendered. Howard's nature imagery is captivating, comparable to that in James Dickey's *Deliverance*. As in Conrad's "Heart of Darkness," the forest mirrors the characters' souls. In both

Dickey and Conrad, a river is the central image. Howard too taps this particular image and utilizes it as a symbol. He is equally adept in the use of other symbols.

In the Pictish village, Zogar Sag calls two behemoths out of the benighted depths of the primeval forest. They are the saber-tooth tiger and the Serpent. These carefully chosen symbols represent different versions of humanity's most ancient and terrible adversaries. The Serpent was present in Genesis as the bane of the first man and woman and endures today as the figure of ultimate evil to the pious. The saber-tooth has been revealed by modern anthropology as the most fearsome predator battled by our troglodyte ancestors for supremacy in the Pleistocene epoch. The irony of this juxtaposition of symbols was not lost on Howard.

The men of the Pictish frontier are a hearty, vital breed, but they are governed by incompetents from afar who do not comprehend the realities of the frontier. The pioneers are placed in a perilous position. They would have a better chance with the proper type of military support, but such support is not forthcoming. Ultimately they succumb to the tide of barbarism that sweeps across the Black River.

Similar scenarios have been repeated throughout history. Both the American campaign in Vietnam and the Soviet campaign in Afghanistan met with costly resistance from indigenous guerrilla fighters. In "Beyond the Black River," Conan counsels Balthus on the realities of the frontier, commenting on the lack of government support:

> "Soft-bellied fools sitting on velvet cushions with naked slave girls offering them iced wine on their knees—I know the breed. They can't see any farther than their palace wall. Diplomacy—hell! They'd fight Picts with theories of territorial expansion. Valannus and men like him have to obey the orders of a set of damned fools. They'll never grab any more Pictish land, any more than they'll ever rebuild Venarium. The time may

come when they'll see the barbarians swarming over the walls of the Eastern cities!"

A week before, Balthus would have laughed at any such preposterous suggestion. Now he made no reply. He had seen the unconquerable ferocity of the men who dwelt beyond the frontiers. (85)

Conan's remark about the barbarians sweeping over the walls of cities foreshadows the story's final statement that barbarism must always ultimately triumph. In a civilized milieu, there are always people like Thomas Aquinas who attempt to establish criteria for "the just war." Hence, there are concerns about "rules of engagement" and "collateral damage." The barbarian, on the other hand, will do whatever is necessary to win his struggle without compunction or conflicting urges of morality.

Howard was compelled to convey this message because he believed that peace is only possible through strength. A puny child cast into a rude, often hostile environment and the prey of local bullies, Howard built his body as a teen until his physical stature and fighting prowess were such as to intimidate any foe. Some would call this paranoia, but Howard well knew that it was his physical strength, boxing skill, bearing of firearms, and willingness to do violence that enabled him to read and write poetry unmolested. Howard knew that strength is what makes all other values possible. That is why he wrote what he wrote.

"Red Nails" (*Weird Tales*, July, August–September, and October 1936; CSC) is the last Conan story Howard wrote and the last major fantasy he completed. On the verge of abandoning fantasy for more commercial endeavors, Howard devoted considerable thought and effort to his final allegorical statement. It was a watershed story to Howard, and in a letter to Clark Ashton Smith he expressed his feelings about it:

> Sent a three-part serial to Wright yesterday: 'Red Nails,' which I devoutly hope he'll like. A Conan yarn, and the grimmest, bloodiest and most merciless story of the series so far. Too much raw meat, maybe, but I merely portrayed what I honestly believe would be the reactions of certain types of people in the situations on which the plot of the story hung ... (REH to Clark Ashton Smith, 23 July 1935; CL 3.367)

The narrative begins in the jungles far to the south of any known civilized lands. Into this forest primeval rides Valeria of the Red Brotherhood, an Aquilonian adventurer and pirate. Howard tells us that "She was tall, full-bosomed and large-limbed, with compact shoulders. Her whole figure reflected an unusual strength, without detracting from the femininity of her appearance. She was all woman" (211).

Valeria is fleeing persecution for killing a would-be rapist. She is followed into this remote region by Conan, a fellow adventurer who is hoping to make her his woman. Conan, as his fans well know, does not have to go out of his way to obtain the favors of the fairest of the fair sex. Obviously, the woman Valeria represents something special to him; like Bêlit, she is a woman of action and would make a fitting mate-woman.

However, Valeria does not welcome Conan's advances, for living as she has among men, she has been routinely subjected to their constant degrading attention and brutish attempts at coercion. Conan is determined to have her, and Valeria is determined to resist. Valeria is as formidable a warrior as many a man, and Conan is at a loss as to how to deal with her. Callous to constant sexual harassment, Valeria is unable to recognize the genuine respect and admiration Conan sincerely expresses toward her when he says, "'I'm not like that Stygian you knifed, and you know it'" (214). Conan and Valeria's antagonism is representative of the battle of the sexes, and Howard describes their confrontation as "a scene at once ludicrous and perilous" (216).

The tense stand-off is interrupted by the more pressing concerns of survival. A monstrous dinosaur attacks, killing their horses. Howard's description of the creature combines physical features of the Spinosaurus and stegosaurus. In the case of the latter, Howard may have been inspired by the memorable depiction of the stegosaurus in the movie *King Kong* (1933). In any event, he portrays the great beast as a natural, albeit unusual, creature as opposed to some fanciful dragon. Valeria and Conan refer to it as a dragon because they don't know what else to call it.

The beleaguered adventurers take refuge from the "dragon" atop a crag it cannot scale. They are trapped without food and water, and Valeria is fearful of slow death by starvation. Conan is stoic. Valeria is relieved to spot some fruit within reach, but Conan's broad experience enables him to recognize it as deadly poison. They formulate and execute a plan to fashion a spear, coat it with poison from the fruit, and drive it into the "dragon's" mouth. As the poison begins to take effect, Conan and Valeria attempt to flee. The monster, blinded and in pain, catches their scent and pursues them. Unable to outrun it, Conan turns to face the charging monstrosity. His sword-stroke only wounds the creature, but diverts its headlong charge so it blindly dashes its brains out against a tree.

Conan and Valeria emerge from the forest and make their way toward a strange walled city they spotted from the crag. As they near it, they are puzzled by the unusualness of the city; there are no grazing herds or cultivated fields and the irrigation system lies in ruins. They can only assume that the city is deserted.

At length they arrive at the door, long since rusted shut. Conan's great strength enables him to open it, and the couple enters a bizarre twilight world. This city, which they come to know as Xuchotl, is a single massive structure completely enclosed and roofed over. A single great hallway runs the length of the city, but there are no other streets or open courtyards. It consists entirely of four tiers of rooms, chambers, and passageways. Xuchotl is constructed mostly of jade, with traces of lapis lazuli, ivory, and other exotic materials. Whenever possible, Howard likens Xuchotl to a modern city. For example, most of the lighting is artificial, and the main source of illumination is "green fire-stones," which Conan recognizes as "'the petrified eyes of those prehistoric snakes the ancients called Golden Serpents'" (229). Xuchotl is thus revealed to be illuminated by a kind of fossil fuel. Such a parallel would readily occur to Howard, who in his youth witnessed the desecration of his frontier environment by Easterners in search of the precious petroleum recently discovered beneath Texas soil.

Conan and Valeria separate to search the seemingly deserted city. Valeria grows uncomfortable: "These silent rooms and halls with their gleaming green clusters of ornaments and burning crimson floors were beginning to depress her" (231). Soon she discovers a small dark man sneaking through the hallways, and before long she is involved in a skirmish between the two factions that dwell at either end of the once populous city.

Conan reappears in time to aid Valeria, who has managed to overcome a warrior armed with a sorcerous artifact that saps the will of all who behold it. Techotl, their newfound ally, gleefully gloats over his slain enemies, prompting Conan to remark, "'Who is this madman?'" (237). Significantly, Howard informs us that Conan notices a latent insanity burning behind the eyes of all the city-dwellers. Techotl urges Conan and Valeria to accompany him to the stronghold of his people, the Tecuhltli. En route, they are attacked in the dark by a monstrous snake-like creature, "the Crawler," which Conan mortally wounds.

Conan and Valeria are admitted to the area held by the Tecuhltli and are welcomed by the rulers of this faction, Olmec and Tascela. The Tecuhltli exult in the news that five of their enemies, the Xotalancas, have been slain. In accordance with a grim custom, five red nails are pounded into an ebony pillar.

V. Conan

Conan and Valeria rest and are given sustenance in the form of the artificially produced food consumed by all in the city. This food is manufactured by some mysterious process the Tecuhltli only vaguely understand. Once again Xuchotl parallels a modern city in which the inhabitants but dimly comprehend the processes by which their food is produced and brought to them.

Olmec tells Conan and Valeria the history of Xuchotl. The city was built long ago by another race that dwelt there for centuries, doing little besides enjoying their leisure to the fullest. The present inhabitants arrived only half a century before, fleeing a revolution in their native land. A slave of the original rulers, Tolkemec betrayed his masters and admitted the newcomers, who, though intellectually and technologically less advanced, nonetheless supplanted the architects of the city. Thus the new people came to rule a city they only dimly understood. The lessons of history were not lost on Howard, for he knew that in its declining days Rome was inhabited by foreign peoples, most of whom spoke no Latin and had no appreciation for the higher culture they supplanted.

The newcomers to Xuchotl were led by two brothers, Tecuhltli and Xotalanc, and by Tolkemec. They took over different areas of the city and for a time lived in peace. However, a feud between the brothers began when Tecuhltli stole Xotalanc's bride. Tolkemec aided and betrayed both sides for his own purposes, until hideously tortured and cast into the city's catacombs to die. Since that time, the blood-feud has dominated all life in the city.

Howard was familiar with feuds and their damaging effects on a society, for he was steeped in the lore of his pioneer ancestors who knew the grim, bloody feuds of Texas and the Carolinas. He related violent accounts of these rivalries in his letters and wrote of them in his westerns. In "Red Nails," feud is described as horrible and utterly detrimental to society, and an added dimension of horror is generated by this feud's urban setting:

> The feud had become a terrible elemental power driving the people of Xuchotl inexorably on to doom and extinction. It filled their whole lives. They were born in it, and they expected to die in it. They never left their barricaded castle except to steal forth into the Halls of Silence that lay between the opposing fortresses, to slay and be slain . . . It was a ghastly, unreal nightmare existence these people lived, shut off from the rest of the world, caught together like rabid rats in the same trap butchering one another through the years, crouching and creeping through the sunless corridors to maim and torture and murder . . . (249)

This ghastly spectacle is paralleled by the gang warfare that exists in the streets of American cities today. Howard knew something of such conditions, having read Herbert Asbury's study, *The Gangs of New York*, published in 1928.

Howard was not solely concerned with the violence-prone behavior of people trapped in an unnatural urban environment, however. In a letter to H. P. Lovecraft, Howard candidly revealed one of his motives in writing "Red Nails":

> I have been dissatisfied with my handling of decaying races in stories, for the reason that degeneracy is so prevalent in such races that even in fiction it can not be ignored as a motive and as a fact if the fiction is to have any claim to realism. I have ignored it in all other stories, as one of the taboos, but I did not ignore it in this story. (REH to H. P. Lovecraft, 5 December 1935; CL 3.393)

By "degeneracy" Howard was primarily referring to homosexuality, although "Red Nails" does contain incidents of bondage and flagellation. Again, homosexuality was not well understood in Howard's day. He appears to concur with a notion that has been postulated by others: homosexuality is in some way linked to urbanization. Broaching this taboo subject was a courageous act on Howard's part and also on the part of Farnsworth Wright, who published the story. Still, Howard rendered the subject commercially viable by presenting its more agreeable aspect, i.e., Sapphic relations between beautiful women. Howard wrote to Lovecraft, "I'd like to know how you like my handling of the subject of lesbianism" (CL 3.393).

The subject is introduced when the princess Tascela ignores Conan as a sexual object and gazes with "burning intensity" at Valeria (243). Both Olmec and Tascela covet Valeria, and an undercurrent of sexual tension becomes manifest. When Conan and Valeria retire to their separate quarters, Valeria grins with "gleeful malice" as she imagines Conan "scowling and muttering with chagrin as he cast himself on his solitary couch" (252).

The sexual aspects of the story become more bizarre when a slave of Tascela, Yasala, attempts to drug Valeria with the black lotus. Angered, Valeria overpowers Yasala, strips her, binds her, and flogs her to make her reveal the motive behind such treachery. Yasala feigns submission and escapes, fleeing into the catacombs. Before Valeria can pursue her, word reaches her that the Xotalancas have breached Tecuhltli defenses.

The balance of power in the city had shifted with the entrance of Conan and Valeria. Previously, Conan had destroyed the Crawler, and Valeria smashed a supernatural artifact used by the Xotalancas. With these weapons lost and the outsiders fighting for their enemies, the Xotalancas have been driven to a desperate attack to end the feud once and for all.

A pitched battle takes place in the great throne room. It ends with the extermination of the Xotalancas. Only Conan, Valeria, Olmec, Tascela, and fifteen Tecuhltli remain alive. Conan and a pair of warriors go to Xotalanc to see if any enemies remain there. Valeria stays behind to have her wounds tended.

With Conan gone, Olmec attempts to force himself on Valeria. He is thwarted by Tascela, who is revealed to be a witch and the stolen bride who originally started the feud. She plans to sap Valeria's vitality to restore her youth. Meanwhile, Conan has entered Xotalanc, where he finds that the Xotalancas preserve the heads of their victims. Olmec had secretly ordered the two warriors to slay Conan. When they attack, Conan kills them and hurries back to Valeria.

On his way, Conan meets Techotl, who had opposed Olmec and Tascela and now crawls in his own life's blood to warn Conan of their treachery. Returning to Tecuhltli, Conan finds Olmec bound to a torture device. Conan releases him when he agrees to lead him to Tascela and Valeria. However, Olmec attempts another betrayal and Conan kills him.

Conan bursts in on Tascela and her followers, who are engaged in an orgiastic ritual in which Valeria is held down on an altar, the object of the ceremony. Conan's leg is caught in one of the steel traps Tascela has concealed near the entrances. He is unable to free himself as Tascela prepares to press her lips against those of the nude Valeria, drawing out her life force as the sycophants gaze on with "hot, lustful eyes" (275). Tascela and her followers move in an orgiastic frenzy while candles fill the room with smoke that is "disturbingly scented" (275). Whether their behavior is induced by a narcotic of some sort or a quasi-religious mania is never made clear.

Tascela is about to bring the ritual to a bloody climax when the grim tableau is interrupted by a specter from the past. Tolkemec has returned from "'Twelve years among the bones of the dead!'" (277). He bears a strange weapon left by the former masters of Xuchotl. It is a crystal-tipped wand that fires arcs of electricity to nearby metal, destroying everything in between.

It is interesting that Howard wished to present this device as a piece of advanced technology that seems to function in accordance with natural laws, rather than as a magical artifact that flouts natural laws. Tolkemec uses the device to decimate the Tecuhltli until only Conan, Valeria, and Tascela remain. Desperate, Tascela frees Conan. Because Tolkemec's weapon is subject to natural law, Conan is able to pinpoint its weakness and slay Tolkemec, even as Valeria avenges herself on Tascela with a dagger.

The last inhabitant of the city is dead. Conan takes Valeria in his arms. This time she does not resist. Scorning the city and its treasure, Conan and Valeria return together to the surrounding wilderness and the world beyond.

One of the most important characters in "Red Nails" is Xuchotl itself. Howard makes it clear that the city, once shaped by man, now shapes humanity. In a city, "north" and "south" are replaced by "uptown" and "downtown"; leagues and miles are replaced by blocks and boroughs.

In Xuchotl, conventional warfare is replaced by the stealth of urban guerrillas. Wind and weather are no longer a factor, but familiarity with the elaborate network of halls and corridors is essential to the inhabitants, just as modern urban delinquents know the value of being "streetwise." Knowledge of agriculture is unimportant to today's city dweller; food appears on supermarket shelves as if by magic. In Xuchotl, Olmec tells Conan and Valeria that their food grows from air.

The people of Xuchotl are held prisoner in the city not just by the "dragons" they believe to surround it, but by their own complacency. They prefer their existence (which Howard portrays as a mad parody of normal life) to living in the natural world. Their numbers are dwindling not only because of the feud, but because they can no longer have children. In their artificial environment, they have lost the vitality and perhaps even the instinct to reproduce. All that the people live for is the feud.

Only Tascela possesses any sort of instinct for survival, and hers is twisted into a parasitic endeavor to prolong her unnatural youth. The beauty and treasure of the city itself are tainted by the malignant presence of the city dwellers, who do not comprehend or care to comprehend the art, architecture, and technology left to them by the builders.

Into this environment are thrust Conan and Valeria, the elemental man and woman. Their slaying of the "dragon" early in the story establishes their status as archetypal heroic figures. Howard felt that the presence of such individuals in a decaying society could make a difference; their vitality could perhaps stem the tide of decay.

Howard's contemporary Aldous Huxley took a more pessimistic view in his 1932 dystopian novel *Brave New World*; his "Savage" is held in contempt by civilization, is shunned, and ultimately commits suicide. However, in "Red Nails," Conan and Valeria's wills, physical prowess, and untainted mental faculties enable them to alter Xuchotl irrevocably, if only by accelerating its entropy and bringing the hideous charade of life therein to its inevitable denouement.

The appearance of Conan and Valeria in Xuchotl brings about its inhabitants' extinction, but not before they have a positive effect on one of them. The first person they meet is the warrior Techotl, who develops a strong emotional attachment to them:

> In the cold, loveless and altogether hideous life of the Tecuhltli his admiration and affection for the invaders from the outer world formed a warm, human oasis, constituted a tie that connected him with a more natural humanity that was totally lacking in his fellows, whose only emotions were hate, lust, and the urge of sadistic cruelty. (263)

Olmec and Tascela are Conan and Valeria's urban counterparts. Each possesses physical strength and force of will far in excess of their fellows: they occupy the dominant positions in their society. Olmec is motivated by his obscene appetites and his will to power. Tascela seems to be representative of a certain breed of modern urban woman. Like them, she seeks to prolong her youth by unnatural means and will stop at nothing to achieve her ends.

In "Red Nails," the sins of the fathers are visited upon the sons. Tecuhltli and Xotalanc were originally the names of the two brothers who went to war against each other over Tascela, thus initiating the feud. The two brothers, aided by Tolkemec, destroyed the original inhabitants of Xuchotl. This is part of a recurring motif in the story.

As the tale opens, Valeria is fleeing the brother of the man she killed. Elsewhere in the story, a Tecuhltli warrior becomes a raving madman when he discovers the preserved heads of his brother and his "father's younger brother" (262). Olmec and Tascela, though not siblings, have become the city's dual rulers, like Tecuhltli and Xotalanc long before, but have a falling out when each lusts for Valeria.

While Howard himself was an only child, he had a close friend in Truett Vinson. About the time "Red Nails" was written, this friendship was put to the test when they became romantic rivals for Novalyne Price. Perhaps this incident prompted the betrayals and recriminations between siblings in "Red Nails."

Howard's tale reaches its climax with the emergence of Tolkemec from the catacombs, where he has survived for twelve years eating corpses and devolving into something less than human. When he appears, his skin is described as possessing a quality of *"scaliness"* (277). It was Tolkemec who offered the forbidden fruit of the jade city to the brothers Tecuhltli and Xotalanc; now his very appearance suggests that of the serpent of Eden. Tascela is shocked by Tolkemec's sudden reappearance, as if he represents fifty years of decadence and decay now catching up with her people. Not surprisingly, it is Conan to whom she turns for salvation from her own depravity. So ends Robert E. Howard's allegory and indictment of modern urban living.

After examining two stories that embody the core of Howard's personal philosophy, we should now examine the validity of his claims. To what extent was Howard justified in asserting that civilization was detrimental to humanity and that a more natural state of tribal barbarism was to be preferred?

It is easy to dismiss Howard as naïve, overly romantic, or a cranky misanthrope dissatisfied with the present social order. As Thomas Hobbes famously pointed out in *Leviathan*, life prior to modern civilization was "solitary, poor, nasty, brutish, and short."

In countless ways, civilization has prolonged and enriched the lives of nearly all in industrialized nations. Plagues and diseases that terrorized our ancestors have been virtually eliminated by modern medicine. Civilized man is safer and more secure than his ancestors. Most citizens of the industrialized West possess comforts and pleasures that the kings of a thousand years ago could not have had for all their wealth and power. Through mass communications, the average man and woman are better informed and enjoy a richer, broader range of experience than their most privileged and learned ancestor of centuries ago.

Civilization, however, does have certain serious drawbacks. Progress, though nurtured by civilization, is, as often as not, also impeded by it. New goods and services intended to better the lot of the common man are often forestalled by businessmen who market those products and systems that are threatened with obsolescence. Scientific and technological advancement is frequently opposed by religion, which has consistently objected to every major discovery or breakthrough as a flouting of divine will. Misapplication of science and technology is frequently assailed. However, the scientific community on the whole is more conscientious and better intentioned than the members of most of our other institutions, which seem to be made up of self-serving parasites.

Leaders of big business award themselves lavish perks and bonuses, while the workers who generate their wealth are dismissed as expendable. Political bureaucracies are prone to corruption and abuse of power. Even the arts can be sapped of vitality by self-aggrandizing dilettantes on one hand and crass commercial concerns on the other. Much of civilization's stability is an illusion, for inevitable periodic upheavals such as the Industrial Revolution tear at the fabric of the system and cause widespread personal misery.

However, one of civilization's drawbacks is less obvious, and this is the one Howard was primarily concerned with. Howard's chief objection to civilization involved the regimentation of society and the stifling of individual autonomy. In modern society, most people are relegated to menial jobs or inane tasks that reduce them to the status of little cogs in a vast and impersonal machine. Only a smaller professional class is able to derive personal satisfaction from rewarding careers. Therefore, most people never achieve their full potential as human beings.

The consequences of this stifling of the individual are staggering. In the United States alone, millions of people suffer from the two most common forms of mental illness: depression and anxiety (www.nimh.nih.gov/health/statistics/index). An array of pharmaceuticals is marketed for the treatment of depression. Some people choose to self-medicate; thirty percent of Americans have been estimated to have had a drinking problem at some point (www.newsweek.com/30-percent-americans-have-had-alcohol-use-disorder-339085). Addiction to illegal narcotics continues to be a concern. In addition, abuse of prescription medications like Valium is widespread. Incidents of domestic violence have reached an alarming rate. Eating disorders traceable to cultural influences afflict millions of women (www.womenshealth.gov/mental-health-conditions/eating-disorders). Suicide is now the tenth leading cause of death in the United States (suicidology.org/facts-and-statistics).

Of course, not all cases of these social dilemmas can be linked to thwarted aspirations, diminished personal autonomy, and similar forms of repression, but these conditions can likely be found among the root causes in a woefully large percentage.

While we need not subscribe to Howard's beliefs in their totality, we must not dismiss his insights completely. One need only acknowledge that civilization has certain drawbacks as a trade-off for its many advantages. And perhaps Howard's message is not that civilization is bad, but that the danger lies in too much civilization. After all, food and sleep are essential to human life, but it is possible to eat and sleep too much. Can there be such a thing as too much civilization, and if so, when is a society "over-civilized"?

A society could be said to be over-civilized, as opposed to decadent, when dogmatic allegiance to abstractions such as universal brotherhood overrules common sense and becomes detrimental to the continued survival and well-being of that society. This occurs when even the most vicious malefactor is deemed worthy of mercy. It occurs when blind pacifism undermines the instinct for self-preservation. It also occurs when the will of the individual is surrendered to the supposedly higher goals of society at large.

In "Beyond the Black River," Conan warned against disastrous governmental policies that resulted in needless bloodshed. In "Red Nails," the lives of the individuals were dominated by their allegiances to a feud they barely understood and never questioned.

In all the stories, Conan's instincts regarding who is deserving of his help and mercy are sound. Rousseau's romantic notions of primitivism are not truly echoed in Howard's work, for Howard never asserted that barbarians are lacking in vice or immune to corruption. Rather, he simply points out, primarily in the Conan stories, that a free individual who is unconfused by abstract notions of no immediate concern to him will behave in a manner more logical, pragmatic, and conducive to survival than one burdened by the intellectual debris of various ideologies, creeds, and beliefs derived from cultural conditioning. This is the core of existentialism.

In the final phase of his career, Conan becomes embroiled in a civil war that results in his ascension to the throne of Aquilonia. Now middle-aged, Conan rules the most powerful kingdom in the west. Howard realized that some stories are better left untold and never actually depicted Conan's taking of the crown.

The first Conan stories to appear in *Weird Tales* were "The Phoenix on the Sword" and "The Scarlet Citadel," in which King Conan's turbulent reign is depicted. "The Phoenix on the Sword" was rewritten from the unsold Kull story, "'By This Axe I Rule!'" Howard fleshed out the story, retaining the conspiracy and assassination attempt, discarding the young lovers, adding several new subplots, and an even more ominous menace. In "The Scarlet Citadel," Conan temporarily loses his kingdom but regains it with the help of a supernatural ally.

Howard incorporated elements of both these early stories and others, such as "Black Colossus," into his only successful novel, *The Hour of the Dragon* (*Weird Tales*, December 1935, January, February, March, and April 1936; BCC). The last of the series chronologically, it brings Conan's saga to a masterful conclusion.

The Hour of the Dragon was commissioned by a British publisher that subsequently went out of business, forcing Howard to sell it for magazine publication. It is a shame that Howard never saw any of his works in book form. *The Hour of the Dragon* would have made an excellent first novel for Howard, enhancing his reputation and spreading his name and fame.

The 71,000 words that comprise *The Hour of the Dragon* offer the reader a grand tour of the Hyborian world, and it is perhaps the best-written episode of the series. The plot is well conceived, for it pits Conan against almost impossible odds as he faces his greatest challenge and confronts his deadliest foe.

The narrative begins when four conspirators use a magical jewel called the Heart of Ahriman to bring life to a three-thousand-year-old mummy of the wizard Xaltotun, the greatest sorcerer of ancient Acheron, an evil empire of necromancers who ruled much of the world before the coming of the Hyborians. In a magic mirror, the conspirators show Xaltotun the image of the enemy they have brought him back from the dead to defeat—King Conan of Aquilonia. Thus, the greatest warrior of an age of warriors is pitted against the greatest sorcerer of an age of sorcerers.

The conspirators use Xaltotun's magic to take over Aquilonia's rival, the neighboring kingdom of Nemedia. Once in power, they launch an invasion of Aquilonia. The Aquilonian armies led by King Conan meet the Nemedian hosts on the field, but on the eve of battle Conan is struck down by Xaltotun's sorcery. During the battle, Xaltotun causes an avalanche that destroys much of the Aquilonian army, including the soldier who impersonated Conan and led the host. The Aquilonians believe their king is dead, but in truth Xaltotun has imprisoned him in Nemedia, keeping him alive to ensure the continuing loyalty of his fellow conspirators.

In Nemedia, Conan is freed from the dungeon by a young female slave. Returning to an Aquilonia ravaged by the Nemedians, Conan finds barons of outlying provinces who will place their armies at his disposal but for the fact that Xaltotun's sorcery makes the Nemedians invincible. Conan learns that the Heart of Ahriman that brought Xaltotun to life can also destroy him and sets out to obtain it.

Conan's quest for the Heart takes up most of the novel. This is the only instance in which Howard utilizes a quest like that of Jason or Odysseus as the crux of a major work, though such quests have since become a staple of modern fantasy. The Heart has been stolen and changes hands many times in the course of the novel. Conan must use every skill he has learned in his long and varied career to recover it.

After doing so, he gathers his allies, raises another army to battle the Nemedians, and confronts his enemies once more. Conan destroys Xaltotun, drives the invaders from the land in defeat, and regains his lost kingdom. The novel closes as Conan vows to make the slave girl who delivered him from his enemies the Queen of Aquilonia.

The Hour of the Dragon is a powerful work that engages the reader on a gut level. Conan's triumph over treachery and ultimate evil was possible only for the hero Conan has forged himself into during the

V. Conan

years he wandered over the world facing every form of human and inhuman menace. Victory springs from Conan's iron will and resolve.

At one point in the story, as Conan rides off on his quest, it occurs to him that he need not risk his life attempting the impossible. Having lost his position of power, he realizes he could simply return to a life of wandering and adventuring in far-off lands as he has always done in the past. Conan's decision to win back his crown despite the impossible odds arrayed against him is the true climax of the novel and, in a way, the entire series.

It may seem that in his final adventure Conan trades freedom for responsibility, but he makes his choice with full awareness of his options. Conan now knows kingship as well as adventuring, and his decision is not that of an average citizen who merely assumes his role in society upon reaching maturity. It is Conan's act of will in making a conscious enlightened choice among the available alternatives that makes all the difference.

It is well that Conan made the choice he did. Unknown to his fellow conspirators, Xaltotun's true ambition far exceeds the conquest of Aquilonia. Using all his vast sorcerous knowledge, Xaltotun plans to set in motion powerful occult forces that will reweave the fabric of reality itself, blotting out the Hyborian world as an eraser removes figures from a blackboard and resurrecting the ancient, unspeakably evil empire of Acheron as though it had never fallen. Thus Conan and his evil counterpart both seek to place the stamp of their wills on the next thousand years of human history.

At the beginning of the novel, Xaltotun is raised from the dead. At the novel's climax, Conan returns from exile, astonishing his foes and subjects alike, for nearly all had believed he had perished. Xaltotun returned from literal death; Conan returns from figurative death at his hands. Xaltotun is destroyed, and his evil plan dies with him. In stopping Xaltotun, Conan has saved the world. The act of saving the entire world, though overused in popular fiction, is nonetheless the ultimate heroic feat. It is a fitting final triumph for Conan.

In the final pages of *The Hour of the Dragon*, Howard describes Conan for the last time in the series: "He loomed gigantically against a background of blood and slaughter, like some grim pagan hero of mythology" (253).

Few deny that Conan is Howard's greatest creation. Reviewing the characters we have examined up to now, it becomes clear that each was a step in the evolution toward Conan. Howard's four main heroes each represent a different type of individual. Bran Mak Morn is the political man whose abiding concern is affecting change in the social order. Solomon Kane is the religious man, the man of faith; his abiding concern is not with the temporal world, but with the advancement of the human spirit. Kull is the thinking man, the philosopher concerned with the true nature and purpose of the universe who endeavors to discern it through his reasoning faculty. Conan is the free, existential man. Politics, mysticism, and philosophy touch his life but do not dominate it. Conan often affects political change, but this is not his driving ambition. Conan's people have a religion, but it does not dictate their morality or affect their lives in any discernible way.

In "Queen of the Black Coast," Conan relates his personal philosophy, one devoid of perplexing quandaries. Conan's ruling passion is life itself, not arbitrary concerns. When Conan rides into battle, he does not ride what Laurence Sterne termed a "hobby horse."

In a time when it is fashionable for literary protagonists to gain notoriety, not for their strengths, but for their all-too-human weaknesses and foibles, reading about Conan is like being scorched by a divine flame. The blood races, and readers feel as if they have awakened from Gurdjieff's "sleep." Suddenly new vistas of meaning and purpose are glimpsed. Heroes have always served this purpose, and reverence for heroic ideals is one of humanity's healthiest instincts.

In a world in which reality diminishes the individual, the timelessness of what Joseph Campbell called the Hero with a Thousand Faces is an expression of undying faith in the importance of what one person can do. In a century when the leading literary lights debased themselves in abject submission before the entropic forces of nihilism and despair, popular writers as diverse as Edgar Rice Burroughs, Ian Fleming, Jerry Siegel and Joe Shuster, Raymond Chandler, and Robert E. Howard were fighting the battle against the death of individuality.

In ancient times mighty heroes strode across people's imaginations in many lands. Greece had Odysseus; Germany had Siegfried; Britain had King Arthur. In America today, Superman is our Hercules and Conan our Beowulf. Conan, with his fondness for money, good living, sex, and adventure, embodies many American values. Conan's self-sufficiency, independence, self-evident physical superiority, luck, and knack for always coming out on top make him an embodiment of the American dream.

To Howard, Conan was an amalgamation of every type of man he had known. To us, Conan is a fusion of every type of hero we have known. A mighty warrior like Jason and Odysseus, Conan is also a rebel like Marlon Brando and James Dean. He combines qualities of the oldest type of hero with those of the newest.

All that Robert E. Howard knew, all that he experienced, all that he envisioned, all that he wrote, led him to beget his ultimate hero, Conan the Conqueror.

VI. Other Fantasies

In addition to the sagas of Conan, Kull, Kane, and Bran Mak Morn, Howard wrote a number of other fantasy stories. Some are set in recognizable historical eras, while others take place in more distant imaginary epochs Howard envisioned.

Two of the latter, a fragment and an essay, are set in Conan's Hyborian Age, and the Picts play a prominent role in both. "Wolves Beyond the Border" comes down to us in the form of two rough drafts. Narrated by a young pioneer, it takes place on the Pictish frontier and could be considered a sequel of sorts to "Beyond the Black River." Transpiring sometime after the Conan story, it concerns a renegade Aquilonian noble who has gone native and is causing unrest along the border. Where Howard previously employed mood and imagery similar to that which occurs in "Heart of Darkness," he now borrows Conrad's plot.

"The Hyborian Age," an ersatz historical essay written by Howard in an attempt to present Conan and his times more convincingly, outlines the forgotten prehistory of the world from Kull's time through the Hyborian Age to the beginnings of extant history. All the races of ancient times are traced back to their Hyborian counterparts. The great empires of our history—Egypt, Greece, Rome—are shown to be echoes of the lost Hyborian Age.

Howard has often been criticized for naming his imaginary realms after mythological and historical locales easily recognizable as such to

VI. Other Fantasies

even moderately well-read persons. While names such as "Stygia" and "Cimmeria" are likely to pass unrecognized by the average modern reader, others such as "Asgard" are familiar to practically anyone. Howard's premise was that all the myths and legends of the ancients derive from garbled memories of the Hyborian Age. Howard realized that such names as "Hyperborea" evoke a sense of antiquity and wonder lacking in artificially constructed terms. He utilized these names with the scrupulous economy of the poet, allowing, for example, the name "Corinthia" to suggest a classic Grecian-like culture and thus avoiding the need for lengthy detailed description. Moreover, many of the names, encountered long before in an obscure passage of Homer or the Bible and subsequently forgotten, evoke a vague sense of familiarity akin to racial memory.

Occasionally, Howard would use these names to forward the thematic elements of his stories. In "A Witch Shall Be Born," the name Constantius was meant to evoke Imperial Rome, but more interesting is his use of exotically familiar names in "The Pool of the Black One."

To summarize the story briefly, Conan climbs aboard a ship commanded by the sullen and taciturn Zingaran, Zaporavo. Immediately Conan covets the captain's mistress Sancha, though he harbors larger ambitions as well. In time Conan wins the hearts of the crew, and when they put ashore on a lost isle, Conan slays the captain in a duel, then claims the ship and the woman too. Not exactly chivalrous behavior on the Cimmerian's part, and to highlight Conan's existential self-reliance (not to mention his Ayn Randian self-interest), Howard references characters from great literature to hammer his moral home.

Howard's "Zingara" is a thinly disguised Spain in its golden age. Also, the name of doomed Captain Zaporavo sounds vaguely like a minor Conquistador on a wild quest for El Dorado, which is similar to Zaporavo's role in "The Pool of the Black One." The name Sancha (mistress of the late Zaporavo and Conan's "sidekick" in this story) is an ironic counterpoint to Sancho Panza in Cervantes's *Don Quixote*. This satire of medieval romances followed the antics of a protagonist suffering from a hopeful and inspiring, but ultimately misguided and deluded, form of chivalry, so it seems that Howard was taking a subtle jab at polite notions of chivalry by referencing Cervantes's character.

While unimpressed with Howard's nomenclature, Lovecraft regarded "The Hyborian Age" highly enough to compare it favorably with Olaf Stapledon's works. The historical sweep of Howard's essay is compelling, and reading it one is captivated by the pageant of "history" as kingdoms and empires succumb to the march of time. The Hyborian civilization, as Conan predicted in "Beyond the Black River," is engulfed by the barbaric Picts, united by a forerunner of Bran Mak Morn, and taught to work iron by a well-meaning missionary.

Other fantasies by Howard serve to illuminate different aspects of his personality and passions. One of his most burning interests was Irish history. As a youth, Howard was engrossed by historical accounts of the Irish clans. While some of his ancestors were Irish, Howard's strong identification with the ancient Celts was based more on an emotional kinship than an ancestral one. Howard was prone to attribute his fits of depression and melancholy to the waywardness of the Celtic nature. He was quite knowledgeable concerning Celtic history and lore, an enthusiasm he shared with his friend Harold Preece, who fondly remembered him as "The Last Celt."

Howard's Celtic tales are marked by a mingling of Celtic history and Celtic myth. The supernatural element of these stories is less pronounced than in the Conan or Kull tales, but is all the more eerie for its subtlety. The prevailing mood is a grim fatalism, which derives in part from a Dark Age milieu devoid of gleaming cities and exotic empires. There are no men of truly heroic stature in these tales, only sullen butchers moved by ancestral feuds and howling in the grip of berserker rages.

Bitter ancestral feuds, brutality, and an oppressive atmosphere of fatalism are all prominent features of a story unpublished in Howard's lifetime titled "The Grey God Passes." This tale is loosely based on the historic Battle of Clontarf in 1014, supposedly the final battle between the Celts and the Vikings for the possession of Ireland. Howard transforms this forgotten historical event into an apocalyptic vision of the Twilight of the Gods.

"The Grey God Passes" (B1) begins as a runaway Gaelic slave of the Norsemen, Conn, meets a mysterious one-eyed stranger garbed in grey and wearing a slouch hat. The stranger addresses Conn by name and tells him of the forthcoming battle, in which Conn's clan will be engaged. The Grey Man gives utterance to a curious soliloquy: "'Now comes the reaping of kings, the garnering of chiefs like a harvest. Gigantic shadows stalk red-handed across the world, and night is falling on Asgaard. I hear the cries of long-dead heroes whistling in the void, and the shouts of forgotten gods. To each being there is an appointed time, and even the gods must die'" (154). Then the stranger shouts to the sky and the Choosers of the Slain—Valkyries of Norse legend—fly before an oncoming gale. Conn flees in fear as the Grey Man looms gigantic against the stormy sky.

At length, Conn meets Dunlang O'Hartigan, who is on his way to Dublin to take part in the battle against the Vikings. All the clans are gathered to make war, and many a fierce warrior is present: King Brian Boru, Donald of Mar, King Malachi O'Neill, Meathla O'Faelin, and others. Some of the warriors named by Howard actually existed. One of the characters, Black Turlogh Dubh of the clan O'Brien, appears in several other Howard stories. These characters are part of an army of twenty thousand Gaels who face an equal number of Vikings led by the chiefs Sigurd and Brodir and their allies. Conn also learns of the beautiful but treacherous Kormlada, once the wife of King Brian, who now conspires with Brodir and Sigurd to be queen of Erin.

On the road to Dublin, Conn and Dunlang meet Eevin of Craglea, Dunlang's lover and a member of a race of fairy-folk not entirely human. She pleads with Dunlang not to go to battle and prophesies his death. When Dunlang refuses to desert his clan, she presents him with armor forged by the lost art of the Romans but tells him this will not save him and that she knows she will never see him alive again. Eevin further prophesies the fates of all the principal characters and the outcome of the battle itself. Like Dunlang, those who hear their fates from Eevin's lips believe her but are not swayed from their plan of action. The Vikings have their soothsayer and he prophesies defeat for them, but they choose not to heed, accepting fate with stoical indifference.

The day of the battle, Good Friday, arrives and the assembled hosts meet on the plains of Clontarf. The battle for Erin is one of the most gripping Howard ever penned. In the end the Vikings are driven from Ireland. As prophesied, death comes to Dunlang, King Brian Boru, Brodir, Donald of Mar, Prince Meathla O'Faelin, and others. Conn the thrall survives the battle, achieving grim satisfaction by killing the man who enslaved him. In the aftermath of battle he meets Turlogh Dubh, who strikes the slave collar from his neck. Looking into the sky, he is startled to see the image of the Grey Man fading away. Black Turlogh tells him that the Grey Man is the Norse god Odin and comments:

> "His children are broken, his altars crumble, and his worshippers fallen before the swords of the South. He flees the new gods and their children, and returns to the blue gulfs of the North which gave him birth. No more will helpless victims howl beneath the daggers of his priests—no more will he stalk the black clouds . . . The Grey God passes, and we too are passing though we have conquered. The days of twilight come on again, and a strange feeling is upon me as of a waning age. What are we all, too, but ghosts waning into the night?" (181–82)

VI. Other Fantasies

At the heart of "The Grey God Passes" is the most lucid illustration of one of Howard's most prevalent themes, one that de Camp refers to as the theme of "universal destruction" (*Dark Valley Destiny* 64). In much of Howard's work, the author laments the impermanence of all things. This is also a keynote of the Norse myths themselves. Ragnarok, the Twilight of the Gods, was the central tenet of the Norse religion. This notion appealed to Howard, and he incorporated it into his own work. In writing "The Grey God Passes," Howard also made use of the Greek notion that the struggles of men are a reflection or extension of the battles between the gods. However, the assertion "as above, so below" is reversed by Howard, for his gods fade away when men cease to believe in them. Howard knew that gods spring from the minds of men and that their powers end with men's loss of belief in them.

Black Turlogh Dubh reappears in "The Dark Man" (*Weird Tales*, December 1931; *B1*). Seen as a young man in "The Grey God Passes," Turlogh is now a renegade outcast, driven from his clan due to internal rivalries. In exile, he is a hardened, bitter warrior who roams the bleak Celtic lands friendless and alone.

"The Dark Man" begins with the appearance of Turlogh on a desolate Irish shoreline lashed by sleet and snow. He commandeers a lone fisherman's boat and sets out across perilous seas to a Norse stronghold in the Hebrides. His mission is one of rescue and, failing that, vengeance. Moira, a kinswoman of Turlogh, has been abducted in a raid by the arrogant Thorfel the Fair, who means to make her his bride.

Stopping briefly on a small island en route, Turlogh discovers the bodies of strange squat dark men and a number of Vikings. As nearly as Turlogh can discern, the strange men died in defense of a statue of a Dark Man, perhaps some sort of god. Turlogh feels compelled to take the statue of the Dark Man and hefts it easily aboard his boat.

Turlogh reaches the island of Thorfel and sneaks ashore while the Vikings feast. As he scouts the camp and attempts to formulate a plan, he spies two Norsemen struggling to carry the statue. His sense of chagrin at the discovery of his boat is overshadowed by his astonishment that two burly Vikings can barely lift the statue he handled with ease. He follows the Vikings to their mead hall and is enraged to discover Moira about to be forcibly married to Thorfel by a Christian priest abducted by the Norseman on a whim. As the mock ceremony is about to begin, Moira snatches Thorfel's dagger and plunges it into her heart, preferring death to defilement by her hated enemy.

Overcome with a berserker rage, Turlogh leaps from his place of concealment and, though hopelessly outnumbered, deals death to the Vikings. Just before he is overwhelmed by sheer numbers, the hall is filled with small dark men like those Turlogh found dead on the island. As the strangers dispatch the remaining Vikings, Turlogh decapitates Thorfel.

When the slaughter has ended, the chief of the strangers speaks to Turlogh. He tells him that they are the last of the Picts and have come in search of their icon, the Dark Man. He says the Dark Man is the statue of their greatest king, Bran Mak Morn, whose spirit they believe inhabits it. The Pictish chief calls Turlogh a friend of the Dark Man and tells him that the statue helped him gain his vengeance. As Turlogh sails away, the priest has a vision of an ocean of blood spilled in brutal warfare.

The theme of "The Dark Man" can be summed up in a single word: hate. Hate drives Turlogh across the icy seas in a small open boat and is his motivation throughout the story. It does not matter to him whether Moira is alive or dead. If alive, he will rescue her and take vengeance; if dead, he will simply take vengeance. Howard tells us that Turlogh's hatred of the Norse is "a burning, living thing, almost an obsession, that at times drove him to the point of insanity" (69). It is not only Turlogh who hates, for hatred of the Norsemen drives Moira to plunge a dagger into her breast. The priest's piety and gentle faith seem feeble things indeed when contrasted with such passionate fury.

"The Dark Man" is as intense as "The Grey God Passes" but much more polished. Rage and violence are unrelenting. The mood and atmosphere of grim despair are reflected in the bleak winter landscape. The tone is bitter, pessimistic, and ultimately fatalistic. At the story's close, the priest cries out in anguish, "'Almighty God, when will the reign of blood cease?'" Turlogh replies, "'Not so long as the race lasts'" (84).

"Not so long as the race lasts"—words that echo and re-echo in readers' minds long after they have put the story down. Howard seems to suggest the unspeakable: not since the archetypal crime of Cain has hate and bloodshed ceased. Killing of man by man has gone on and will continue, regardless of what social or economic conditions prevail. Neither religion nor science has been able to stem the red tide of history. Howard knew this and, unlike most of us, did not shy away from this truth. Some suggest he reveled in it. Such indictments, however, have always been leveled at those artists who chose to deal with subjects that are not particularly pretty, and they often appear absurd to later generations. D. H. Lawrence was assailed for the frank sexuality of his novels, Jack London for his realism, Faulkner and James M. Cain for portraying the seamy side of life. Censure of this sort seems to be the lot of the taboo-breaking artist.

Beyond his fascination with Picts and Celts, another of Howard's most fervent interests centered on the allied concepts of reincarnation and "racial memory." Howard's father was familiar with many religious doctrines and was widely read in mysticism and the occult. Dr. Howard shared this interest with his son, and both gave some credence to the doctrine of reincarnation.

The concept of "racial memory" is similar to what psychologist Carl Jung has termed the "collective unconscious." According to Jung, the collective unconscious is the seat of humanity's religious aspirations and contains dreams and symbols from the whole history of humankind. Jung asserted that these symbols possess lives of their own. We have previously seen that both Solomon Kane and Kull were afforded such glimpses. Howard, however, could not have learned of the concept from Jung, for the psychologist did not begin to formulate his theories until the 1920s, and his writings were not available in English until after Howard's death. He probably encountered the concept of racial memory in Jack London's *Before Adam*.

Reincarnation is the theme of the next three stories we shall examine. Each represents a different approach to the subject, and together they show how powerfully this concept gripped Howard's imagination.

"The Valley of the Worm" (*Weird Tales*, February 1934; B1) is considered by many to be Howard's best story and is frequently anthologized. It has been cited as the quintessential Howard story by Rick McCollum in his essay "'The Valley of the Worm': A Gathering of Howard's Essential Creative Themes." Themes and motifs dealt with individually in other Howard stories are all present here. McCollum's tally cites the following: *Racial Drift, The Picts, Reincarnation, The Physical Superiority of the Barbarian, The Moral Superiority of the Barbarian, Bloodshed and Battle as a Commonplace Event, Hate and Revenge, Lost Civilizations, Unnatural Enemies, One Strong Man Against All Odds, Beneath the Earth Lurks Horror, Serpents and Apes*. "The Valley of the Worm" is therefore essential reading for readers new to Howard as well as those with a scholarly interest in his writings.

The themes of both reincarnation and racial memory are especially notable. Howard modeled this tale to a certain extent after Jack London's last and most ambitious novel, *The Star Rover*. However, this story's primordial savagery and passionate intensity, as well as the startling clarity of its vision, make it uniquely Howardian.

"The Valley of the Worm" is the narrative of James Allison, a modern man wasting away from a debilitating disease who can vividly recall his past incarnations. Howard wrote other stories and fragments loosely connected by this common narrator. One especially, "The Garden of Fear," is a provocative tale in its own right, but it and the other Allison narratives have long been overshadowed by "The Valley of the Worm."

The tale begins with Allison's assertion that the narrative he is about to relate is the archetypal story of the dragon-slayer, the basis of all our myths of this type from Siegfried to St. George. Allison tells us that the actual event transpired so long ago that the continents have changed their shapes a score of times and even the constellations in the sky have shifted. He admits that geologists and anthropologists alike would call him mad, but at the same time boldly states that he intuitively knows the truth.

The shape that Allison's spirit wore in that distant epoch was that of a mighty warrior, Niord of the Æsir. Repeatedly, Allison tells us that he will interpret some of Niord's thoughts and motives from a modern viewpoint, "so the saga of Niord will not be a meaningless chaos to you" (260). Howard makes clear through Allison that the way of life and way of thinking of people so close to humanity's primordial origins is nearly incomprehensible to today's civilized people.

Niord's saga takes place during the first great racial drift of "that restless race men once called Nordheimr and later Aryans, and today name by many names and designations" (260). De Camp has pointed out that there was never really such a thing as an "Aryan race"; the term "Aryan" properly refers to the family of languages also known as the Indo-European group. However, Howard, like most people of his time, used the term "Aryan" as a synonym for "Nordic" and subscribed to the belief that a single race carried its language across the entirety of what is now Europe and Asia.

During the great drift of Niord's people, they come to a fertile jungle clime and do battle with and defeat a tribe of small, dark men. These men are, of course, the Picts. Niord befriends Grom, a Pict they take prisoner, and the Æsir make peace with them. Niord and Grom go hunting together, and on one occasion Niord single-handedly kills a saber-tooth in a fierce struggle. Though severely wounded, he recovers to the amazement of all.

As Niord convalesces, some of the Æsir separate peaceably to form their own tribe. They settle in an area called the Valley of the Broken Stones, shunned by the Picts. Grom tells Niord of the terrible tragedy that befell the Picts who first came to the Valley; they were wiped out by some hideous monstrosity lurking somewhere in the Valley's mysterious ruins. Sometime later, Niord goes to the Valley to visit his kin, only to find them exterminated by some monstrous thing that has left a trail of slime. Niord vows to avenge his people and conceives a plan.

Niord goes into the jungle in search of Satha, the great serpent, a beast as terrible as "old saber-tooth" (270). More massive than the largest boa constrictor, Satha also possesses venom far deadlier than any cobra. Niord sets a trap and lures Satha into it. He beheads the serpent and coats the heads of his arrows in the venom. Then he paints himself, breaks his spear, and sings his death song.

Niord returns alone to the forbidden Valley and, entering the ruins, draws the monster from its subterranean lair. Its appearance is heralded by a shaggy anthropomorphic creature piping obscenely on a magic flute. Niord slays the creature, but the flute continues to pipe as the Worm crawls forth. Taking up a vantage point atop a stone pillar, Niord is struck by the sheer horror of the Worm:

> . . . I . . . looked on the spawn of nightmare. From what subterranean hell it crawled in the long ago I know not, nor what black age it repre-

sented. But it was not a beast, as humanity knows beasts. I call it a worm for lack of a better term. There is no earthly language that has a name for it. I can only say it looked somewhat more like a worm than it did an octopus, a serpent, or a dinosaur.

It was white and pulpy, and drew its quaking bulk along the ground, worm-fashion. But it had wide flat tentacles, and fleshy feelers, and other adjuncts the use of which I am unable to explain . . . Its forty eyes, set in a horrific circle, were composed of thousands of facets of as many scintillant colors which changed and altered in never-ending transmutation. But all through interplay of hue and glint, they retained their evil intelligence—intelligence there was behind those flickering facets, not human nor yet bestial, but a night-born demoniac intelligence such as men in dreams vaguely sense throbbing titanically in the black gulfs outside our material universe. In size, the monster was mountainous . . . (276)

Niord fires all his poison arrows into the Worm's shambling bulk and, discerning no effect, leaps upon its back and begins to hack at it with his sword. A tentacle flings Niord hundreds of feet into the air, and he lands with bone-splintering impact to lie broken and shattered. As his life ebbs, he sees the Worm convulse in its death throes and tumble back into the pit from which it crawled. Grom rushes to Niord's side, and Niord tells him to spread the tale of his victory far and wide. Then, "while Grom howled and beat his hairy breast, death came to me in the Valley of the Worm" (278).

"The Valley of the Worm" is beautifully rendered. Howard treats this epic saga in fitting manner and chooses every word meticulously, giving readers the impression they are reading prose-poetry. The story's many vivid images stand out as poetic symbols as well as archetypes. As in "Beyond the Black River," the saber-tooth and the Serpent represent different versions of humanity's ancient foes. Here Howard directly links Satha with the biblical Serpent, saying, "in later ages Satha becomes the veritable devil of the white races, and the Stygians first worshipped, and then, when they became Egyptians, abhorred him under the name of Set, the Old Serpent, while to the

Semites he became Leviathan and Satan" (270-71).

Niord himself is the archetypal hero whose countenance is reflected in those of Tyr, Seigfried, Beowulf, and many others. The Worm he strives against is utterly alien and destructive to all earthly life; it is what Poe called the Conqueror Worm, the embodiment of death.

In addition to the universal archetypes represented, Howard adds his personal archetypal figure of the eternal Pict. The Pict who appears in all Howard's story-cycles virtually unchanged from epoch to epoch is a constant symbol for man as a part of nature. In "The Valley of the Worm," a Pict is witness to humanity's triumph over death. The entire story is a denial of death, from its very premise of reincarnation to its denouement of the epic struggle of man against monster. Niord perishes in the struggle, but only to be reincarnated again and again and again, both as all the myriad incarnations of James Allison and as every heroic myth-figure of Western civilization.

While the reincarnation tales narrated by James Allison concern the deeds of some member of the so-called Aryan race, Howard departs from this trend in a later work unpublished during his lifetime entitled "The Thunder-Rider" (*WT*). The narrator of the tale is John Garfield, who is not even a "white man." Though raised in white society, Garfield is a Comanche, a member of the only "barbaric" race of which Howard had firsthand knowledge. He has never known any other ways except those of civilization. He was educated in America's universities and is prosperous in the world of commerce. However, beneath the stoic mask of an Indian's face, he seethes with resentment and a dim longing he can barely understand.

Howard, speaking through Garfield, once again assails civilization, with more bitter malice than usual. Garfield rails against "the most highly artificialized civilization the planet has ever known," a society that "crushes all dreams and turns men and women into whimpering automatons" (389).

Garfield has accepted the advantages of civilization: he is prosperous and well educated, a respected member of the community. In truth he despises white civilization but avails himself of its comforts because the life of his ancestors is forever denied him.

Garfield's inner turmoil threatens to overwhelm his reason; sometimes he feels himself in the grip of a "primitive murderous urge" (391). While still a child, he was troubled by disturbing dreams of savage strife and an indomitable warrior who rode the prairies. As he grew older, he began to feel a restlessness he felt only blood would quench. In desperation, Garfield seeks the help of an aged Comanche medicine man.

The medicine man tells him that it is the spirits of the men he once was that trouble him, and only by achieving full memory of his past incarnations can his sanity be saved. To attain this memory, Garfield must submit to a terrible ordeal similar to that depicted in the film *A Man Called Horse*. The medicine man cuts slits in the muscles of Garfield's back and draws rawhide thongs through the slits. Garfield is then suspended in mid-air from a tree by these thongs. The red haze of his agony fades into a vision and forever after John Garfield possesses full memory of his past life as Iron-Heart, the Thunder Rider.

The rest of the narrative concerns Iron-Heart's exploits, in particular his adventure in a strange haunted land. Though moody and atmospheric, this supernatural adventure tale lacks the intensity of the story's first half.

The opening segment of "The Thunder-Rider" is a deeply personal statement on Howard's part. The loathing of civilization, the atavistic childhood dreams, and the urge to do violence were all personally experienced by Howard himself. Howard's disdain for modern society is evident in all his major works. His dreams of alien, unfamiliar landscapes peopled by savage inhabitants formed the basis of many of these same stories. His violent urges are documented in the de Camps' biography: as a youth, Howard was dismissed from his school basketball team for use of excessive force. John Garfield also tried to sublimate his violent urges through sports but found that athletics only aggravated them.

Garfield tells us that the medicine man was "offering me a solution—a substitute for a violent life in my present existence—a safety valve for the innate ferocity that lurks at the bottom of my soul" (393). Garfield's safety valve was an escape into visions of a violent past life. Howard's safety valve was the violent fantasies into which he thrust himself. These valves are opened at great cost. Garfield's vision is awakened by voluntarily undergoing torture.

Though the so-called "Sun rituals" actually existed, a likely source of Howard's inspiration was the ordeal of the protagonist of London's *The Star Rover*. Darrell Standing is a professor who murders a colleague in a fit of atavistic rage. In San Quentin, Standing undergoes grueling torture that induces a trance wherein time melts away and he remembers his past lives.

Howard himself, however, paid a heavy price when his safety valve was closed. "The Thunder-Rider" is believed to be the last story he wrote, with the exception of "Nekht Semerkeht." It was written almost a year after "Red Nails"; that is, after Howard had ostensibly abandoned the fantasy field for more reliable markets. His main economic concern at that time was to provide medical care for his dying mother. The de Camps considered Howard's writing a stabilizing influence in his life, and the loss of his main means of self-expression during a time of great upheaval undoubtedly further handicapped Howard's ability to cope with the loss of his beloved parent.

"'For the Love of Barbara Allen'" (*B1*) is yet another story not published until long after Howard's death. It also concerns reincarnation, but this gentle, poignant tale is a radical departure from the bulk of Howard's output. It merits attention for being the only love

VI. Other Fantasies

story Howard wrote aside from "Queen of the Black Coast." Although this brief tale seems overly romantic in our more sophisticated era, and the denouement is realized long before the climax, it delivers considerable emotional impact.

Like the previous story, "'For the Love of Barbara Allen'" contains autobiographical elements, but in this case feelings of hostility and aggression are replaced by quiet nostalgia for Howard's post oaks homeland, and the Old South his family hailed from. Howard also had a keen interest in the folk music of the region. He informed Lovecraft:

> In the Scotch-Irish settlement of Holly Springs [Arkansas] where William Benjamin Howard settled in 1858, they still sang songs that carried the tang of the heather, though the singers were generations removed from the old country. Forty years ago such songs were popular there, as "Barbary Allen", "William Hall, a young Highlander", "The Wearin' of the Green", "Little Susie, the pride of Kildare", "Shamus O'Brien" . . . (REH to H. P. Lovecraft, c. November 1930; CL 2.141)

Howard had earlier corresponded with noted expert Robert W. Gordon. At the time, Gordon edited a column in *Adventure* magazine entitled "Old Songs That Men Have Sung," and later served as head of the Archive of American Folk Song at the Library of Congress. With the present tale, a folk song is central to the plot.

The story opens as the narrator, young John Grimes, listens to his grandfather sing the folk song "'For the Love of Barbara Allen'":

> Barbara Allen! An echo of a distant and forgotten homeland among the post-oak covered ridges of a barren land. In my mind I saw the settlers forging westward from the Piedmont, over the Alleghenies and along the Cumberland River—on foot, in lumbering wagons drawn by slow-footed oxen, on horseback—men in broadcloth and men in buckskin. The guitars and the banjos clinked by the fires at night, in the lonely log cabins, by the stretches of river black in the starlight, up on the long ridges where the owls hooted. Barbara Allen—a tie to the past, a link between today and the dim yesterdays. (251)

The grandfather recalls how his brother Joel always sang this song to his sweetheart, Rachel Ormond, before the brothers went off to the Civil War with General Nathan Bedford Forrest's Confederate forces. The old man then recounts Joel's death in a cavalry charge. Rachel never got over her grief and, now an old woman, lies dying in her nearby home.

The conversation is interrupted by the noise of horses fighting in the barn. When young John goes to quiet them, he is knocked unconscious by a horse's kick. He awakens clad in the gray uniform of the Confederacy, under the command of General Nathan Bedford Forrest. In reality, both of Howard's own grandfathers actually served under Forrest during the Civil War. Famed as a master of tactics, Forrest was also a large, powerful man and ferocious fighter who killed thirty men in single combat. It seems likely that Forrest was one of the prototypes Howard had in mind while creating Conan.

In the story, Forrest leads a charge against Union troops, and young John Grimes realizes that he is living the battle he just heard his grandfather recount. He realizes that he is Joel Grimes just as a Union bullet strikes him dead. John reawakens back in the barn with certain knowledge that he was once Joel Grimes.

Young John rushes to Rachel's side as she breathes her last. She immediately recognizes him as Joel and asks him to play "'For the Love of Barbara Allen'" one last time. Though he has never played a guitar before, he is suddenly able to as he sings her favorite song to her. As he finishes the song a string snaps and Rachel Ormond lies dead.

By this point in the story, the reader has been lulled into a sentimental, romantic mood, thinking it wonderful that the lovers should be reunited one last time. However, Howard closes the story with two terse sentences that upset this mood: "'She waited long for him; now she must wait somewhere else. That's the hell of war; it upsets the balance of things and throws lives into confusion that eternity can not make right'" (255).

VI. Other Fantasies

Howard thus chooses to end his romance on a bitter note of irony as his familiar theme of cosmic tragedy intrudes, shattering the complacent atmosphere of sentiment which pervades the story. Howard is not exactly known for antiwar statements. The battle-weariness experienced by his heroes is usually physical, not an emotional revulsion against the bloodshed. Here, however, he portrays war as a cosmic tragedy, a disruptive force in the universe.

The last of Howard's fantasies examined here is something of a departure. The novel *Almuric* is set on an unknown planet on the far side of the universe. Unique among Howard's works, *Almuric* is neither a heroic fantasy in the usual sense nor is it hard science fiction. Rather, it is a part of a subgenre sometimes referred to as "sword and planet." Sword and planet sagas typically involve earthmen transported to other worlds. There they engage in hand-to-hand combat using swords and similar weapons, even in technologically advanced societies. Sword and planet heroes include Edwin Lester Arnold's Gulliver Jones, Alex Raymond's Flash Gordon, Leigh Brackett's Eric John Stark, and John Norman's Tarl Cabot. But of them all, the most prominent and influential is Edgar Rice Burroughs's John Carter of Mars.

Howard's agent, Otis Adelbert Kline, was also the author of several noteworthy sword and planet novels. These swashbucklers, though shameless in their imitation of Burroughs, were nonetheless extremely popular. While the high-paying *Argosy* consistently turned down Howard's best efforts, Kline's Burroughs copies were enthusiastically welcomed. Kline's *Buccaneers of Venus* was chosen over "Worms of the Earth" to receive a cover illustration for *Weird Tales*. At some point, Howard felt moved to follow his agent's example and try his hand at a sword and planet tale.

The composition of *Almuric* cannot be accurately dated. It may have been written as early as 1934, but it has also been thought that it was written in the late, post-fantasy phase of Howard's career. If the latter is true, this would suggest that Howard was still eager to write fantasy and was seeking a way to do so profitably. In any case, Howard abandoned the project. It was published posthumously in *Weird Tales* in 1939 thanks to the efforts of Howard's father and Otis Adelbert Kline. The version of the novel that has come down to us is a composite of a first draft and an incomplete, more polished second draft. This accounts for the uneven quality of the novel.

Like many of Burroughs's novels and Kline's subsequent imitations, *Almuric* concerns the adventures of a terrestrial human transported to another planet. This earthman is Esau Cairn, and the novel's foreword details the circumstances surrounding Cairn's teleportation to a distant world. Cairn is a misfit, a man born out of his time. Mightier than any other man on earth, Cairn's proper place is in a more primitive era. Fleeing from the police after killing a crooked politician, Cairn takes refuge in the remote laboratory of a scientist who offers him an escape route. Cairn becomes a human guinea pig and allows himself to be teleported to another planet—the primordial world of Almuric.

Finding himself naked and unarmed, Cairn must survive in the hostile wilderness of Almuric, becoming tougher in the process. Eventually he joins a tribe of primitive people after first proving his worth. The novel declines in quality after a promising beginning as Cairn, now known as Iron-Hand, unites Almuric's humans and leads them in a final war against their hereditary enemies, a cruel race of winged men.

Although *Almuric* is an imitation of an imitation, some of the writing in the early portion of the novel is outstanding. This is due to autobiographical elements and deeply felt personal convictions that creep in despite Howard's commercial intentions. In the foreword, the scientist who rescues Cairn from execution by a society to which he can never belong describes him at length:

VI. Other Fantasies

> Many men are born outside their century; Esau Cairn was born outside his epoch. Neither a moron nor a low-class primitive, possessing a mind well above the average, he was, nevertheless, distinctly out of place in the modern age. I never knew a man of intelligence so little fitted for adjustment in a machine-made civilization . . .
> He was of a restless mold, impatient of restraint and resentful of authority. Not by any means a bully, he at the same time refused to countenance what he considered to be the slightest infringement on his rights. He was primitive in his passions, with a gusty temper and a courage inferior to none on this planet. His life was a series of repressions. Even in athletic contests he was forced to hold himself in, lest he injure his opponents. Esau Cairn was, in short, a freak—a man whose physical body and mental bent leaned back to the primordial.
> Born in the Southwest, of old frontier stock, he came of a race whose characteristics were inclined toward violence, and whose traditions were of war and feud and battle against man and nature . . . (56-57)

The similarities between Cairn and Howard himself should by now be obvious. Cairn, however, has the advantage of being a physical superman who would actually have a chance for survival in such a savage, hostile world.

The first chapter of the novel proper deals with Cairn's solitary existence in Almuric's wilderness. The many hardships and privations he endures, the torments of hunger, thirst, heat, and cold, are rendered by Howard in unromantic terms. Cairn's unashamed confession that he almost wept with joy to see the sun rise after his first freezing night on Almuric is particularly moving. Nonetheless, Cairn comes to thrive and exult in his primitive existence, and Howard makes some of his most salient points in favor of the simple life of the primitive as opposed to the empty, habit-filled existence of a modern, faceless automaton:

> I was living the life of the most primitive savage; I had neither companionship, books, clothing, nor any of the things which go to make up civilization. According to the cultured viewpoint, I should have been most miserable. I was not. I reveled in my existence. My being grew and expanded. I tell you, the natural life of mankind is a grim battle for ex-

istence against the forces of nature, and any other form of life is artificial and without realistic meaning.

My life was not empty; it was crowded with adventures calling on every ounce of intelligence and physical power. When I swung down from my chosen eyrie at dawn, I knew that I would see the sun set only through my personal craft and strength and speed . . . I was fully alive. That phrase has more meaning than appears on the surface. The average civilized man is never fully alive; he is burdened with masses of atrophied tissue and useless matter. Life flickers feebly in him; his senses are dull and torpid. In developing his intellect he has sacrificed far more than he realizes.

I realized that I, too, had been partly dead on my native planet. But now I was alive in every sense of the word; I tingled and burned and stung with life to the finger tips and the ends of my toes. Every sinew, vein, and springy bone was vibrant with the dynamic flood of singing, pulsing, humming life. My time was too much occupied with food-getting and preserving my skin to allow the developing of the morbid and intricate complexes and inhibitions which torment the civilized individual. To those highly complex persons who would complain that the psychology of such a life is over-simple, I can but reply that in my life at that time, violence and continual action and the necessity of action crowded out most of the gropings and soul-searchings common to those whose safety and daily meals are assured them by the toil of others . . . (73-74)

In this manner, Howard shows us that Cairn has undergone a profound spiritual transformation in accompaniment to his growing physical prowess.

Unfortunately, the novel gradually declines in quality from this high point. Howard had created his own distinctive brand of fantasy and may have felt ill at ease employing another author's format. He set *Almuric* aside and did not pick it up again.

In the last year of his life, Howard felt compelled to abandon fantasy altogether due to practical concerns. However, if "The Thunder-Rider" is any indication, he never stopped looking for a way back to it. Fittingly, his very last story, begun less than a month before his death and never finished, was a fantasy.

VII. Horror Stories

The bulk of Howard's fantasy appeared in *Weird Tales*, a magazine devoted primarily to chilling tales of vampires, werewolves, witches, ghosts, and other familiar figures of Gothic horror. *Weird Tales* was the first magazine to publish Howard's work, doing so at a time when he was submitting a wide variety of fiction to a number of pulp titles in vain.

Wishing to follow up his initial success, Howard fashioned a number of horror tales in a more or less traditional mold with an eye to becoming a regular contributor to "The Unique Magazine." However, even after he had established himself as the popular creator of Solomon Kane, Conan, et al., Howard still contributed an occasional tale of supernatural horror to its pages.

Howard became quite adept at creating short vignettes of the supernatural. H. P. Lovecraft, a scholar and exponent of horror fiction as well as a master practitioner, said of Howard: "Not only did he excel in pictures of strife and slaughter, but he was almost alone in his ability to create real emotions of spectral fear and dread suspense" ("In Memoriam: Robert Ervin Howard" 125). Howard had ample raw material to draw upon in the form of legends, folk tales, and local superstitions related to him during childhood. He learned of zombies and voodoo from "Aunt Mary" Bohannon, a black cook employed by his family when they lived in Bagwell in East Texas. As an adult, he vividly recalled the tales of Celtic lore told by his grandmother, Eliza Howard:

All the gloominess and dark mysticism of the Gaelic nature was hers, and there was no light and mirth in her. Her tales showed what a strange legion of folklore grew up in the Scotch-Irish settlements of the Southwest, where transplanted Celtic myths and fairy tales met and mingled with a sub-stratum of slave legends. My grandmother was but one generation removed from south Ireland, and she knew by heart all the tales and superstitions of the folks, black and white, about her ... (REH to H. P. Lovecraft, c. September or October 1930; CL 2.90)

Howard's earliest horror stories made use of the traditional themes of witchcraft and lycanthropy. His werewolf story "Wolfshead" (*Weird Tales*, April 1926) gained him his first cover illustration for *Weird Tales*. It was an inducement to keep his hand in the horror genre. "Wolfshead" was followed by "Sea Curse" (*Weird Tales*, May 1928), an atmospheric tale set in a remote fishing village on a barren coast. It concerns a witch's vengeance on the two town bullies who caused her niece's suicide. A related story, "Out of the Deep," not published in Howard's lifetime, tells of a clammy horror that rises from the briny depths to stalk the streets of the same town.

In 1930, Howard began his spirited correspondence with fellow *Weird Tales* contributor H. P. Lovecraft. Generally acknowledged as the greatest horror author of the twentieth century, Lovecraft is best known for such stories as "The Dunwich Horror," "The Call of Cthulhu," and "The Shadow over Innsmouth." These are part of a loosely connected cycle making use of common background lore. Critic S. T. Joshi has dubbed Lovecraft's fictional mythology "the Lovecraft Mythos," but it is more commonly known to readers as "the Cthulhu Mythos."

To give his mythos greater resonance and a sense of authenticity, Lovecraft encouraged colleagues such as Howard to make use of elements of the mythos in their own fiction. August Derleth, Clark Ashton Smith, Frank Belknap Long, and the young Robert Bloch also took Lovecraft at his word, and this famous story cycle took form in the pages of *Weird Tales*.

Lovecraft's mythos centers on the lore of a pantheon of vastly powerful extraterrestrials called the Old Ones who ruled the earth long ago, and whose presence is still felt on the outer fringes of human consciousness. Their minions still lurk in the dark corners of the world, and one day the Old Ones will return to take dominion. Revelations concerning these entities and their minions can be found in rare and forbidden occult tomes such as the *Necronomicon*. In some stories, obscure writings or artifacts related to the Old Ones are discovered, while in others the beings themselves are actually encountered. Whatever the case, horrifying revelations concerning the universe and man's place in it are borne upon the protagonist. Certain stories by Howard, Smith, and others make only marginal use of mythos references, but others make more integral use of Lovecraft's concepts and lore.

"The Black Stone" (*Weird Tales*, November 1931; HS) is one of Howard's best-known horror stories and his most satisfying excursion into the realm of Lovecraftian horror. In this story an unnamed narrator recounts his visit to a prehistoric monolith called the Black Stone, located near a tiny village in a remote area of Hungary. He had learned of its existence while studying a rare occult book, *Nameless Cults* by a German mystic named von Juntz. Other references to the Stone are found in the mad poet Justin Geoffrey's "The People of the Monolith."

In Hungary, the narrator ignores the warnings of the locals and spends Midsummer's Night at the foot of the Black Stone. He falls into a trance-like sleep and witnesses the obscene rites of a strange people. An infant is sacrificed, its brains dashed out against the Stone, and finally the narrator sees "a huge monstrous toad-like *thing*" (171) squatting atop the monolith. The next morning he awakens with his sanity shaken but intact. Research reveals that all he witnessed actually transpired centuries before. As the story closes, the narrator ponders, "But what of the other fiendish possibilities hinted at by Von Juntz . . . *what nameless shapes may even now lurk in the dark places of the world?"* (175).

"The Black Stone" is a fine horror story and superior to the general run of Lovecraft imitations. The other Howard tales in which Lovecraftian concepts are central are "The Thing on the Roof" and an unfinished story, "The House in the Oaks," while marginal Cthulhu Mythos references occur in "Dig Me No Grave," "The Children of the Night," "The Fire of Asshurbanipal," and several additional stories. Howard expressed doubts concerning the effectiveness of "The Black Stone" due to his uneasiness in writing in another author's style. He soon abandoned his Mythos fiction, but his creations von Juntz, *Nameless Cults*, and the mad poet Justin Geoffrey remain entrenched in Mythos lore.

Howard was correct in his assessment of his Mythos writings, for in attempting to write a Lovecraftian pastiche Howard had to sacrifice some of the elements that made his own work unique. Howard's protagonists are usually fierce fighters equipped to destroy, or at least contain, the horrors they confront. Only when he writes in a Lovecraftian vein are Howard's protagonists passive witnesses relating the horrific events that have transpired. Lovecraft himself had adopted this approach very designedly in the sense that he intended for horrifying episodes to flow over and envelop the protagonist, just as they do to a dreamer in the throes of an actual nightmare. This makes for compelling horror fiction, but to Howard, at heart a writer of action, it was anathema. Thomas Reid pinpointed the fundamental differences between the outlooks of Lovecraft and Howard: "Howard's is a position of optimism, and Lovecraft's a statement of utter cynicism and pessimism. Their themes are, however, identical. They write, in archetypal and epic terms, of man's struggle against that which is utterly destructive and evil. Howard's primordial heroes most often win. Lovecraft's are invariably crushed" (30).

A number of Howard's other horror stories derived from folk tales about the "little people." As previously noted, Howard was fascinated by Celtic mythology. He was familiar with legends of fairies, leprechauns, goblins, and elves, as well as the then-current anthropological theories concerning their basis in fact. These theories posited that Europe was once inhabited by a pygmy-like race that was supplanted and absorbed by the ancestors of modern Europeans. Howard blended these theories with the myths themselves to formulate such stories as "Worms of the Earth," discussed earlier, as well as "The Children of the Night," "People of the Dark," and "The Little People."

Howard also set several horror stories in his own American Southwest. These include "The Man on the Ground," "The Dead Remember," "Old Garfield's Heart," and "The Horror from the Mound" (*Weird Tales*, May 1932).

"The Horror from the Mound" (*HS*) concerns an impoverished dirt farmer, dwelling alone in a tiny cabin, who unearths a vampire while searching for treasure in a forbidden Indian burial mound. With its stark depiction of the farmer's hardscrabble existence, the story is notable for its brooding atmosphere of loneliness, despair, and isolation. However, a more significant distinction may be that it is a very early example of a popular genre now known as the "weird western."

As the name suggests, the weird western combines a western setting with elements of horror, fantasy, or science fiction. Noteworthy entries in the genre include the novels *The Circus of Dr. Lao* by Charles G. Finney, *The Hawkline Monster: A Gothic Western* by Richard Brautigan, *The Haunted Mesa* by Louis L'Amour, and Stephen King's *Dark Tower* series. Examples also include the television program *The Wild, Wild West* and the comic book *Jonah Hex*, as well as motion pictures such as the Gene Autry serial *The Phantom Empire*, *The Beast of Hollow Mountain*, *Billy the Kid vs. Dracula*, *The Valley of Gwangi*, *Cow-*

boys & Aliens, and El Topo.

Howard's most interesting weird western is, perhaps, "The Valley of the Lost." Published posthumously, this tale combines the Southwestern regional setting with a variation of the "little people" theme. Its background is the Reynolds–McCrill feud, which Howard modeled after the bloody Texas feuds with which he was familiar.

The story begins as John Reynolds is fleeing an ambush by the McCrills. He takes refuge in Lost Valley, an area shunned by the Indians as haunted. He is followed by the ambushers, and shoots one from a hidden vantage point. Thinking Reynolds has fled once more, the ambushers hide the body of their kinsman in a nearby cave and set off on the route they think Reynolds has taken.

Reynolds, having exhausted his ammunition, seeks to obtain that on the gunbelt of the body in the cave. He enters the cave and, while groping in the darkness, tumbles through a trap-door. Almost immediately, he is attacked by the corpse of the man he has slain. Killing his foe once more, he is mystified by a strange noise. Following it to its source, he finds an altar adorned with the statue of a feathered serpent. This icon is worshipped by a horde of hideous snake-men that capture Reynolds. These dwarfish, repellent creatures use their telepathic powers to relate their history to him.

Once they were a mighty race inhabiting a city in the Lost Valley. They were obliterated by prehistoric humans and driven underground. Ages passed; their city crumbled to dust. The descendants devolved into an obscene parody of what the race once was. Only their hate sustains them, and they avenge themselves on occasional hapless humans by using their arcane arts to compel the dead to attack the living.

As the vision fades, Reynolds seizes the statue of their god and threatens to destroy it if the snake-men harm him. He escapes into the outer world and hides just as the ambushers return to claim their dead. They enter the cave and are slain horribly. Reynolds takes some dynamite from one of their saddlebags and uses it to seal the cave forever. Then, sickened and horrified by the terrible knowledge he has gained, he shoots himself in the head.

Unlike most of Howard's horror stories, which are written solely to entertain, "The Valley of the Lost" embodies a personal statement. The bitter hatreds of Reynolds's feud are rendered meaningless by the burden of his newfound knowledge, much as Bran Mak Morn's hatred of the Romans was nullified by his similar encounter with the worms of the earth. So terrible is this knowledge that the entire universe is tainted by it:

> John Reynolds walked slowly away; and suddenly the whole horror swept upon him and the earth seemed hideously alive under his feet, the sun foul and blasphemous over his head. The light was sickly, yellowish and evil, and all things were polluted by the unholy knowledge locked in his skull, like hidden drums beating ceaselessly in the blackness beneath the hills.
>
> He had closed one Door forever but what other nightmare shapes might lurk in the hidden places and the dark pits of the earth, gloating over the souls of men? His knowledge was a reeking blasphemy which would never let him rest, for ever in his soul would whisper the drums that throbbed in those dark pits where lurked demons that had once been men. He had looked on ultimate foulness, and his knowledge was a taint because of which he could never stand clean before men again or touch the flesh of any living thing without a shudder. If man, molded of divinity, could sink to such verminous obscenities, who could contemplate his eventual destiny unshaken? And if such beings as the Old People existed, what other horrors might not lurk beneath the visible surface of the universe? He was suddenly aware that he had glimpsed the grinning skull beneath the mask of life, and that that glimpse made life intolerable. All certainty and stability had been swept away, leaving a mad welter of lunacy, nightmare and stalking horror.
>
> John Reynolds drew his gun and his horny thumb drew back the heavy hammer. Thrusting the muzzle against his temple, he pulled the trigger. The shot crashed echoing through the hills, and the last of the fighting Reynoldses pitched headlong. (287–88)

Like Reynolds, Howard too was aware of "the grinning skull beneath the mask of life," and Reynolds's suicide prefigures Howard's own.

In addition to his native Southwest, Howard made use of another regional setting of which he had some knowledge, the Deep South. In Howard's horror tales of the South, the gloomy forbidding pine woods and bayous become a presence, the nighted depths of the forest reflecting the dark side of human passion and grim secrets concealed within. Rusty Burke referred to these tales as Howard's "Piney Woods" stories. Piney Woods stories include "Black Hound of Death," "The Shadow of the Beast," "The House of Suspicion," "Moon of Zambebwei," "Black Canaan," and "Pigeons from Hell."

"Pigeons from Hell" was written in late 1934 and published posthumously (*Weird Tales*, May 1938; HS). The title derives from an image present in many of the ghost stories Howard heard during boyhood, "the old deserted plantation mansion, with the weeds growing rank about it, and the ghostly pigeons flying up from the rails of the verandah" (REH to H. P. Lovecraft, c. September 1930; CL 2.90). This remarkable tale is perhaps Howard's best-known horror story. It was the first of his stories to be adapted into another medium; in 1961 it was televised as an episode of Boris Karloff's *Thriller* series. In 2008 the tale was rather too freely adapted into a disappointing graphic novel published by Dark Horse.

The story opens as two New Englanders, John Branner and his friend Griswell, are traveling in the South and spend the night in a deserted manor house like those Howard so often heard described during childhood. Griswell awakens from a troubled sleep to see Branner walking up the stairs in a trance. He is horrified when Branner returns, no longer alive but an animated corpse gripping the bloody axe that had split his skull. Griswell flees the house in a blind panic and runs aimlessly into the woods.

In his headlong flight, he meets the county's sheriff, Buckner,

VII. Horror Stories

who investigates the house and finds Branner cold and motionless on the floor. Griswell is implicated in his friend's murder, but the sheriff gives him the benefit of the doubt and doggedly attempts to clear him. Buckner is inclined to give some credence to Griswell's bizarre tale due to the ominous reputation of the manor, which was once the residence of a family from the West Indies, the Blassenvilles. One night in 1890, the last of the Blassenvilles, Elizabeth, fled from the house and never returned. The manor has lain deserted ever since and is shunned by the local black folk.

The following evening Buckner and Griswell go to the hut of an ancient voodoo man, Jacob, seeking information about the house and the Blassenvilles. Jacob tells of the extinct family who were known for their cruelty and of Celia Blassenville who mistreated her mulatto maid, Joan. He then begins to ramble incoherently about voodoo, about the god Damballah, and about zombies and their female counterparts, zuvembies. Finally, he tells how Joan participated in voodoo rites. While reaching for firewood, Jacob is bitten by a poisonous snake and soon dies, meeting the very fate he feared would overtake him for revealing the secrets of Damballah.

Buckner and Griswell conclude that Joan transformed herself into a zuvembie to exact vengeance on Celia Blassenville and her nieces. They resolve to spend the night in the Blassenville manor to learn the truth. That night Griswell has another strange dream and is drawn up the stairs in the grip of a hypnotic trance. Buckner follows him, and when a figure appears at the top of the stairs, he shoots it. The sheriff and Griswell follow a bloody trail to a secret room where they find the withered corpses of the Blassenville sisters. Lying dead in the room is the zuvembie Buckner had shot—not the mulatto maid Joan, but "'the creature that once was Celia Blassenville'" (448). Joan's vengeance was not to become a zuvembie, but to make Celia one.

The "Pigeons from Hell" of the story's title are ghostly birds that sometimes flock mysteriously about the decaying manor; legend has it that they are the souls of the Blassenvilles let out of Hell. The legacy of the Blassenvilles is one of cruelty and hatred. The embodiment of this legacy is the zuvembie Celia, an unnatural thing neither alive nor dead that exists only to inflict more pain. The prevailing mood of the story is one of apprehension at the uncovering of secrets too sordid and terrible to be brought to light.

"Pigeons from Hell," with its decaying Southern family, sexual sadism, gruesome murder, and evil psychotic spinster, brings to mind the disturbing works of William Faulkner. The image of the undead Celia existing for decades in a room filled with the corpses of her nieces is reminiscent of Faulkner's story "A Rose for Emily," in which a widow sleeps with the corpse of her husband. Sexual sadism is present in many of Faulkner's novels and echoed in Howard's work.

In "Pigeons from Hell," an ex-slave recalls how Miss Celia tied Joan naked to a tree and whipped her. The axe-murder in "Pigeons from Hell" is no more unpleasant than the fates that befall many of Faulkner's characters. At one point in the story, Howard says of Griswell: "He had thought of the South as a sunny, lazy land washed by soft breezes laden with spice and warm blossoms, where life ran tranquilly to the rhythm of black folk singing in sun-bathed cottonfields. But now he had discovered another, unsuspected side—a dark, brooding, fear-haunted side, and the discovery repelled him" (430). This passage neatly sums up the prevailing themes of Faulkner's work.

The source of both the supernatural trappings in "Pigeons from Hell" and Joan's torture by Celia was a childhood acquaintance of Howard's. Howard reminisced at length in a letter to Lovecraft:

> As regards African-legend sources, I well remember the tales I listened to and shivered at, when a child in the "piney woods" of East Texas . . . There were quite a number of old slave darkies still living then. The one to whom I listened most was the cook, old Aunt Mary Bohannon . . . Mistreatment of slaves is, and has been somewhat exaggerated, but old Aunt Mary had the misfortune, in her youth, to belong to a man whose wife was a fiend from Hell. The young slave

women were fine young animals, and barbarically handsome; her mistress was frenziedly jealous. You understand. Aunt Mary told tales of torture and unmistakable sadism that sickens me to this day when I think of them . . .

She told many tales, one which particularly made my hair rise . . . A young girl going to the river for water, met, in the dimness of dusk, an old man, long dead, who carried his severed head in one hand . . .

Another tale she told I have met with often in negro-lore . . . Two or three men—usually negroes—are travelling in a wagon through some isolated district—usually a broad, deserted river-bottom. They come on to the ruins of a once thriving plantation at dusk, and decide to spend the night in the deserted plantation house. This house is always huge, brooding and forbidding, and always, as the men approach the high columned verandah, through the high weeds that surround the house, great numbers of pigeons rise from their roosting places on the railing and fly away. The men sleep in the big front room with its crumbling fire-place, and in the night are awakened by a jangling of chains, weird noises and groans from upstairs. Sometimes footsteps descend the stairs with no visible cause. Then a terrible apparition appears to the men who flee in terror . . . (REH to H. P. Lovecraft, c. September 1930; CL 2.88-89)

"Pigeons from Hell" is a story in which the horror of zombies and voodoo mingles with the horror of human degeneracy and wanton cruelty.

In addition to his Piney Woods tales, Howard wrote other horror stories, such as "Black Country" and "The Dream Snake," set on the dark continent of Africa. As in the Solomon Kane stories, Africa is portrayed more metaphorically than physically. Howard is consistent in his depiction of the jungle as a brooding, evil presence alive with malignant menace. In "The Valley of the Worm," Niord encounters a tribe of Picts dwelling in the jungle and says of them:

> Already they were exhibiting hints of characteristics I have noted among black savages in jungle countries, though they had dwelt in these environs only a few generations. The abysmal jungle was engulfing them, was obliterating their pristine characteristics and shaping them in its own

horrific mold. They were drifting into headhunting, and cannibalism was but a step which I believe they must have taken before they became extinct. These things are natural adjuncts to the jungle; the Picts did not learn them from the black people, for then there were no blacks among those hills. (B1 262)

Howard's most interesting African story is one of the first he sold to *Weird Tales*, "The Hyena" (March 1928). "The Hyena" is narrated by a young man from the southern United States, brought up regarding blacks as inferiors, who comes to work on a ranch on the African coast. He develops a dislike for a local fetish man who is tall, virile, and muscular and inspires in the narrator feelings of physical inferiority. His emotions are further befuddled when an attractive young woman comes to visit the ranch. The narrator timidly worships the woman from afar, while the black fetish man openly covets her with thinly veiled lust. The fetish man is finally revealed as a were-hyena and destroyed. This early story mingles supernatural horror with elements of racial and sexual tension, a formula Howard made more skillful use of in a much later story, the piney woods tale "Black Canaan."

"Black Canaan" (*Weird Tales*, June 1936; HS) was originally based on the legend of Kelly the Conjure-Man. According to a legend from the Ouachita pinelands of Arkansas, Kelly was a mysterious black man who dwelt in the region during the 1870s and held a powerful sway over the ex-slaves of the area. Howard recounted the legend to Lovecraft in a December 1930 letter. With Lovecraft's encouragement, Howard wrote an article, "Kelly the Conjure-Man," in 1931. It was submitted unsuccessfully to the *Texaco Star*, the company paper of Texaco which had previously published a similar article by Howard, "The Ghost of Camp Colorado."

In "Black Canaan" Kelly is transfigured into a conjure-man named Saul Stark. Because of editorial difficulties, Howard was displeased with the final version of the story, remarking that he had to "cut . . . the guts out of it." (REH to August Derleth, 9 May 1936; CL 3.439). Nevertheless, it remains one of Howard's most gripping tales of primeval supernatural forces.

The narrative starts in New Orleans, where Kirby Buckner is accosted by a withered black crone who whispers the ominous words, "'Trouble on Tularoosa Creek!'" (379). Buckner immediately realizes that his backwoods homeland is in peril and instantly departs for the Canaan country of his birth. He arrives after midnight and sets out on horseback through the bayous to the town of Grimesville. En route he encounters a mysterious "quadroon girl" who mocks him (381). Buckner is struck by her provocative beauty and strange urges stir within him:

> I had never before paid any attention to a black or brown woman. But this quadroon girl was different from any I had ever seen. Her features were regular as a white woman's, and her speech was not that of a common wench. Yet she was barbaric, in the open lure of her smile, in the gleam of her eyes, in the shameless posturing of her voluptuous body. Every gesture, every motion she made set her apart from the ordinary run of women; her beauty was untamed and lawless, meant to madden rather than to soothe, to make a man blind and dizzy, to rouse in him all the unreined passions that are his heritage from his ape ancestors. (381)

The woman calls forth several large blacks from hiding to kill Buckner, but he shoots one and kills another with a bowie knife. As a third flees, he notices that the girl has disappeared.

Buckner joins his fellow white men but finds himself strangely reluctant to speak of the black woman. He learns that the local blacks are now being led by a strange conjure-man, Saul Stark, who has vowed to kill all the whites in Grimesville and set up a black empire in America. All are apprehensive concerning the imminent "uprising," and Buckner tells us that "The blacks had risen in 1845, and the red terror of that revolt was not forgotten, nor the three lesser rebellions before it . . . The fear of a black uprising lurked forever in the depths of that forgotten back-country; the very children absorbed it in their cradles" (384). The scion of an important family, Buckner is looked to for leadership in the time of crisis.

The men of Grimesville have captured a frightened black man, Tope Sorley, and were about to interrogate him when Buckner arrived. Buckner, loath to beat the truth out of Tope, attempts to calm the terrified man, who dreads the vengeance of Saul Stark should he betray the conjure-man. He fears that Stark will use his magical powers to "'put me in de swamp!'" (386). Promises of protection persuade Tope to tell them of Stark's ambitions. Buckner decides to confront Stark.

Traveling to Stark's cabin, Buckner finds that Stark is gone but instinctively realizes that he has left some sort of supernatural entity within the cabin to guard it and does not enter. As he returns to his fellows, Buckner once again meets the quadroon girl. She taunts him and, though he is armed, he cannot bring himself to shoot her. "'I have made such magic as none but a Bride of Damballah can make,'" she gloats (394). She tells him that that very night she will summon him to her, and that he will be powerless to resist. Deep down the white man knows it is true. He will witness the Dance of the Skull before meeting a horrible fate.

The witch-woman melts mysteriously into the swamp and Buckner, panic-stricken, rides away. Along the trail Buckner meets Jim Braxton, a friend who has come looking for him. Buckner admonishes Braxton to return to Grimesville and let him find and face Stark alone, but Braxton refuses to allow his friend to face the danger on his own. As the sun sets, Buckner feels himself drawn to the black settlement at Goshen, unable to resist or even speak of the spell to Braxton. He attempts to warn his friend away several times, but to no avail.

Arriving at Goshen, the two men encounter the witch. Buckner is paralyzed, but Braxton acts and shoots at her. Once more she

VII. Horror Stories

vanishes, and they find no body. Suddenly they are attacked by something in the swamp they cannot see clearly, and Jim Braxton is killed.

Buckner, totally helpless in the grip of the voodoo spell, finds himself watching the orgiastic rites of Damballah from a copse of trees. The witch who called herself a Bride of Damballah appears, her body swaying rhythmically to the obscene music. Buckner realizes that she is the source of Stark's power, and at the end of the ceremony the conjure-man will consolidate his rule over the blacks.

However, as the Bride of Damballah finishes her dance she collapses, dead, for Braxton's bullet had struck home, hitting her in the heart. Only her evil power had kept her alive this long. As she expires, Buckner feels the spell laid upon him lift. The blacks flee in panic, the uprising is broken, and Buckner stalks out of the swamp and kills Stark. Afterwards, Buckner learns what was meant by Tope Sorley's cryptic words, "'He'll put me in de swamp!'" He discovers that Stark magically altered the bodies of his enemies, transforming them into mindless amphibious horrors. He keeps the burden of this terrible knowledge to himself.

The most striking thing about "Black Canaan" is its racial element, presented in unabashed frankness with no regard for delicate sensibilities. Throughout the story, the omnipresent racial tension threatens to erupt into violence, bloodshed, and ghastly horror. Primitive emotions dominate the story; one of them is hate, another is lust.

The lust that the Bride of Damballah awakens in Buckner is something he can neither control nor bring himself to mention to his fellow white men. The spell by which he is summoned to his doom is merely an extension of the dark passions already awakened, and once again Buckner can neither control himself nor communicate his dilemma to others. The struggles of black against white and man against woman are overshadowed by Buckner's internal struggle, as feelings of helplessness, rage, and shame vie with his terror of his own libidinous urges.

Howard's personal fascination with black women is evident in several works besides "Black Canaan," most notably the Solomon Kane story "The Moon of Skulls" and certain poems. In Howard's time black women were commonly perceived as being more highly sexed, hence both more available and sexually interesting. For Howard, there was also the allure of the barbaric and exotic.

It seems doubtful that "Black Canaan," a story brimming with more racial and sexual tension than the average prison, could even be published if written today. The ugly epithet "nigger" is used throughout the story with alarming frequency. (As narrator, Kirby Buckner recounts its use by others and uses it himself in conversing with peers, but uses "black" or "negro" when addressing the reader directly.) Howard employs it and additional unflattering terms for blacks in other Piney Woods stories, but more sparingly. "Black Canaan," with its central theme of impending race war, is by far the roughest. The draft version that Howard felt compelled to "cut . . . the guts out" is rougher still.

Unfortunately, this has left Howard open to damaging charges of racism. Judged by today's standards, he was as guilty of racism as most white people of the time. He was not above the casual use of ethnic slurs in his private correspondence. Even so, Howard was by no means a virulent racist by the standards of his own day. There is no evidence that he harbored any sort of active hostility toward blacks or other minority groups.

Moreover, we do find Howard groping toward a more enlightened attitude, fittingly enough, through his art. In his autobiographical novel, *Post Oaks and Sand Roughs*, Howard relates how his fictional alter ego "found it easier to write of primitive peoples and was especially fond of using the negro as a subject" (145). While he did make some use of ethnic stereotypes, then a staple of pulp fiction and the vaudeville stage, Howard also portrayed blacks sympathetically in a number of stories. If at times condescending, he still expressed a sincere interest and curiosity concerning them. His personal library included four novels in the once-popular *Miss Minerva* series by Emma Speed Sampson; these were similar to Booth Tarkington's *Penrod* novels, only featuring African-American characters. Howard's collection included *Miss Minerva on the Old Plantation* (1923), perhaps not the best source of information concerning African-American life. However, in regard to the African-American folktales of the sort that inspired "Pigeons from Hell," Howard told Lovecraft, "I wish I had the time and money to go carefully through the Old South and gather negroid traditions systematically" (REH to H. P. Lovecraft, c. September 1930; CL 2.96). One wishes that he had indeed been able to document black folklore more thoroughly, since it is almost certain that such lore has by now been irretrievably lost.

The most notable black character in Howard's fiction is, perhaps, N'Longa, the conjure-man who served as Solomon Kane's mentor in Africa. Howard also wrote several stories featuring black heavyweight champion Ace Jessel as the protagonist. In one of his weird westerns, "The Dead Remember," an innocent black couple is murdered by a drunken cowboy, who suffers their vengeance from beyond the grave.

In his important essay, "The Old Deserted House: Images of the South in Howard's Fiction," Rusty Burke posits that Howard was, consciously or unconsciously, attempting to work through his prejudices in his Piney Woods fiction. In "Pigeons from Hell," the source of the evil is the Blassenville family—and by extension the plantation system. Even in "Black Canaan" Saul Stark and the Bride of Damballah are interesting characters who hold the upper hand, while the whites of Grimesville are stereotypically narrow and ignorant. The story concludes with Kirby Buckner sharing an unspoken bond with the black people of Canaan due to the horrible knowledge they share.

One can therefore conclude that, as a Southerner who died in 1936, Howard could be considered a racist only in the sense that every white Texan was at the time. Any racism on his part was more in the nature of a casual attribute as opposed to a defining characteristic. Of course, it does not help Howard's reputation that the editor of *Action Stories* changed the title of one of his Oriental adventures from "The House of Peril" to "Blow the Chinks Down." However, this does serve to illustrate the prevailing attitudes of the day. It should also be noted that with "The Thunder-Rider," discussed previously, Howard conveyed a story sympathetic to a Comanche—sheer heresy in his region at the time.

Howard's horror stories frequently appear in anthologies alongside those of Lovecraft, Robert Bloch, Henry S. Whitehead, Seabury Quinn, and other notables whose reputations rest solely on their efforts in the horror genre. Howard's output was not confined to a single genre; the horror story was one genre among many in which Howard worked. Yet the readers of *Weird Tales* consistently applauded Howard's work in the traditional horror tale as well as his own unique brand of fantasy. Though comprising only a small percentage of Howard's total output, his horror stories are among his best-remembered works today.

Howard became a professional writer through the pages of *Weird Tales*. Like many another fledgling writer, he was able to hone his skill with the horror story, as such stories require a convincing atmosphere, adept description, and well-timed narrative pacing. It is upon these and other elements that the success of a horror story rests, and the author who fails to master them will quickly fade from the reader's memory.

Howard's relationship with H. P. Lovecraft was a fruitful one, not merely for Howard's personal intellectual development, but for his fiction as well. Lovecraft's vision of cosmic horror was put to its most effective use by Howard, not in his horror stories, but in his heroic fantasies. Abominations from beyond the gulfs of time and space are among the menaces that Howard's heroes strive against. That Howard's characters endure and Lovecraft's are crushed is due to the central position of the hero in the former's work.

While the human race is roughly equivalent to a colony of ants in the gaze of the horrific entities conjured by Lovecraft in his fiction, in most of Howard's horror stories the horrors are inextricably linked to humanity. In these tales there is never a ghost without a murder, the details of which are not long withheld. There is almost a cause-and-effect relationship between the horrors of the temporal world and those of the spiritual one. Howard is at his best depicting human beings caught in the clutches of dark supernatural forces. Whether or not they prevail, it is their struggles that are the crux of the story.

For Howard, the human soul is the prime mover in the universe. In all his fiction, significant change for better or worse is the result of human effort. His horror stories reflect the dark side of this thesis. Obscene passion, bitter hatred, wayward impulses, twisted ambition, morbid obsessions, wanton cruelty, and loathsome degeneracy are the poisons in the well from which Howard's horrors spring.

VIII. OTHER PROSE AND POETRY

Howard resolved to become a writer at an early age because he loathed the drudgery of a routine job and valued his independence highly. In the 1920s and '30s, motion pictures and broadcast media were in their infancies, and the main source of entertainment for the middle and lower classes was reading. Paperback books were as yet unborn, and reading entertainment for the masses was furnished by that errant child of the publishing industry, the pulp magazine.

Pulp magazines sprang from the "penny dreadfuls" and dime novels of the Victorian era and were called "pulps" because of the cheap paper on which they were printed. Publishing empires were founded on these ten-cent periodicals, and by the late twenties approximately 250 titles were on sale at any given time.

Every conceivable type of story was told, as evidenced by the dazzling array of titles that crowded the newsstands. There were hero pulps such as *The Shadow*, *Doc Savage*, *The Spider*, and *G-8 and His Battle Aces*, as well as adventure anthologies such as *Argosy*, *Adventure*, *Blue Book*, and *Top-Notch*. There were numerous detective pulps, with *Black Mask* and *Dime Detective* among the most prominent, but also including *Private Detective*, *Hollywood Detective*, *Ten Detective Aces*, *Strange Detective Stories*, and *Super-Detective Stories*, to name but a few. Competitors of *Weird Tales* included *Dime Mystery Magazine*, *Terror Tales*, *Horror Stories*, *Thrilling Mystery*, *Ghost Stories*, and *Strange Tales*.

Sports pulps were popular: *Fight Stories, Dime Sports Magazine, Jack Dempsey's Fight Magazine, Sport Story Magazine*. Many pulps were devoted to westerns: *Wild West Weekly, Cowboy Stories, Western Aces, Quick-Trigger Western, Frontier Stories, Pioneer Western*. There were spicy stories, sailor stories, aviation pulps, jungle pulps, and magazines devoted to every interest: *Railroad Stories, Super Science Stories, Terence X. O'Leary's War Birds, Speakeasy Stories, Zeppelin Stories, Strange Suicides*.

During the pulp era, it was easier for a person to earn a living as a writer than today. One needed only to be able to fashion a coherent narrative, gauge editorial needs, and of course meet the grueling pace demanded by an industry that customarily paid about a penny a word. Regardless of the literary merit of the pulps, people who grew up with them, because they read for entertainment, were more functionally literate than those born in more recent decades. The short story as a literary form has been on the decline since the pulps' demise and has been kept alive by science fiction anthologies and other digest-sized magazines descended from the pulps.

The product of a working-class background, Howard approached writing pragmatically, regarding it as a business more than as a mode of self-expression. In addition to penning the tales that bore the stamp of his personal vision, Howard was not averse to producing standard material for purely commercial reasons. Regular payment for this fiction granted him financial security and peace of mind that enabled him to devote time to those tales for which he is most noted.

As a teenager embarking on his chosen profession, Howard set his sights on the high-paying prestigious pulps such as *Argosy, Blue Book*, and *Top-Notch*. He wrote his first story intended for publication at the age of fifteen and submitted it to *Adventure*. For the next three years, he endeavored to break into the pulps and succeeded at eighteen with his first sales to *Weird Tales*. Howard tried his hand at many types of stories during his fledgling period, but his goal in those early

VIII. Other Prose and Poetry

years was to become a contributor to the adventure pulps.

Magazines such as *Adventure* and *Argosy* featured stories set in the far-flung corners of the world that concerned the exploits of lone soldiers-of-fortune in search of treasure, exotic women, lost cities, and above all adventure. Howard admired the works of such authors as Talbot Mundy and Harold Lamb and sought to join their ranks. He attempted to do so with the first character he ever conceived of, an adventurer named Francis X. Gordon, whom he created when he was ten years old.

In his teens Howard began setting down the adventures of Francis Xavier Gordon, also known as "El Borak." Early short stories about El Borak included "El Borak," "The Coming of El Borak," "The Shunned Castle," and "The Land of Mystery." None of these stories saw print in Howard's lifetime. The early version of the character was embryonic, and he put Gordon aside for a time. Years later, as a seasoned professional, Howard resurrected Gordon in a new series of tales. These were successful and in 1934 and 1935 appeared in Street & Smith's prestigious *Top-Notch*.

Francis X. Gordon was a footloose rover cut from the same cloth as those in the works of Lamb, Mundy, and others. He was probably named for the British hero Charles George Gordon (1833-1885), known as Chinese Gordon, who died defending the Sudan. His exploits were most likely inspired by those of T. E. Lawrence, whose campaign against the Turks in Arabia was widely publicized during Howard's boyhood.

This second series of El Borak adventures, written at the peak of Howard's career, contains all the earmarks of his most vivid prose. In them, we learn that Francis X. Gordon was once a Texas gunfighter who found the Wild West too tame. His tempestuous nature draws him to the desolate outlands and colorful bazaars of the Middle East. In Afghanistan and Arabia, his deadly skill with both the sword and the gun earns him the name El Borak, "the swift." Fluent in native tongues and steeped in the native cultures, El Borak is also a shrewd judge of character and a master tactician. Combined with his considerable fighting prowess, these qualities help make the American adventurer a legend in distant lands.

Howard also wrote a few stories about a similar character, Kirby O'Donnell, a brawling Irish-American who finds his true home in the wilds of Afghanistan. O'Donnell goes completely native, rarely having occasion to speak English. Secure in his false identity as a wandering Kurd, O'Donnell is able to search for treasure in remote regions barred to westerners.

Howard's mature Middle Eastern tales are in many ways comparable to the Conan stories. The action is vigorous and unrelenting, the characterization well defined and believable. The plots are ably crafted, eschewing stock situations and often revealing a subtle complexity. Some of the tales concern political intrigue between European powers endeavoring to extend their influence into the Near East and use the barbaric natives as pawns.

Particularly notable are Howard's historical epics. Though comprising only a relatively small percentage of the author's total output, they are among his best work.

Howard, of course, was fascinated by the past and as man and boy immersed himself in the pages of history. When he was a student, history was the only subject he excelled in. As a writer, he was eager to turn his hand to historical fiction:

> There is no literary work, to me, half as zestful as rewriting history in the guise of fiction. I wish I was able to devote the rest of my life to that kind of work. I could write a hundred years and still there would be stories clamoring to be written, by the scores. Every page of history teems with dramas that should be put on paper. A single paragraph may be packed with action and drama enough to fill a whole volume of fiction work. (REH to H. P. Lovecraft, c. September or October 1933; CL 3.130)

VIII. Other Prose and Poetry

The opportunity arose in 1930 when *Weird Tales* launched a companion magazine, also edited by Farnsworth Wright, called *Oriental Stories*. The contents of *Oriental Stories* consisted primarily of Arabian Nights–style romances and exotic tales of the Near and Far East. Howard's contributions did not reflect the light-hearted tone of the bulk of the magazine's contents. These stories, usually set around the period of the Crusades, are among his grimmest and most vividly realistic stories.

"Red Blades of Black Cathay" was the lead story in the February-March 1931 issue of *Oriental Stories*. It concerns Godric de Villehard, a Norman Crusader, and his search for the fabled lost kingdom of Prester John. Godric runs afoul of Genghis Khan and ultimately leads a rag-tag army of Easterners against the Mongol chieftain. The story climaxes with one of the best battle sequences Howard ever wrote.

The next two stories Howard wrote for *Oriental Stories* were "Hawks of Outremer" and "The Blood of Belshazzar." The hero of both these tales is one Cormac Fitzgeoffrey, a bitter Irish knight, adventurer, and Crusader whom Howard described as the grimmest character he ever created. Fitzgeoffrey is a man of great physical strength and almost maniacal ferocity. In one of the stories he grips an enemy's wrist and squeezes it so hard that blood squirts out of the victim's fingertips. Such is the stark brutality and intensity of this pair of tales that reading them can be an unsettling experience.

"The Sowers of the Thunder," published in the Winter 1932 issue of *Oriental Stories*, is about another Irish adventurer, Cahal O'Donnel. A saga of betrayal and revenge, the story tells of O'Donnel's suffering at the hands of his former love, whose treachery cost him the throne of Ireland and forced him into exile. O'Donnel is reunited with his penitent lover as she dies on a battlefield near Jerusalem. "Lord of Samarcand," in the Summer 1932 issue, concerns the Mongol conqueror Tamerlane and his defeat of the Turks in 1402.

Oriental Stories was an ill-fated publishing venture, being of limited commercial appeal and launched just as the Great Depression was getting underway. After nine issues it was floundering, and an attempt was made to rescue it. It was retitled *Magic Carpet* and its format was altered slightly.

"The Lion of Tiberias" appeared in the July 1933 issue of *Magic Carpet*. This tragic tale of slavery and retribution spans decades and tells of the fall and rise of John Norwald. Sold into slavery by the Moslem conqueror Zenghi, he languishes at the oars of a galley before escaping to enact his revenge. The story contains a love interest as a subplot, a nicety lacking in most of Howard's historical tales.

Magic Carpet lasted only five issues. In the final issue, January 1934, one of Howard's finest historical stories appeared. "The Shadow of the Vulture" takes place at the siege of Vienna in 1529, where the Ottoman Empire's expansion was checked by the forces of the West. The main characters are Suleyman I; Mikhal Oglu, Suleyman's personal assassin; Red Sonya of Rogatine, a fiery Russian adventuress; and Gottfried von Kalmbach, a European knight, drunkard, and misanthrope.

The siege and the events surrounding it are seen through the tired, bloodshot eyes of Von Kalmbach himself. Many of Howard's heroes are drinkers, but Von Kalmbach is the only one explicitly portrayed as an alcoholic. He is plagued by doubts about himself and his role in the human drama being played out in Vienna, and the doubts are banished only when he dons armor and takes to the battlefield. Von Kalmbach fights because he must, because there is some peace for him in the primitive fury of combat, and he returns from the battle purged, at least for a little while.

With the cancellation of *Magic Carpet*, Howard was bereft of a market for his historical works and turned his attention to other genres and markets. Two historical tales were published posthumously in another short-lived publication, *Golden Fleece*. Howard himself observed, "I could never make a living writing such things . . . the markets are too scanty, with requirements too narrow, and it takes me so long to complete one" (REH to H. P. Lovecraft, c. September or October 1933; CL 3.130). However, as L. Sprague de Camp pointed out (*Dark Valley Destiny* 331), Howard would have become a best-selling author had he lived until the 1950s, for at that time historical novels came into vogue.

Howard strove for historical accuracy, and his occasional lapses and inaccuracies were more a matter of literary license than ignorance. Though he sometimes took liberties with the finer details of actual events, Howard captured the spirit of the times, rendering the realities of medieval life and warfare quite accurately. Howard chose to debunk the myth of the knight in shining armor, preferring to give a more truthful portrayal of violent men vying for power. Yet all the characters are eclipsed by the relentless march of time itself. Howard envisioned an era in history filled with brutality, strife, human misery, plague and pestilence, infusing it with a vital theme of his works: his recurrent lament that the entirety of humanity's pageantry, ambition, suffering, and sacrifice are, in the end, meaningless.

Little has been written about the historical phase of Howard's career. Perhaps the most perceptive and eloquent appraisal came from the late Roy G. Krenkel in his introduction to a collection of these stories:

> One reads Howard distantly, as through a mist of time—fleeting glimpses, lightning sharp, are caught of marching men in grim armor, of battlements stormed by savage hordes, of whispered intrigues in tapestried candlelight. As from afar we hear the summons of the oliphant, the ring of steel on steel, the screams of the dying; too vast—too terrible—to grasp as reality, and, somehow, the more "real" for all of that! What emerges, sharp and clear, is the mood. (10)

Howard was able to infuse such vision into these works because of his immersion in the pageant of bygone eras. As he himself said, "The future of the race interests me little; the present but a little more than;

the past, greatly . . . I live in the dust of the past and my dreams are seldom of present or future, but I am ever-treading roads of the dim ages" (REH to Harold Preece, 20 October 1928; CL 1.274).

In 1929, the year before he began writing historical fiction, Howard cracked his first market other than *Weird Tales*. With his first sale to *Fight Stories*, he began a several-year stint as an author of boxing stories. Howard was an avid fan of the sport of prize-fighting and was himself an amateur boxer. Coming of age in the era of Gene Tunney and Jack Dempsey and admiring physical prowess as he did, it was natural that Howard should become a boxing enthusiast.

Howard, like many a noted author before and after him, celebrated this human drama of physical conflict in his fiction. The genre of the boxing story was originated by Jack London in his novel *The Game* (1905), and stories such as "A Piece of Steak." Literary notables such as Ring Lardner, Norman Mailer, and Joyce Carol Oates have seen the sport of prize-fighting as a metaphor for the human condition. The spectacle of the prize-fight, in which an individual must overcome a formidable opponent to obtain the good things life has to offer, is the struggle of everyman reduced to the most basic possible terms.

In Howard's day, the pulp magazine jungle offered ample opportunity for publication of stories of this type. So diversified was the pulp magazine industry that there were titles devoted to football and baseball as well as boxing. However, the boxing story preceded the pulps and survived their demise. It alone, of the many types of sports stories written during the pulp era, is regarded as a legitimate vehicle for literary expression. This is doubtless because boxing is the struggle of individuals rather than members of a team. The striving of the lone fighter endures as the subject of numerous motion pictures from *Body and Soul* to *Raging Bull*.

The type of boxer most admired by Howard is exemplified by the hero of his story, "The Iron Man" (originally titled "Iron Men"), which appeared in the June 1930 issue of *Fight Stories*. Mike Brennon, the "Iron Man" of the title, achieves recognition not for his fighting skills but for his ability to withstand punishment. In this story and similar ones by Howard, tenacity and courage are deemed more laudable than either physical prowess or pugilistic skill. Howard's admiration for iron men with the ability to stoically endure life's brutal knocks reveals the high value he placed on a quality he may have felt lacking in himself.

Howard wrote numerous boxing stories, the majority belonging to a series about a merchant seaman and amateur boxer named Sailor Steve Costigan. These stories are narrated in the first person by Costigan himself, an uneducated, gullible, thick-headed, but basically good-natured sailor whose running commentary on his exploits provided the earliest glimpse of Howard's heretofore unsuspected sense of humor. The descriptions of the fights themselves contain Howard's usual force and vigor, but the often inane circumstances leading up to Costigan's battles are light-hearted and comical.

Sailor Steve Costigan's exploits take place in the far-flung corners of the world. At various ports of call, Costigan is likely to find himself battling in local fight clubs where sailors and other wayfarers congregate. Stories of sailors and the sea were very popular during the era of the pulps; set in exotic locales and dealing with high adventure, they appealed to the romanticism of the times. The world was a much larger, more mysterious place then, and names like Hong Kong and Singapore were able to evoke in readers images of opium dens and swashbuckling action that we of today can barely imagine in our Americanized world. Often, as in the case of Howard, no attempt was made to portray these locations as they really were, mainly because the authors of these stories were scarcely more knowledgeable than the readers themselves.

In addition to the Sailor Costigan fight stories, Howard wrote several straight adventure yarns set on the high seas. In the final post-fantasy stage of his career in 1936, Howard entered the lucrative "spicy stories" market. In the 1930s, a pulp house called Culture Publications began a line of magazines that featured fairly standard genre stories with an added element of "naughty" sex, tame by today's standards. The first of these was *Spicy Detective Stories*, and it was soon followed by *Spicy-Adventure*, *Spicy Mystery*, and *Spicy Western*. For *Spicy-Adventure*, Howard created the South Seas adventurer Wild Bill Clanton. Five Clanton stories appeared in 1936 and 1937 under the by-line Sam Walser.

The sex in a "spicy" story was by no means explicit. While a prelude to sexual activity is described in some detail, the act itself is indicated by a line space or a discreet fade-out. The writers of these stories, hemmed in by various taboos, had to be skilled in innuendo and the description of beautiful women and intimate feminine apparel. It was the trappings of sex—the exotic locale, the circumstances, the passionate dialogue, the heroine's garments and boudoir—that provided the erotic titillation in the spicy pulps. Howard made effective use of these elements and others in his contributions to *Spicy-Adventure Stories*.

Howard's most manifestly commercial fiction was the ill-conceived "weird detective" stories he briefly experimented with. The dregs of his writing, they are neither traditional puzzle mysteries nor hard-boiled crime dramas in the Hammett/Chandler mold. In these stories, Howard combined elements of the familiar private detective story with those sometimes found in the "weird menace" pulps: secret societies, Thuggee assassins, exotic poisons, bound-and-gagged damsels in distress, archaeological treasures, and the ominous menace of the "yellow peril." The protagonist of most of these tales is the tough, burly detective Steve Harrison, an investigator attached to the police who operates independently in the "Oriental quarter" of an unnamed city. Some of Harrison's adventures take him further afield, even into the foreboding "piney woods." Howard was uncomfortable working in the genre, however, and was dismissive of his efforts in the field. He felt moved to remark, "I have definitely abandoned the detective field, where I never had any success anyway, and which represents a type of story I actively detest. I can scarcely endure to read one, much less write one" (REH to H. P. Lovecraft, 13 May 1936; CL 3.461). Even so, the best of these stories do bear the distinctive mark of Howard's bracing, fast-paced action and therefore offer a modicum of light reading entertainment.

Howard's westerns, on the other hand, have been widely lauded. Many readers consider his western fiction to be his best work aside from his fantasies, and some even rank it above his more famous work. Though steeped in the history and lore of the West, Howard did not begin writing westerns until late in his career. In all, Howard wrote more than forty westerns, only four of which were written before 1933.

His western tales fall into several categories; the aforementioned "weird westerns," standard Zane Grey-type westerns, and wildly humorous yarns in the Texas tall tale tradition. Howard's humorous westerns comprise the bulk of his western output and were written as episodes in a series about one of several characters, the best known of which is Breckinridge Elkins of Bear Creek, Nevada.

Breckinridge Elkins is a huge, powerful, but rather thick-headed and naïve frontiersman. His penchant for getting into trouble is usually the result of either trying to impress the beauteous Glory McGraw or some other alluring young lady, or of his attempts to help some irresponsible kinsman who has gotten himself into a predicament. Though he is generally amiable and good-natured, Breck's great strength usually wreaks havoc upon the various outlaws, rustlers, buffalo hunters, card-sharps, and conniving city-slickers of whom he runs afoul in the course of his exploits. Episodes usually close with a tallying of bruises, broken bones, and busted heads.

The Breckinridge Elkins westerns are the best example of Howard's humorous writing and as such are essential to a balanced view of the often grim creator of Bran Mak Morn and Cormac Fitzgeoffrey. The humor in these tales consists primarily of the broad physical slapstick so despised by intellectuals. This sort of humor, however, is the most universally appealing type, crossing all boundaries of class and culture. Like the Three Stooges short features they so resemble, Elkins's misadventures evoke laughter where more sophisticated fare would be regarded with puzzled bewilderment. Of course, this violent physical slapstick does express a certain amount of aggression on the part of its creator, and most likely it enabled many a Depression-era reader to let off some steam as well.

The Elkins series appeared in every issue of *Action Stories* beginning in early 1934 and continuing after Howard's death until January 1937, when the editorial backlog was exhausted. So popular were these western comedies that editors of other magazines solicited Howard to create a similar series for them. In 1936 the most prestigious of all pulps, *Argosy*, commissioned a series of this type. Howard complied with several exploits of Pike Bearfield, attaining his long-sought goal of becoming a regular in *Argosy* only months before his death.

These tales of Breckinridge Elkins, Pike Bearfield, and another character, Buckner J. Grimes, preserve the flavor of the traditional tall tale of American folklore. Moreover, with their frequent emphasis on strong family ties, they offer a better picture of frontier life than do Howard's more standard westerns.

Westerns such as "Knife, Bullet, and Noose," "The Last Ride," and "Law-Shooters of Cowtown" are for the most part not appreciably different from the westerns of Max Brand, Zane Grey, Luke Short, and countless other purveyors of western fiction. Howard, however, considered the short novel *The Vultures of Wahpeton* one of his best works. The plot concerns the machinations of a sinister outlaw faction to exploit a gold mining boom town.

Howard strove constantly during the last years of his life to de-romanticize the western genre and bring it more in line with the true West that he knew so well. Consequently, his westerns feature such disreputable figures as scalp-hunters, bushwhackers, buffalo hunters, and corrupt law-enforcement officers. This ran contrary to the sanitized image of the Old West presented in the stories and motion pictures of Howard's day and long thereafter. The genre was then defined by the clean-cut western films of Gene Autry, Hopalong Cassidy, and The Three Mesquiteers. Writing for such markets as *Cowboy Stories* and *Western Aces*, Howard was constrained by editorial policy and public taste as to the amount of realism he could introduce into his westerns.

The richest source of authentic western lore in Howard's writings is to be found in his letters. There, to any interested correspondent, he would relate little-known facts and legends about western history and detail the hardships and privations of frontier life:

> How few people give any thought to the history of even their own locality! Why, it was from the Concho River, only about a hundred miles from here that John Chisum started to New Mexico in 1868, with his herd of ten thousand cattle, his caravan of wagons and his army of hard-bit Texas cowpunchers, yet his name is hardly known in this country. John Chisum was born in Tennessee and grew up in East Texas. He was an empire builder if ever one lived. To read New Mexican history of the 70's it would seem that he supported the territory—people either worked for John Chisum or stole cattle from him! In the days of his greatest power his herd numbered more than a hundred thousand head ... He was a figure of really heroic proportions, a builder of empires, yet he was by instinct merely a hard-headed business man. Nothing dramatic about John Chisum, and maybe that's why history has slighted him in favor of fruitless but flashing characters who blazed vain trails of blood and slaughter across the West. John Chisum never even buckled a gun on his

hip in his life; he was a builder, not a destroyer. (REH to H. P. Lovecraft, c. January 1931; CL 2.172)

> I have spent most of my time in the hard, barren semi-waste lands of Western Texas, and since infancy my memory holds a continuous, grinding round of crop failures—sandstorms—drouths—floods—hot winds that withered the corn—hailstorms that ripped the grain to pieces—late blizzards that froze the fruit in the bud—plagues of grasshoppers and boll weevils that stripped the cotton. I remember year-long drouths that killed the very mesquite trees, when the streams ran dry and the cattle ate cactus until their mouths and bellies were stuck full of the spines, and then lay down and died when even the cactus was gone. (REH to Farnsworth Wright, c. June/July 1931; CL 2.225)

> Authorities class the Comanches as members of the Shoshonean race, which also includes the Shoshones, Utes, and Pawnees. But I wouldn't have cared to tell an old-time Comanche that he was of the same blood as the Utes; a knife in the guts would have been the probable retort. Their legends made them blood-kin with the Apaches, whom ethnologists name Athabascans, along with the Navajos. Yet the Comanches and Apaches seem to have had many points in common, though much intermarrying might explain that. At any rate the Comanches were the most skillful horse-thieves on the continent, not even excepting the white rustlers that worked between El Paso and New Orleans back in the '70's. (REH to August Derleth, c. January 1933; CL 3.4)

It is a shame that Howard was not able to make more use of this wealth of authentic lore and first-hand knowledge in his fiction.

In his introduction to the first collection of Howard's fantasy tales, *Skull-Face and Others*, August Derleth expressed the opinion that, had he lived, Howard would have become "an important American regionalist" (viii). Derleth, whose most distinctive work was his Midwestern regional fiction, over-esteemed the value of regional writing. As previously noted, it is more likely that historical fiction would have in time become Howard's main literary occupation since the historical novel became much in vogue during the 1950s. And yet, the darker, grittier western films of Sam Peckinpah, Sergio Leone, and John Ford would have created a wider audience for more realistic western fiction. Certainly, such westerns as Howard would have later written would have borne a more distinctive imprint of his first-hand knowledge of the American West.

Engraved on Howard's tombstone is the epitaph, "Author and Poet." It is fitting that the description "poet" should be inscribed on the stone marking Howard's final resting place, for he was as much a poet as he was a storyteller. Indeed, as with Clark Ashton Smith, the bulk of his poetry predates the bulk of his prose. Howard could be said to have been a poet first, if not foremost.

Howard was introduced to poetry at his mother's knee. In his maturity he enjoyed the poetry of Robert W. Service, Poe, Kipling, the Benéts, Tennyson, Swinburne, Lord Dunsany, G. K. Chesterton, Oscar Wilde, and Longfellow. He considered Sappho the finest woman poet and counted her among the greatest poets who ever lived.

Howard corresponded regularly with Clark Ashton Smith, who in his youth was associated with the Carmel artists' colony that included Ambrose Bierce and George Sterling, and who was at that time regarded as the West Coast's most promising young poet. While a student at Brownwood, Howard was encouraged in his own poetical efforts by Lexie Dean Robertson, already an accomplished poet and later to become Poet Laureate of Texas.

Howard began composing poetry in earnest while a student. Most of his verse was written in his early twenties: by 1930 he had all but ceased writing poetry to concentrate on his expanding professional markets. Howard wrote more than seven hundred poems, only a small percentage of which was published in his lifetime.

Concerning the construction of his verse, Howard maintained, "I know nothing at all about the mechanics of poetry—I couldn't tell you whether a verse was anapestic or trochaic to save my neck" (REH to H. P. Lovecraft, c. August 1931; CL 2.264). While perhaps unfamiliar with the terminology of meter and rhyme, Howard was nonetheless adept in their use.

Howard was a self-taught poet who learned his craft like the skalds of old. Like the eddas and epics of antiquity, Howard's poems possess a surging rhythm that is more often simple than complex. His command of the language is such that common words are linked in remarkable passages that resonate with power. The vigor of these passages is directed into a disciplined structure that is uncomplicated and straightforward.

Howard wrote lyrical poetry more often than narrative and employed a variety of poetic forms. He penned sonnets, for example, but avoided the more rigid structures such as haiku and sestinas. One of his later poems, "Cimmeria," written in 1932, makes effective use of blank verse. Howard had a good ear for rhythm and rhyme, and his poetical style was one of forthright honesty devoid of affectation. The themes he chose were highly personal ones, reflecting his love of nature, metaphysical beliefs, fascination with the opposite sex, and love of history and the exotic, as well as his obsessions with death, hate, and violence. All these themes Howard infused with his unswerving conviction and unrelenting emotional intensity.

The majority of Howard's poems published in his lifetime appeared in *Weird Tales*. Consequently, poems such as "The Moor Ghost," "Dead Man's Hate," "Arkham," and "The Song of the Bats" deal with horror and the supernatural. These well-crafted mood pieces served as filler in the pages of *Weird Tales*. Other poetry appeared as story headings or was featured in the body of the stories themselves. Howard also wrote a few poems about his famous creations, such as "Solomon Kane's Homecoming" and "The King and the Oak," a ballad of Kull. These poems formed the basis of the first collection of Howard's poetry, *Always Comes Evening* (1957).

A related type of verse, seen less often during Howard's life, concerns dreams and visions. "Altars and Jesters," a panoramic vision of heaven and hell, is an unrestrained flight of fancy, echoing the "drug-inspired" poetry of Baudelaire. In "Cimmeria," a poem about racial memory, Howard stresses the strength of his vision with the first line, "I remember" (CP 247). Poems such as these often deal not just with visions, but with the intensity of the visionary experience itself. Howard saw "black alleys gape" and "heard strange surges boom"; he "fled from crimson eyes and black unearthly wings" and "watched the dragons come, fire-eyed, across the world" (CP 223).

Howard's vision often encompassed scenes from the antiquity he cherished. Some of his historical poems deal with the pomp and pageantry of the ancient world, such as "Belshazzar" and "The Gates of Babylon." Most, however, concern strife and warfare: "Song Before Clontarf," "Marching Song of Connacht," "Viking's Trail," "The Road to Rome," "To Harry the Oliad Men," "The Gold and the Grey."

The theme of inevitable destruction is often present in Howard's historical verse. "Haunting Columns," "The Dust Dance," "Oh Babylon, Lost Babylon" and others lament the passing of mighty empires. In some of the poems, these kingdoms fade before the passing of time; in others, they come crashing down in red ruin. "Shadows on the Road" is a haunting vision of fallen Rome. "A Word from the Outer Dark" warns of the inevitable triumph of the Dark Barbarian over civilization.

Hate, violence, and bloodshed figure prominently in much of Howard's most powerful verse. Poems such as "Mark of the Beast," "Tarantella," and "The Feud" reflect Howard's belief that aggression is the driving force behind human history. Howard's disgust with the human race is expressed in "Black Dawn," "Hymn of Hatred" and "To All Sophisticates." Though he wrote a number of erotic poems exalting women and sex, in poems such as "To a Woman" and "A Song for All Women" the female is not exempt from Howard's misanthropic hatred.

The most revealing of all Howard's poetry concerns his weariness with life and obsession with death. In the poem "Always Comes Evening," he tells us

> I rode the moon-mare's horses in the glory of my youth,
> Wrestled with the hills at sunset—till I met brass-tinctured Truth.
> Till I saw the temples topple, till I saw the idols reel,
> Till my brain had turned to iron, and my heart had turned to steel.
> Satan, Satan, brother Satan, fill my soul with frozen fire,
> Feed with hearts of rose-white women ashes of my dead desire.
> For my road runs out in thistles and my dreams have turned to dust,
> And my pinions fade and falter to the raven wings of rust . . . (CP 146)

Howard considered himself "A scarred old man, masked in the guise of youth" (CP 360). He regarded life as "a liar and a drear-eyed whore" (CP 412) and remarked, "I'll reel through a few more years somehow. Then I'll quit them altogether" (CP 291).

Howard's harsher critics have both dismissed his work as inconsequential junk and assailed it as the product of a disturbed mind, but the one thing that no one has ever doubted is that Howard wrote from the heart. His poetry, written solely for self-expression, was uninfluenced by commercial considerations or even by the need to relate a narrative. In it, we find the soul of the real Robert E. Howard laid bare. Howard was a poet and a lover of poetry, and these words he wrote at the end of his life were verse:

> All fled—all done, so lift me on the pyre.
> The feast is over and the lamps expire.

IX. Conclusion

Serious attention to Howard's work in literary and academic circles has been a long time in coming. At first, Howard criticism was a kind of grass-roots movement, almost exclusively the province of non-academic writers. In recent years, however, distinguished academics such as Dr. Mark Hall of the University of California at Berkeley, Prof. Frank Coffman of Rock Valley College, Prof. Charles Gramlich of Xavier University of Louisiana, Dr. Jeffrey Kahan of the University of La Verne, Dr. Patrice Louinet, and Dr. Lauric Guillaud of the University of Nantes, France, have all made significant contributions to Howard studies.

Such was certainly not always the case. In the not-so-distant past, critics, academics, and other intellectuals tended to be extremely dismissive of Howard, and indeed many remain so. Because Howard wrote to earn a living, he has been dismissed as a pulp hack; because his works were unabashedly written to entertain, they have been deemed empty of deeper significance.

From yet another negative perspective, because he exhibited evidence of mood disorders and suicidal tendencies, some have likened his more intense writings to the ravings of a madman. Still others have seen in Howard's exaltation of mighty-thewed warriors and athletes evidence of latent homosexuality, or have regarded it as a denial of the human intellect. Sadist, fascist, and arrested adolescent are all charges that have been leveled against him. All told, Howard has possibly been more misunderstood than any writer since Nietzsche.

To what extent Howard was or was not a fascist, etc. is subject to debate. However, the extreme negative reaction in certain circles indicates an additional factor beyond the intrinsic elements of the work itself—some raw nerve piqued by Howard's message perhaps.

Howard has frequently been assailed for the bloodshed in his work, and no doubt many writers, critics, and scholars (leading more placid lives than the average working adult) find the violence disconcerting. Also, the sheer physicality of Howard's work is in itself offensive to them. The single most consistent motif in Howard's fiction—a constant that crosses all genres, surfacing in fantasies, westerns, even comedies—is his emphasis on the physical. Physical prowess and/or conflict lie at the heart of virtually the whole of Howard's prose.

Many intellectuals, by training, inclination, and habit, regard the mind as humanity's most significant attribute and tend to dismiss physical ability as being of comparatively little importance. By stressing the physical side of humanity's nature, Howard tends to alienate thinkers (including his friend Lovecraft at times) in much the same way that Walt Whitman's singing of the "body electric" caused him to be reviled by contemporary critics. This is both unfortunate and unnecessary, for to regard the physical and sensuous as the antithesis of the intellectual and spiritual is an all-or-nothing fallacy. In Howard's case, the extreme negative reaction of some intellectuals may just be a rationalization of their own fears and feelings of inadequacy in the realm of the physical.

By stressing physical superiority, Howard appears to imply that "might makes right," a notion repugnant to the thinker. While without validity in an ethical argument, physical might, for practical purposes, is what spreads ideologies and conceptions of morality. The "peaceful" religions of Christianity and Islam have both been forced on pagans and infidels at swordpoint. The rising tide of Nazism was checked, not by the League of Nations, but by the guns of the Allies on the battlefield.

Howard's heroes also work their wills by virtue of their preeminent physical might. Bran Mak Morn drives invaders from his land by forging his people into a force to be reckoned with; his downfall comes when he resorts to subterfuge. Solomon Kane rights wrongs and punishes evildoers by the strength of his sword arm. King Kull strives against the soul of all silence with bone and sinew. Conan's physical superiority wins him a world and all it has to offer.

It is important to note that in Howard's writings, strength is used to further the will of an individual, not that of a nation or creed. It is here that the charge of "fascism" against Howard crumbles.

In a fascist regime, the will of the individual is surrendered to that of the state. Howard was such an ardent individualist that employment by others was anathema to him. In his writings, the will of an individual is often shown to be stronger than that of some tribe, mob, or other group. Howard's greatest heroes exhibit not only more powerful bodies, but also sharper minds and brighter spirits than the mass of men, and these attributes are linked by an iron will. Thus we find the second constant in Howard's writing to be the central position of the individual—the hero.

Howard's reverence for individuality was a key factor in his adopting the conflict between civilization and barbarism as his major theme. As society becomes more civilized, the individual becomes more and more dependent on others for food, clothing, and shelter. The individual today is relegated to a specific function, working in harmony with millions of others performing their functions. While the individual's standard of living has been bettered in this manner, Howard felt that his spirit had not been enhanced but diminished.

The physicality of Howard's work and the central position of the individual therein are intrinsic elements more properly considered "subtext" rather than "theme." However, the boons of barbarism as opposed to the drawbacks of civilization comprise a message that Howard consciously endeavored to impart in much of his major work. This theme is clearly evident to even the most casual reader of the Conan stories. Certainly, this alone is sufficient to refute the allegation that Howard's stories, so strong on mood, action, and atmosphere, are barren of ideas.

On receiving a poem dedicated to him from an admirer, Howard wrote the poet, Emil Petaja, saying: "You seem to grasp the motif of my stories, the compelling idea-force behind them which is the only excuse for their creation, more completely than any one I have yet encountered. This fine sonnet reveals your understanding of the abstractions I have tried to embody in these tales" (REH to Emil Petaja, 17 December 1934; CL 3.259-60). Many of the themes and ideas that we have studied owe their presence in the stories to an artistic sincerity and personal conviction as great as those of any writer who ever lived. Others were unconsciously culled from various dreams, nightmares, anxieties, fancies, and visions, and are conveyed with the surer hand of instinct.

While Howard's aversion to civilization and love of the barbaric are the result of conscious consideration, his other great theme of universal destruction stems from traits deeply ingrained in his personality. Howard was obsessed by thoughts of death and suicide even as a teen, a time when most youths are oblivious to their own mortality.

In his prose and poetry, death and destruction are personified in the bleak, desolate landscapes of such stories as "Worms of the Earth" and "The Dark Man," and such poems as "Cimmeria." Turlogh O'Brien and other of Howard's Celts mutter grim lamentations about the inevitable end that comes to all things. The Celts and Picts, so beloved by Howard, had turned to dust centuries before his birth. Everything Howard truly loved—the clangor of swords, the songs of

IX. Conclusion

Sappho, the mysterious Orient, the Wild West—was part of the past. He knew that someday he, too, would be dust.

Many of Howard's serious readers are overwhelmed by the images of destruction and doom that he renders so convincingly. To them, these stark specters of doom and annihilation are as gripping as Conan's adventures in search of treasure and excitement are to the more casual reader. However, it would be a mistake to cast Howard as a nightmare-haunted scribe of dark, somber visions like a Poe or Gogol.

There is much life and laughter in Howard—the carousing and wenching of Conan, the rollicking exploits of Breckinridge Elkins—but, ironically, most of it is to be found in his later works, those written in the last four years of his life. Howard's historical tales, Celtic fantasies, and poetry were all written before 1932; the Conan stories, reincarnation fantasies, and humorous westerns were written afterwards.

It almost seems as if Howard's mental outlook improved with age. In the fantasies, we see a departure from the sometimes morbid obsessions of Bran Mak Morn, Kane, and Kull in the later character Conan, a life-loving extrovert. Undoubtedly, writing proved to be therapeutic to Howard, serving as a cathartic outlet for the visions that hammered at the inside of his skull. That others found his tales entertaining, and editors and fellow writers thought highly of them, must have been a source of profound gratification for him. In time, Howard might have brought his mood swings under control, but unfortunately circumstances conspired to undermine his emotional stability.

In mid-1935, Howard was forced by financial necessity to abandon fantasy fiction, his primary means of self-expression. His most pressing concern at the time was, of course, providing medical care for his ailing mother. Howard's sacrifice of his art was not sufficient to prolong the life of the human being to whom he felt closest. Had Howard been able to continue writing fantasy and had his mother lasted a few more years, he might have been in a less vulnerable emotional state. As it was, he took his own life at age thirty when her death was at hand.

A few weeks before his suicide, Howard began one last fantasy story, entitled "Nekht Semerkeht." It concerns a fictional Spanish conquistador, Hernando de Guzman, and his search for gold in the New World. Early in the story Guzman, lost in the wilderness, contemplates his plight and the meaning of life and death:

> Men rationalize the blind instinct of self-preservation, and build glib aircastles explaining why it is better to live than to die, when their boasted—but ignored—intellect is, in every phase, a negation of life. But civilized men hate and fear their instincts, as they hate and fear every heritage from the blind, squalling pit of primordial beginnings that bred them. Dogs, apes, elephants, these creatures obey instincts and live only because instinct bids them live. Man's urge toward life is no less blind and reasonless, but, abhorring his kinship with those creatures who had the misfortune not to be made in the Deity's image—having no prophets to declare it—fondles his favorite delusion that *he* is guided wholly by reason, even when reason tells him it is better to die than to live. It is not the intellect he boasts that bids him live, but the blind, black, unreasoning beast-instinct. (*Pictures in the Fire* 172)

Albert Camus's lengthy essay "The Myth of Sisyphus" concerns the philosophical implications of suicide and begins by asking questions similar to those posed by Howard's protagonist. Camus's conclusions derive from philosophical considerations that Howard, in "Nekht Semerkeht," regards as "wisps of mist, phantoms conjured up by men to explain the unexplainable" (173). Guzman chooses life over death because "in his being there was implanted too deeply a blind black urge to live, that was in itself question and answer, desire and goal, beginning and end, and the answer to all the riddles in the universe" (173).

To Howard himself, Life and Death were two titans locked in eternal combat. In *Almuric*, Esau Cairn exclaims, "'I tingled and burned and stung with life to the finger tips and the ends of my toes. Every sinew, vein, and springy bone was vibrant with the dynamic flood of singing, pulsing, humming life" (74). In "The Valley of the Lost," John Reynolds becomes "suddenly aware that he had glimpsed the grinning skull beneath the mask of life, and that that glimpse made life intolerable" (*HS* 288). In his poetry, Howard laments that "Life is a liar and a drear eyed whore— / Death has his hand upon a silent Door" (*CP* 412). His alter ego, Conan of Cimmeria, bellows back, "'I live, I burn with life, I love, I slay, and am content'" (*CCC* 133).

It was only in his final days, in a story he didn't bother to finish, that Howard regarded life as mere biological activity, death as the cessation of same, and the will to live as "blind unreasoning beast-instinct." When Howard lost the light of fantasies and visions, oblivion swallowed him. Howard is dead, but his heroes live on. Howard sought death and the peace it offered. Conan embraces life replete with all its strife and conflict. Perhaps it is not so surprising after all that Conan's fame far outstrips his creator's.

Howard's last story, "Nekht Semerkeht," like many another of his tales, languished unpublished in his personal effects to see print only decades after the author's death. Abandoned by Howard, it was completed by Andrew J. Offutt and published in 1977. A more authentic version, combining two drafts by Howard, was not published until 2005.

Sadly, the fate of Howard's final tale reflects the fate of his writing in general. Of the various pastiches and posthumous collaborations of Howard's fiction, the less said, the better. Howard's body was barely cold when the public first made it known that there was a market for additional Conan stories by other authors. Some readers of *Weird Tales* requested that the editor commission a new writer to continue the saga. Farnsworth Wright, in his wisdom, declined to do so. In the October 1937 issue of *Weird Tales*, he published a letter from an English reader, Reginald A. Pryke, that reads in part:

> Howard the great, the incomparable, the master. Howard, whose tales were breathless sagas snatched vibrant with life from the scalds of old. Howard, who lifted his characters out of the dust and decay of times forgotten, breathed eager, lusting, laughing, fighting life into them, clapped swords in their fists, and sent them tramping the witch-haunted, battle-strewn roads. . . . Revive Conan? Never, never, never! No, the sagas are finished . . . Let each true lover of the great barbarian dream his own tales of battle, love and brooding witchcraft. Any other course savors of sacrilege. Read and read again what has been written, but let no other man try and wield that pen or gird on that sword. Bury them with him. He will sleep the quieter . . . (508)

The relative merits of individual pastiches aside, all of them may be considered superfluous. Raymond Chandler defined a classic in this manner: "Within its frame of reference, which is the only way it should be judged, a classic is a piece of writing which exhausts the possibilities of its form and can hardly be surpassed" (xi). Using these criteria, Robert E. Howard's fantasies are certainly classics, a yardstick by which all similar tales are judged. But they are also much more.

Colin Wilson devotes a chapter of his widely heralded study, *The Outsider*, to visionaries such as Blake, Yeats, and Van Gogh. In this chapter, appropriately entitled "The Outsider as Visionary," Wilson relates a Taoist parable from Chaung Tzu about a duke and his wheelwright.

In the parable, the wheelwright sees the duke reading and inquires about the book's contents. The duke replies he is reading the works of the sages. "The lees and scum of bygone men," remarks the wheelwright. The duke demands an explanation for this curious comment, and the wheelwright tells him that there is an aspect to the art of wheel-making that he cannot put into words, cannot even pass on to his own son. He concludes that it was the same with the sages; all that was truly worth handing down has died with them and what remains is merely "the lees and scum of dead men" (Wilson, *The Outsider* 204).

No one can ever see or know all that went through Howard's head, and it therefore seems incredible that his starkly rendered images of strife and conflict, remote places and times, are but the shadows and reflections of what he "saw"—"the lees and the scum." But had Howard remained mute, he would have been, in the final analysis, merely a dreamer. It is because he built windows through which the rest of us might glimpse what he saw so clearly that he was an artist.

WORKS CITED

A. Primary

Almuric. In *Adventures in Science Fantasy*. n.p.: Robert E. Howard Foundation Press, 2012. 55-193.

The Best of Robert E. Howard, Volume One: Crimson Shadows, New York: Del Rey, 2007.

The Black Stranger and Other American Tales. Lincoln: University of Nebraska Press/Bison Books, 2005.

The Bloody Crown of Conan. New York: Del Rey, 2004.

Bran Mak Morn: The Last King. New York: Del Rey, 2005.

The Collected Letters of Robert E. Howard. n.p.: Robert E. Howard Foundation Press, 2020.

The Collected Poetry of Robert E. Howard. n.p.: Robert E. Howard Foundation Press, 2008.

The Coming of Conan the Cimmerian. New York: Del Rey, 2003.

The Conquering Sword of Conan. New York: Del Rey, 2005.

The Horror Stories of Robert E. Howard. New York: Del Rey, 2008.

Kull: Exile of Atlantis. New York: Del Rey, 2006.

Pictures in the Fire: Remaining Weird Tales and Esoterica. n.p.: Robert E. Howard Foundation Press, 2018.

Post Oaks and Sand Roughs. In *Post Oaks and Sand Roughs & Other Autobiographical Writings*. n.p.: Robert E. Howard Foundation Press, 2019. 96-230.

Robert E. Howard's Western Tales. n.p.: Robert E. Howard Foundation Press, 2013.

The Savage Tales of Solomon Kane. New York: Del Rey, 2004.

"The Wandering Years: A History of the Howard Family and Its Branches." In *Post Oaks and Sand Roughs & Other Autobiographical Writings*. n.p.: Robert E. Howard Foundation Press, 2019. 3-12.

B. Secondary

Blake, William. *The Marriage of Heaven and Hell*. 1793. New York: Oxford University Press, 1975.

Brownmiller, Susan. *Against Our Will: Men, Women and Rape*. New York: Simon & Schuster, 1975.

Burke, Rusty. "The Old Deserted House: Images of the South in Howard's Fiction." *The Dark Man: The Journal of Robert E. Howard Studies* No. 2 (July 1991): 13-21.

Chandler, Raymond. *Trouble Is My Business*. 1939. New York: Ballantine, 1972.

de Camp, L. Sprague. *Literary Swordsmen and Sorcerers: The Makers of Heroic Fantasy*. Sauk City, WI: Arkham House, 1976.

de Camp, L. Sprague; Catherine Crook de Camp; and Jane Whittington Griffin. *Dark Valley Destiny: The Life of Robert E. Howard*. New York: Blue Jay Books, 1983.

Derleth, August. "Foreword" to *Skull-Face and Others* by Robert E. Howard. Sauk City, WI: Arkham House, 1946.

Ellis, Novalyne Price. *One Who Walked Alone*. West Kingston, RI: Donald M. Grant, 1986.

Hays, H. R. "Superman on a Psychotic Bender." *New York Times Book Review* (29 September 1946): 34. (Review of *Skull-Face and Others*)

Howard, Dr. I. M. *The Collected Letters of Doctor Isaac M. Howard*. n.p.: Robert E. Howard Foundation Press, 2011.

Knight, George (Don Herron). "Robert E. Howard: Hard-Boiled Heroic Fantasist." In *The Dark Barbarian*, ed. Don Herron. Westport, CT: Greenwood Press, 1984. 117-33.

Krenkel, Roy G. "Introduction" to *The Sowers of the Thunder* by Robert E. Howard. West Kingston, RI: Donald M. Grant, 1973.

Leiber, Fritz. "Howard's Fantasy," In *The Dark Barbarian: The Writings of Robert E. Howard, A Critical Anthology*, ed. Don Herron. Westport, CT: Greenwood Press, 1984. 3-15.

Lovecraft, H. P. "In Memoriam: Robert Ervin Howard." In *Miscellaneous Writings*. Ed. S. T. Joshi. Sauk City, WI: Arkham House, 1995. 123-26.

———. "The Rats in the Walls." In *Collected Fiction: A Variorum Edition.* New York: Hippocampus Press, 2015. 1.374-396.

———. *Selected Letters.* Ed. August Derleth, Donald Wandrei, and James Turner. Sauk City, WI: Arkham House, 1965-76. 5 vols.

McCollum, Rick. "'The Valley of the Worm': A Gathering of Howard's Essential Creative Themes." In *The Fantastic Worlds of Robert E. Howard,* ed. James Van Hise. Yucca Valley, CA: James Van Hise, 1997. 14-21.

Nietzsche, Friedrich. *Beyond Good and Evil.* Tr. Walter Kaufmann. New York: Vintage, 1966.

Perry, Alvin Earl. "A Biographical Sketch of Robert Ervin Howard." In *The Last Celt,* ed. Glenn Lord. West Kingston, RI: Donald M. Grant, 1976. 65-66.

Preece, Harold. "The Last Celt." In *The Last Celt,* ed. Glenn Lord. West Kingston, RI: Donald M. Grant, 1976. 93-102.

Pryke, Reginald A. Letter to "The Eyrie." *Weird Tales* 30, No. 4 (October 1937): 508.

Rand, Ayn. *The Romantic Manifesto.* New York: Signet, 1975.

Reid, Thomas R. "Cultural Trends in Literature." *The Dark Man: The Journal of Robert E. Howard Studies* No. 2 (July 1991): 30-32.

Schultz, Mark. *Robert E. Howard's Conan of Cimmeria: A Sketchbook.* London: Wandering Star, 2001.

Scithers, George H. "Balthus of Cross Plains." In *The Conan Grimoire,* ed. L. Sprague de Camp. Baltimore: Mirage Press, 1972. 25-28.

Wilson, Colin. *The Occult.* New York: Random House, 1971.

———. *The Outsider,* Boston: Houghton Mifflin, 1956.

BIBLIOGRAPHY

I. The Works of Robert E. Howard

The following is by no means a complete roster of all the hardcover and paperback editions of Howard's work. Due to the multiplicity of different editions of his writings, such an extensive bibliography could easily fill a separate volume. Glenn Lord's now-dated *The Last Celt* (1976) is a lengthy volume of biographical and bibliographical data concerning Howard and his work, and the better part of it is devoted to a listing of this sort. The list below is a selective catalogue. The editions cited are mostly free of editorial revision and, to the extent possible, comparatively recent. For the reader's convenience, they are listed here in roughly the order that their contents are discussed within the text of the present study. For reference, each book's contents are listed following the volume's title and publication data. In some cases, the contents overlap. Stories of Conan, Kull, etc., may also appear in miscellaneous fiction collections. Also, a book like Bison Press's *Boxing Stories* will offer a good representative sampling of Howard's work in this genre, while the multi-volume *Fists of Iron* from the Robert E. Howard Foundation Press presents the complete works.

Bran Mak Morn

Bran Mak Morn: The Last King. New York: Ballantine Books/Del Rey, 2005. Contents: Foreword by Gary Gianni; Introduction by Rusty Burke; "Men of the Shadows," "Kings of the Night," "A Song of the Race," "Worms of the Earth," "The Dark Man," "The Lost Race," Poem; *Miscellanea*: Notes on Miscellanea, "The Little People," "The Little People—Typescript," "The Children of the Night," "Bran Mak

Morn," "Bran Mak Morn—Manuscript, Synopsis," "Worms of the Earth—Draft Version," Fragment, Poem—Previously Unpublished, Untitled; *Appendices:* "Robert E. Howard and the Picts: A Chronology," "Robert E. Howard, Bran Mak Morn and the Picts" by Rusty Burke and Patrice Louinet, Notes on the Original Howard Texts, Sketches by Gary Gianni.

Solomon Kane

The Savage Tales of Solomon Kane. New York: Ballantine Books/Del Rey, 2004. *Contents:* Foreword by Gary Gianni; "In Memoriam: Robert Ervin Howard" by H. P. Lovecraft; "Skulls in the Stars," "The Right Hand of Doom," "Red Shadows," "Rattle of Bones," "The Castle of the Devil," "Death's Black Riders," "The Moon of Skulls," "The One Black Stain," "The Blue Flame of Vengeance," "The Hills of the Dead," "Hawk of Basti," "The Return of Sir Richard Grenville," "Wings in the Night," "The Footfalls Within," "The Children of Asshur," "Solomon Kane's Homecoming," "Solomon Kane's Homecoming (Variant)"; *Appendices:* "A Short Biography of Robert E. Howard" by Rusty Burke; Sketches by Gary Gianni; Notes on the Original Howard Texts.

King Kull

Kull: Exile of Atlantis. New York: Ballantine Books/Del Rey, 2006. *Contents:* Foreword by Justin Sweet; Introduction by Steve Tompkins; Untitled Story (previously published as "Exile of Atlantis"), "The Shadow Kingdom," "The Mirrors of Tuzun Thune," Untitled Draft, "The Cat and the Skull," "The Screaming Skull of Silence," "The Striking of the Gong," "The Altar and the Scorpion," "The Curse of the Golden Skull," "The Black City" (Unfinished Fragment), "'By This Axe I Rule!,'" "Swords of the Purple Kingdom," "The King and the Oak," "Kings of the Night"; *Miscellanea:* The "Am-ra of the Ta-an" Fragments ("Summer Morn," "Am-ra the Ta-an," "The Tale of Am-ra," Untitled and Unfinished Fragment, Untitled and Incomplete Fragment), "The Shadow Kingdom" (Draft), "Delcardes' Cat," "The King and the Oak" (Draft); *Appendices:* "Atlantean Genesis" by Patrice Louinet, Notes on the Original Howard Texts.

Conan

The Coming of Conan the Cimmerian. New York: Ballantine Books/Del Rey, 2003. *Contents:* Foreword by Mark Schultz; Introduction by Patrice Louinet; "Cimmeria," "The Phoenix on the Sword," "The Frost-Giant's Daughter," "The God in the Bowl," "The Tower of the Elephant," "The Scarlet Citadel," "Queen of the Black Coast," "Black Colossus," "Iron Shadows in the Moon," "Xuthal of the Dusk," "The Pool of the Black One," "Rogues in the House," "The Vale of Lost Women," "The Devil in Iron"; *Miscellanea:* "The Phoenix on the Sword" (first submitted draft), "Notes on Various Peoples of the Hyborian Age," "The Hyborian Age," Untitled Synopsis, Untitled Synopsis ("The Scarlet Citadel"), Untitled Synopsis ("Black Colossus"), Untitled Fragment, Untitled Synopsis, Untitled Draft, Hyborian Names and Countries, Hyborian Age Maps; *Appendices:* "Hyborian Genesis" by Patrice Louinet, Notes on the Conan Typescripts and the Chronology, Notes on the Original Howard Texts.

The Bloody Crown of Conan. New York: Ballantine Books/Del Rey, 2004. *Contents:* Foreword by Gary Gianni; Introduction by Rusty Burke; "The People of the Black Circle," *The Hour of the Dragon,* "A Witch Shall Be Born"; *Miscellanea:* Untitled Synopsis ("People of the Black Circle"), The Story Thus Far, Untitled Synopsis, Untitled Draft, Untitled Synopsis (*The Hour of the Dragon*), Notes on *The Hour of the Dragon,* Untitled Synopsis ("A Witch Shall Be Born"); *Appendices:* "Hyborian Genesis Part II" by Patrice Louinet, Notes on the Conan Typescripts and the Chronology, Notes on the Original Howard Texts.

The Conquering Sword of Conan. New York: Ballantine Books/Del Rey, 2005. *Contents:* Foreword by Gregory Manchess; Introduction by Patrice Louinet; "The Servants of Bit-Yakin" (previously published as "Jewels of Gwahlur"), "Beyond the Black River," "The Black Stranger," "The Man-Eaters of Zamboula," "Red Nails"; *Miscellanea:* Untitled Notes, "Wolves Beyond the Border" (Draft A), "Wolves Beyond the Border" (Draft B), "The Man-Eaters of Zamboula" Synopsis, "Red Nails" Draft; *Ephemera:* Letter to P. Schuyler Miller, Map of the Hyborian Age; *Appendices:* "Hyborian Genesis Part III" by Patrice Louinet, Notes on the Conan Typescripts and the Chronology, Notes on the Original Howard Texts.

Other Fantasy and Horror

Adventures in Science Fantasy. n.p.: Robert E. Howard Foundation Press, 2012. *Contents:* "The Science Fiction of Robert E. Howard" by Michael A. Stackpole; *Adventures in Science Fantasy:* "The Last Laugh,"

"The Gondarian Man," "The Supreme Moment," "The People of the Black Coast," "King of the Forgotten People," *Almuric*, "The Challenge from Beyond"; *Miscellanea*: "A Twentieth Century Rip Van Winkle," "The Iron Terror," "The Last Man," "The Last White Man," "A Room in London," "The Man Who Went Back," Untitled Synopsis ("Hunwulf).

The Black Stranger and Other American Tales. Lincoln: University of Nebraska Press/Bison Books, 2005. *Contents*: Introduction by Steven Tompkins; "The Black Stranger," "Marchers of Valhalla," "The Gods of Bal-Sagoth," "Nekht Semerkeht," "Black Vulmea's Vengeance," "The Strange Case of Josiah Wilbarger," "The Valley of the Lost," "Kelly the Conjure-Man," "Black Canaan," "Pigeons from Hell," "Old Garfield's Heart," "The Horror from the Mound," "The Thunder-Rider," "The Classic Tale of the Southwest," "The Grim Land."

The Horror Stories of Robert E. Howard. New York: Ballantine Books/Del Rey, 2008. *Contents*: Foreword by Greg Staples; Introduction by Rusty Burke; "In the Forest of Villefere," "A Song of the Werewolf Folk," "Wolfshead," "Up, John Kane!," "Remembrance," "The Dream Snake," "Sea Curse," "The Moor Ghost," "Moon Mockery," "The Little People," "Dead Man's Hate," "Casonetto's Last Song," "The Touch of Death," "Out of the Deep," "A Legend of Faring Town," "Restless Waters," "The Shadow of the Beast," "The Dead Slaver's Tale," "Dermod's Bane," "The Tavern," "Rattle of Bones," "The Fear That Follows," "The Spirit of Tom Molyneaux," "The Hills of the Dead," "Dig Me No Grave," "The Song of a Mad Minstrel," "The Children of the Night," "Musings," "The Black Stone," "The Thing on the Roof," "The Dweller in Dark Valley," "The Horror from the Mound," "A Dull Sound as of Knocking," "People of the Dark," "Delenda Est," "The Cairn on the Headland," "Worms of the Earth," "The Symbol," "The Valley of the Lost," "The Hoofed Thing," "The Noseless Horror," "The Dwellers under the Tomb," "An Open Window," "The House of Arabu," "The Man on the Ground," "Old Garfield's Heart," "Kelly the Conjure-Man," "Black Canaan," "To a Woman," "One Who Comes at Eventide," "The Haunter of the Ring," "Pigeons from Hell," "The Dead Remember," "The Fire of Asshurbanipal," Fragment, "Which Will Scarcely Be Understood"; *Miscellanea*: "Golnar the Ape," "Spectres in the Dark," "The House," Untitled Fragment; *Appendix*: Notes on the Original Howard Texts.

Beyond the Borders. New York: Baen Books, 1996. *Contents:* "The Voice of El-Lil," "The Cairn on the Headland," "Casonetto's Last Song," "The Cobra in the Dream," "Dig Me No Grave," "The Haunter of the Ring," "Dermod's Bane," "King of the Forgotten People," "The Children of the Night," "The Dream Snake," "The Hyena," "People of the Black Coast," "The Fire of Asshurbanipal."

Eons of the Night. New York: Baen Books, 1996. *Contents:* Introduction (from a letter to H. P. Lovecraft, 1933); "The House of Arabu," "The Garden of Fear," "The Grey God Passes" (as "The Twilight of the Grey Gods"), "Spear and Fang," "Delenda Est," "Marchers of Valhalla," "Sea Curse," "Out of the Deep," "In the Forest of Villefere," "Wolfshead."

Trials in Darkness. New York: Baen Books. 1996. *Contents:* "The Dead Remember," "Black Canaan," "Kelly the Conjure-Man," "The Valley of the Lost," "The Man on the Ground," "Black Hound of Death," "'For the Love of Barbara Allen,'" "The Hoofed Thing," "Moon of Zembabwei," "The Horror from the Mound."

Francis X. Gordon (El Borak) / Kirby O'Donnell

El Borak and Other Desert Adventures. New York: Ballantine Books/Del Rey, 2010. *Contents:* Artists' Forewords by Jim Bradstreet and Jim & Ruth Keegan; Introduction by Steve Tompkins; "Swords of the Hills," "The Daughter of Erlik Khan," "Three-Bladed Doom," "Hawk of the Hills," "Blood of the Gods," "Son of the Hawk," "Son of the White Wolf," "Gold from Tartary," "Swords of Shahrazar," "The Trail of the Blood-Stained God," "The Fire of Asshurbanipal"; *Miscellanea:* "Three-Bladed Doom," Untitled Fragment; *Appendices:* "Gunfighters of the Wild East" by David A. Hardy, Notes on the Original Howard Texts.

Historical Fiction

Lord of Samarcand and Other Adventure Tales of the Old Orient. Lincoln: University of Nebraska Press/Bison Books, 2005. *Contents:* Introduction by Patrice Louinet; "Red Blades of Black Cathay" (with Tevis Clyde Smith), "Hawks of Outremer," "The Blood of Belshazzar," "The Sowers of the Thunder," "Lord of Samarkand," "Timur-Lang," "The Lion of Tiberias," "The Shadow of the Vulture," "Gates of Empire," "The Road of the Eagles," "Hawks over Egypt," "The Road of Azrael"; *Miscellanea:* "The Slave Princess" (synopsis), "The Slave Princess" (unfinished draft), "Two against Tyre" (unfinished draft), "The Track of Bohemund (unfinished draft), "The Shadow of the Hun" (unfinished draft), "He knew de Bracy . . ." (untitled fragment), "The wind from the Mediterranean . . ." (untitled fragment), Recap of Harold Lamb's "The Wolf Chaser," "The Persians had all fled . . ." (untitled draft).

Sword Woman and Other Historical Adventures. New York: Ballantine Books/Del Rey, 2011. Contents: Artist's Foreword by John Watkiss; Introduction by Scott Oden; "Spears of Clontarf," "Hawks over Egypt," "The Outgoing of Sigurd the Jerusalem-Farer," "The Road of Azrael," "The Lion of Tiberias," "Gates of Empire," "Hawks of Outremer," "The Blood of Belshazzar," "Red Blades of Black Cathay," "The Sowers of the Thunder," "The Skull in the Clouds," "A Thousand Years Ago," "Lord of Samarcand," "Timur-Lang," "Sword Woman," "Blades for France," "The Shadow of the Vulture," "The Road of the Eagles"; *Miscellanea*: Untitled Fragment ("The Track of Bohemund"), Untitled Fragment ("The Slave-Princess"), Untitled Fragment ("The Slave-Princess"), Untitled Fragment ("He knew de Bracy . . ."), Untitled Fragment ("The wind from the Mediterranean . . ."), Recap of Harold Lamb's "The Wolf Chaser," Untitled Fragment ("The Persians had all fled . . ."), "The Sign of the Sickle," "Mistress of Death"; *Appendices*: "Howard's Journey" by Howard Andrew Jones, Notes on the Original Howard Texts.

Boxing Stories

Boxing Stories. Lincoln: University of Nebraska Press/Bison Books, 2005. Contents: Introduction by Chris Gruber; "In the Ring," "The Pit of the Serpent," "The Bull Dog Breed," "The Champion of the Forecastle," "Waterfront Law," "Texas Fists," "The Fightin'est Pair," "Vikings of the Gloves," "Cultured Cauliflowers," "A New Game for Costigan," "Hard-Fisted Sentiment," "When You Were a Set-Up and I Was a Ham," "The Spirit of Tom Molyneaux," "Crowd-Horror," "Iron Men" (unedited version of "The Iron Man"), "Kid Galahad," "Fists of the Desert," "They Always Come Back," "Kid Lavigne Is Dead."

Waterfront Fists and Others: The Collected Fight Stories of Robert E. Howard. Holicong, PA: Wildside Press. 2003. Contents: "Kid Lavigne Is Dead," "Dula Due to Be Champion," "The Apparition in the Prize Ring," "The Pit of the Serpent," "The Bulldog Breed," "Sailor's Grudge,"

"Fist and Fang," "The Iron Man," "Winner Take All," "Waterfront Fists," "Champ of the Forecastle," "Alleys of Peril," "Texas Fists," "Circus Fists," "Vikings of the Gloves," "Night of Battle," "The Slugger's Game," "General Ironfist," "Sluggers of the Beach," "Alleys of Darkness."

Fists of Iron: The Collected Boxing Fiction of Robert E. Howard, Round 1. n.p.: Robert E. Howard Foundation Press, 2013. Contents: "The Brute Eternal" by Christopher Gruber; "The Spirit of Tom Molyneaux," "Double Cross," "The Weeping Willow," "The Right Hook," "The Voice of Doom," "Crowd-Horror," "Iron Men" (unedited version of "The Iron Man"), "The Mark of a Bloody Hand," "They Always Come Back," "The Trail of the Snake"; Poems: "Kid Lavigne Is Dead," "Aw, Come On and Fight!," "The Cooling of Spike McRue," "Fables for Little Folks," "The Champ," "Slugger's Vow," "In the Ring," Untitled ("And Dempsey climbed into the ring . . ."), Untitled ("They matched me up that night . . ."), "Down the Ages," "John L. Sullivan," "Jack Dempsey," Untitled ("We are the duckers of crosses . . ."), Untitled ("All the crowd . . ."), "When You Were a Set-up and I Was a Ham"; Early Tales, Variants and Fragments: "The Spirit of Brian Boru," "A Man of Peace," "The Atavist" (unfinished), "Cupid vs. Pollux," "The Spirit of Tom Molyneaux" (alternate version), untitled fragment ("I had just hung . . ."), "The Ferocious Ape" (fragment), untitled fragment ("Spike Morrissey . . ."), untitled fragment ("The tale has always been . . ."), "The Ghost Behind the Gloves" (fragment)," Lobo Volante" (fragment), "Night Encounter" (incomplete), "The Folly of Conceit" (unfinished), "Iron Men" (first version); Articles: "Dulla Due to Be Champion," "The Punch," "Men of Iron"; Odds and Ends: Untitled document, incomplete, perhaps from an essay, "Jeffries Versus Dempsey," "The Funniest Bout," Boxing material from Howard's self-published The Right Hook; Appendix: "The Lord of the Ring" (part 1) by Patrice Louinet.

Fists of Iron: The Collected Boxing Fiction of Robert E. Howard, Round 2. n.p.: Robert E. Howard Foundation Press, 2014. Contents: "Tall Lying in the Far East: Robert E. Howard, Sailor Steve Costigan, and the Narrative Idyll" by Mark Finn; "The Pit of the Serpent," "By the Law of the Shark," "The Bull Dog Breed," "Sailors' Grudge," "Fist and Fang," "Winner Take All," "Waterfront Fists," "The Champion of the Forecastle," "Alleys of Peril," "Waterfront Law," "Hard-Fisted Sentiment," "The Yellow Cobra," "A Student of Sockology," "Texas

Fists," "The Fightin'est Pair," "Cultured Cauliflowers"; *Appendix*: "Blue River Blues," "Sailors' Grudge" (outline), "The Battling Sailor" (incomplete, originally untitled), Untitled ("It was the end . . ."), Untitled ("The night Sailor Steve Costigan . . ."), "Alleys of Peril" (synopsis), Untitled Mike O'Brien fragment ("Help! Help! They're murdering me!"); "The Lord of the Ring" (part 2) by Patrice Louinet.

Fists of Iron: The Collected Boxing Fiction of Robert E. Howard, Round 3. n.p.: Robert E. Howard Foundation Press, 2014. Contents: "Big Talk Don't Bust No Chins" by Chris Gruber; "Circus Fists," "Vikings of the Gloves," "Night of Battle," "Sailor Costigan and the Yellow Cobra," "Sailor Costigan and the Jade Monkey," "Alleys of Darkness," "Sailor Costigan and the Destiny Gorilla," "A New Game for Costigan," "A Two-Fisted Santa Claus," "The Slugger's Game," "General Ironfist," "Sluggers of the Beach," "The Honor of the Ship" (originally untitled), "Alleys of Treachery"; *Appendix*: "Night of Battle" (synopsis), "Sailor Costigan and the Turkish Menace" (incomplete), "Sailor Costigan and the Turkish Menace" (synopsis), "Sailor Costigan and the Jade Monkey" (3rd person version), "Alleys of Darkness" (synopsis), "Sailor Costigan and the Destiny Gorilla" (synopsis), "A New Game for Costigan" (synopsis), "A Two-Fisted Santa Claus" (synopsis), "The Slugger's Game" (synopsis), "General Ironfist" (synopsis), "Sluggers of the Beach" (synopsis), "Iron-Clad Fists" (synopsis), "Alleys of Treachery" (synopsis); "The Lord of the Ring" (part 3) by Patrice Louinet.

Fists of Iron: The Collected Boxing Fiction of Robert E. Howard, Round 4. n.p.: Robert E. Howard Foundation Press, 2015. Contents: "A Boy and His Dog" by Mark Finn; *Kid Allison*: "The Man with the Mystery Mitts," "Kid Galahad," "College Socks," "The Wildcat and the Star," "Fighting Nerves" (Kid Allison version); *Mike Dorgan and Bill McGlory*: "The House of Peril," "One Shanghai Night," "The Tomb of the Dragon"; *Other Tales*: "The Sign of the Snake," "The Fighting Fury," "Fighting Nerves" (Jim O'Donnel version), "Fists of the Desert," "Fists of the Revolution." *Miscellanea*: "The Jinx," "Fistic Psychology," "The Drawing Card," Untitled fragment ("'Huh,' I was so . . ."), "A Tough Nut to Crack" (Allison version), "A Tough Nut to Crack" (Clarney version), "One Shanghai Night" (synopsis), Untitled notes (Knute Hansen); "The Lord of the Ring" (part 4) by Patrice Louinet.

Detective Stories

Graveyard Rats and Others. Holicong, PA: Wildside Press, 2003. Contents: "Black Talons," "Fangs of Gold," "The Tomb's Secret," "Names in the Black Book," "Graveyard Rats," "Black Wind Blowing."

Steve Harrison's Casebook. n.p.: Robert E. Howard Foundation Press, 2011. Contents: "Hard-Boiled in Texas," by Don Herron; "Lord of the Dead," "The People of the Serpent," "The Teeth of Doom," "The Black Moon," "The Voice of Death," "The House of Suspicion," "Names in the Black Book," "The Silver Heel," "Graveyard Rats"; *Miscellanea:* "The Mystery of Tannernoe Lodge," Untitled Synopsis ("Steve Harrison received a wire . . ."), "The Silver Heel" (synopsis), "Graveyard Rats" (draft).

Westerns

The End of the Trail: Western Stories. Lincoln: University of Nebraska Press/Bison Books, 2005. Contents: Introduction by Rusty Burke; "Golden Hope Christmas," "The Extermination of Yellow Donory," "The Judgement of the Desert," Gunman's Debt," "The Man on the Ground," "The Sand-Hills' Crest," "The Devil's Joker," "Knife, Bullet and Noose," "Law-Shooters of Cowtown," "The Last Ride" (with Robert Enders Allen), "John Ringold," "Vultures of Wahpeton," "Vultures of Wahpeton" (alternate ending), "Vultures Sanctuary," "The Dead Remember," "The Ghost of Camp Colorado," "The Strange Case of Josiah Wilbarger," "Beyond the Brazos River," "Billy the Kid and the Lincoln County War," "The Ballad of Buckshot Roberts."

The Riot at Bucksnort and Other Western Tales. Lincoln: University of Nebraska Press/Bison Books, 2005. Contents: Introduction by David Gentzel; "Mountain Man," "Meet Cap'n Kidd," "Guns of the Mountains," "The Peaceful Pilgrim," "War on Bear Creek," "The Haunted Mountain," "The Feud Buster," "The Riot at Cougar Paw," "Pistol Politics," "No Cowherders Wanted," "The Conquerin' Hero of the Humbolts," "A Gent from the Pecos," "Gents on the Lynch," "The Riot at Bucksnort," "Knife River Prodigal," "A Man-Eating Jeopard."

Robert E. Howard's Western Tales. n.p.: Robert E. Howard Foundation Press, 2013. Contents: "Robert E. Howard: Western Pulp Pioneer," by James Reasoner; *Western Tales:* "Drums of the Sunset," "John Ringold" (verse), "The Extermination of Yellow Donory," "Old Faro Bill" (verse), "The Judgement of the Desert," "The Sand-Hill's Crest" (verse),

"Gunman's Debt," "The Devil's Joker," "The Feud" (verse), "Knife, Bullet and Noose," "Law-Shooters of Cowtown," "Over the Rio Grandey" (verse), "Wild Water," "Cowboy" (verse), "The Last Ride" (with Robert Enders Allen), "The Vultures of Wahpeton," "Vultures' Sanctuary," "Ace High" (verse), "The Ballad of Buckshot Roberts" (verse); *The Weird West:* "The Horror from the Mound," "The Valley of the Lost," "The Man on the Ground," "Old Garfield's Heart," "The Thunder-Rider," "The Dead Remember"; *Essays:* "The Strange Case of Josiah Wilbarger," "The Ghost of Camp Colorado"; *Miscellanea:* "Six-Gun Interview" (unfinished), Untitled ("I met him first at the Paradise Saloon . . ."), "The Killer's Debt" (fragment), Three Synopses ("Gunman's Debt," "Wild Water Timing," "The Devil's Joker" [alternate version]), Untitled Synopsis ("The Vultures of Wahpeton"); *Juvenilia:* "A Faithful Servant," "'Golden Hope' Christmas," "The Sonora Kid—Cowhand," "The Sonora Kid's Winning Hand," "Red Curls and Bobbed Hair," Untitled ("Madge Meraldson . . ."), Unititled ("The Hades Saloon . . ."), Untitled ("The Blazing Sun . . ."), Untitled ("The way it came about . . ."), Untitled ("The hot Arizona sun . . ."), Untitled ("Steve Allison settled . . ."), "Brotherly Advice," "Desert Rendezvous," "The West Tower," "'Drag'" (a.k.a. Untitled: "It was a strange experience . . ."); Notes on the text.

The Adventures of Breckinridge Elkins, Volume 1: The Complete Short Stories and Tall Tales. n.p.: Robert E. Howard Foundation Press, 2016. Contents: "Tickled Ribs and Slapped Knees," by Mark Finn; "Mountain Man," "Guns of the Mountains," "A Gent from Bear Creek," "A Stranger in Grizzly Claw," "The Road to Bear Creek," "A Elkins Never Surrenders," "War on Bear Creek," "The Haunted Mountain," "The Feud Buster," "Cupid from Bear Creek," "The Riot at Cougar Paw," "The Apache Mountain War," "Pilgrims to the Pecos," "Pistol Politics," "Evil Deeds at Red Cougar," "Gents on the Rampage," "Gents in Buckskin," "Politics at Lonesome Lizard," "Sharp's Gun Serenade"; *Miscellanea:* "Six-Gun Interview," "A Gent from Bear Creek" (draft), Untitled Synopsis ("The Road to Bear Creek"), Untitled Synopsis ("Evil Deeds at Red Cougar"), Untitled Synopsis ("Gents on the Rampage").

The Adventures of Breckinridge Elkins, Volume 2: Featuring A Gent from Bear Creek, *Pike Bearfield, Buckner J. Grimes, and More.* n.p.: Robert E. Howard Foundation Press. 2017. Contents: "Make 'Em Laugh: Howard's Humorous Westerns," by James Reasoner; *A Gent from Bear*

Creek (novel); *Bearfield Elston:* "A Elston to the Rescue"; *Buckner J. Grimes:* "Knife River Prodigal," "A Man-Eating Jeopard," "Ring-Tailed Tornado"; *Pike Bearfield:* "A Gent from the Pecos," "Gents on the Lynch," "The Riot at Bucksnort," "While the Smoke Rolled"; *Miscellanea:* "West Is West," "Mayhem and Taxes" (unfinished), "The Peaceful Pilgrim," Letter: March 1935 (Byrne to Cooper), Untitled Synopsis ("Ring-Tailed Tornado"), Letter draft: 21 April 1936 (to Byrne), "The Diablos Trail" (unfinished), Untitled Synopsis ("A Gent from the Pecos"), Untitled Synopsis ("Gents on the Lynch"), Untitled Synopsis ("While the Smoke Rolled").

"Spicy" Stories

The She Devil. New York: Ace Fantasy Books, 1983. *Contents:* "She Devil," "Ship in Mutiny," "The Purple Heart of Erlik," "The Dragon of Kao Tsu," "Murderer's Grog," "Desert Blood," "Guns of Khartum," "Daughters of Feud."

Spicy Adventures. n.p.: Robert E. Howard Foundation Press, 2011. *Contents:* Introduction by Patrice Louinet; *Spicy Adventures:* "The Girl on the Hell Ship" (a.k.a. "She Devil") "Ship in Mutiny," "Desert Blood," "The Purple Heart of Erlik," "The Dragon of Kao Tsu," "Murderer's Grog," "Guns of Khartum," "Daughters of Feud"; *Miscellanea:* Untitled Synopsis ("John Gorman . . ."), "The Girl on the Hell Ship" (draft), Untitled Synopsis ("Ship in Mutiny"), "Ship in Mutiny" (draft), List of Characters ("Desert Blood"), Untitled Synopsis ("The Purple Heart of Erlik"), Untitled Synopsis ("Daughters of Feud").

Miscellaneous Fiction Collections

The Best of Robert E. Howard, Volume One: Crimson Shadows. New York: Ballantine Books/Del Rey, 2007. *Contents:* Foreword by Jim & Ruth Keegan; Introduction by Rusty Burke; "The Shadow Kingdom," "The Ghost Kings," "The Curse of the Golden Skull," "Red Shadows," "The One Black Stain," "The Dark Man," "The Marching Song of Connacht," "Kings of the Night," "Recompense," "The Black Stone," "The Song of a Mad Minstrel," "The Fightin'est Pair," "The Grey God Passes," "The Song of the Last Briton," "Worms of the Earth," "An Echo from the Iron Harp," "Lord of the Dead," Untitled, "'For the Love of Barbara Allen,'" "The Tide," "The Valley of the Worm," "The Dust Dance": Selections, Version II, "The People of the Black Circle," "A Word from the Outer Dark," "Hawk of the Hills,"

"Sharp's Gun Serenade," "Lines Written in the Realization That I Must Die"; *Appendices:* "Robert E. Howard: Twentieth Century Mythmaker" by Charles Hoffman, "A Short Biography of Robert E. Howard" by Rusty Burke, Notes on the Original Howard Texts.

The Best of Robert E. Howard, Volume Two: Grim Lands. New York: Ballantine Books/Del Rey, 2007. *Contents:* Foreword by Jim & Ruth Keegan; Introduction by Rusty Burke; "'By This Axe I Rule!,'" "The King and the Oak," "The Mirrors of Tuzun Thune," "The Tower of the Elephant," "Which Will Scarcely Be Understood," "Wings in the Night," "Solomon Kane's Homecoming," "Lord of Samarcand," "Timur-Lang," "A Song of the Naked Lands," "The Shadow of the Vulture," "Echoes from an Anvil," "The Bull Dog Breed," "Black Harps in the Hills," "The Man on the Ground," "Old Garfield's Heart," "Vultures of Wahpeton," "Gents on the Lynch," "The Grim Land," "Pigeons from Hell," "Never Beyond the Beast," "Wild Water," "Musings," "Son of the White Wolf," "Black Vulmea's Vengeance," "Flint's Passing," "Red Nails," "Cimmeria"; *Appendices:* "Barbarian at the Pantheon Gates" by Steven Tompkins, Notes on the Original Howard Texts.

Pictures in the Fire: Remaining Weird Tales and Esoterica. n.p.: Robert E. Howard Foundation Press, 2018. *Contents: Complete Stories:* "'For the Love of Barbara Allen,'" "Two Against Tyre," "The Voice of El-Lil," "Spear and Fang," "Black Canaan" (early version), "The Cobra in the Dream," "The Ghost in the Doorway," "A Thunder of Trumpets," "The Shadow of Doom," "The Haunted Hut," "Under the Baobab Tree," "The Hyena," "Black Country"; *Fragments, Drafts, and Other Esoterica:* "Nekht Semerkeht," Untitled ("As he approached . . ."), "The Abbey," "Age Lasting Love" (with outline), "The Devil's Woodchopper," "The Door of the World," "Redflame," "Serpent Vines," Untitled Synopsis ("Black Canaan"), "The Isle of the Eons," "The Brand of Satan," "Dagon Manor," "Dear Mrs. Shane," "Fate Is the Killer," "Incongruity," "The Jade God," "The Slayer," "Through the Ages," "The Wings of the Bat," Untitled ("'You,' said Shifty Griddle . . ."), Untitled ("Better a man should remain . . ."), Untitled ("From the black, bandit-haunted mountains . . ."), Untitled ("I'm writing this . . ."), Untitled ("Old Man Jacobson . . ."), Untitled ("The matter seemed so obvious . . ."), Untitled ("The next day I was sluggish . . ."), "Songs of Bastards," "Bastards All!," "Pictures in the Fire," "The Dominant Male," "Miss High Hat," "Etched in Ebony," Untitled

("'Arrange, Madame, arrange!'"), "Letter of a Chinese Student" (1 and 2), "For the Honor of the School"; *Poetry:* "A Rattlesnake Sings in the Grass," "The Masque," "A High Land," "Whence Cometh Erlik?," "Lost Nisapur," "Abhorrent Gods," "A Song of Praise," "The Tale of Glory," "The Race without Name," "Let me dream by a silver stream," "My Animal Instinct," "The Wind Blows," "The Wind Blows" (variant).

Poetry

Always Comes Evening. Sauk City, WI: Arkham House, 1957. Contents: "Fragment," "Song of a Mad Minstrel," "Remembrance," "The Moor Ghost," "Dead Man's Hate," "The Ride of Falume," "Arkham," "Crete," "Desert Dawn," "The Riders of Babylon," "The Harp of Alfred," "Moon Mockery," "A Song out of Midian," "The Ghost Kings," "Forbidden Magic," "Recompense," "The Song of the Bats," "Ships," "The King and the Oak," "Futility," "Autumn," "The Poets," "Easter Island," "Black Chant Imperial," "An Open Window," "Lines Written in the Realization That I Must Die," "The Gates of Nineveh," "The Hills of Kandahar," "Which Will Scarcely Be Understood," "The Soul Eater," "The Dream and Shadow," "The Last Hour," "Haunting Columns," "The Singer in the Mist," "Always Comes Evening," "Emancipation," "Invective," "Hymn of Hatred," "Prince and Beggar," "The Tempter," "The Road of Azrael," "A Song of the Don Cossacks," "To a Woman," "Retribution," "Solomon Kane's Homecoming," "Song at Midnight," "One Who Comes at Eventide," "Rune," "Men of the Shadows," "Song of the Pict," "Chant of the White Beard," "Nisapur," "Babylon," "Niflheim," "The Gods of Easter Island," "The Heart of the Sea's Desire," "The Voices Waken Memory," "Moon Shame," "Babel," "Laughter in the Gulfs," "A Crown for a King."

Singers in the Shadows. West Kingston, RI: Donald M. Grant, 1970. Contents: "Zukala's Hour," "The Sea-Woman," "The Bride of Cuchulain," "The Stranger," "Rebel," "White Thunder," "The Men That Walk with Satan," "Thus Spake Sven the Fool," "The Witch," "Sacrifice," "Hadrian's Wall," "Night Mood," "Shadows," "The Lost Galley," "The Fear That Follows," "The Tavern," "Destination," "The Road to Hell," "Attila Rides No More," "The Twin Gates."

Echoes From an Iron Harp. West Kingston, RI: Donald M. Grant, 1973. Contents: "Age Comes to Rabelais," "Belshazzar," "But the Hills Were

Ancient Then," "Cimmeria," "A Dawn in Flanders," "The Day That I Die," "Dreams of Nineveh," "The Dust Dance," "The Dweller in Dark Valley," "Earth-Born," "Fables for Little Folk," "'Feach Air Muir Lionadhi Gealach Buidhe Mar Or,'" "Futility," "Heritage," "Illusion," "John Ringold," "Kid Lavigne Is Dead," "The Kissing of Sal Snooboo," "A Lady's Chamber," "The Last Day," "Lost Altars," "Memories," "A Moment," "Moonlight on a Skull," "Not Only in Death They Die," "Private Magrath of the A.E.F.," "Reuben's Brethren," "Roundelay of the Roughneck," "The Sands of Time," "The Sea," "The Skull in the Clouds," "Skulls and Dust," "Skulls over Judah," "Slumber," "A Song of Defeat," "The Song of Horsa's Galley," "A Song of the Legions," "A Song for Men That Laugh," "A Sonnet of Good Cheer," "Sonora to Del Rio," "Surrender," "Tarantella," "Thor's Son," "Timur-Lang," "To Certain Orthodox Brethren," "A Vision," "A Warning," "Where Are Your Knights, Donn Othna?," "Who Is Grandpa Theobold?," "The Years Are as a Knife."

Shadows of Dreams. Hampton Falls, NH: Donald M. Grant, 1989. Contents: "Shadows of Dreams," "Flaming Marble," "A Weird Ballad," "A Warning to Orthodoxy," "Whispers," "A Riding Song," "Castaway," "Black Seas," "Silence Falls on Mecca's Walls," "Keresa, Kerasita," "Whispers on the Nightwinds," "Nights to Both of Us Known," "To Lyle Saxon," "Symbols," "A Stirring of Green Leaves," "The Gladiator and the Lady," "A Song of the Anchor Chain," "The Path of the Strange Wanderers," "I Praise My Nativity," "Ballade," "Destiny," "Stay Not from Me," "The Last Words He Heard," "The Ecstacy of Desolation," "Musings," "Dreaming in Israel," "The Dust Dance," "A Challenge to Bast," "The Odyssey of Israel," "Romany Road," "Twilight on Stonehenge," "The Call of Pan," "Samson's Broodings," "The Road to Babel," "The Dreams of Men," "A Far Country," "To a Nameless Woman," "Song of a Fugitive Bard," "A Poet's Skull," "A Fable for Critics," "Love," "Song From an Ebony Heart," "Love's Young Dream," "A Ballad of Beer," "John Brown," "Abe Lincoln," "Surrender."

The Collected Poetry of Robert E. Howard. n.p.: Robert E. Howard Foundation Press, 2008.

Robert E. Howard: Selected Poems. Frank Coffman, ed. 2009. Rockford, Il: Mind's Eye HyperPublishing, 2012.

Autobiographical

The Collected Letters of Robert E. Howard. n.p.: Robert E. Howard Foundation Press, 2008 (2nd ed. 2020). 3 vols.

A Means to Freedom: The Letters of H. P. Lovecraft and Robert E. Howard. Ed. S. T. Joshi, David E. Schultz, and Rusty Burke. New York: Hippocampus Press, 2009. 2 vols.

Post Oaks and Sand Roughs. Hampton Falls, NH: Donald M. Grant, 1990.

Post Oaks and Sand Roughs & Other Autobiographical Writings. n.p.: Robert E. Howard Foundation Press, 2019. Contents: "The Wandering Years," "An Autobiography," "What I Did to Help Win the War," "In His Own Image," "Some People Who Have Had Influence over Me," "A Touch of Trivia," "To a Man Whose Name I Never Knew," "The Galveston Affair," "The Beast from the Abyss," untitled play ("A typical small town drugstore . . ."), "Spanish Gold on Devil Horse," *Post Oaks and Sand Roughs,* "Sunday in a Small Town," "Ambition in the Moonlight," "Musings of a Moron," "Irony," "What I Did in Vacation," "What My Signature Means to Me," "The Recalcitrant," untitled story ("Mike Costigan, writer and self-avowed futilist, . . ."), "The Splendid Brute," "The Paradox," "The Ivory Camel," "Spanish Gold on Devil Horse" (early draft), *Post Oaks and Sand Roughs* (early draft), "The Seven-Up Ballad" (poem), "Dula Due to be Champion," "Letters from Mom," Unsigned contract, Letter to *Argosy All-Story Weekly,* Spring 1929, Letter to Farnsworth Wright, June/July 1931, Letter to Wilfred Blanch Talman, September 1931, Letter to *Dime Sports,* June 1936.

II. Robert E. Howard Criticism

A. Biography

de Camp, L. Sprague, Catherine Crook de Camp, and Jane Whittington Griffin. *Dark Valley Destiny: The Life of Robert E. Howard.* New York: Bluejay Books, 1983.

Ellis, Novalyne Price. *Day of the Stranger: Further Memories of Robert E. Howard.* West Warwick, RI: Necronomicon Press, 1989.

———. *One Who Walked Alone: Robert E. Howard, The Final Years.* West Kingston. RI: Donald M. Grant, 1986.

Finn, Mark. *Blood and Thunder: The Life and Art of Robert E. Howard*. Austin, TX: MonkeyBrain Books, 2006.

Lord, Glenn, ed. *The Last Celt: A Bio-Bibliography of Robert Ervin Howard*. West Kingston, RI: Donald M. Grant, 1976.

Smith, David C. *Robert E. Howard: A Literary Biography*. n.p.: Pulp Hero Press, 2018.

B. Criticism and Scholarship

Critical Studies

Blosser, Fred. *Ar-i-e'ch and the Spell of Cthulhu: An Informal Guide to Robert E. Howard's Lovecraftian Fiction*. n.p.: Pulp Hero Press, 2018.

———. *Savage Scrolls: Scholarship from the Hyborian Age, Volume One*. n.p.: Pulp Hero Press, 2017.

———. *Western Weirdness and Voodoo Vengeance: An Informal Guide to Robert E. Howard's American Horrors*. n.p.: Pulp Hero Press, 2018.

Derie, Bobby. *Weird Talers: Essays on Robert E. Howard and Others*. New York: Hippocampus Press, 2019.

Louinet, Patrice. *The Robert E. Howard Guide*. Tallahassee, FL: Skelos Press, 2018.

Schultz, Mark. *Robert E. Howard's Conan of Cimmeria: A Sketchbook*. n.p.: Wandering Star, 2001.

Anthologies

Herron, Don, ed. *The Dark Barbarian: The Writings of Robert E. Howard, A Critical Anthology*. Westport, CT: Greenwood Press, 1984. Contents: Acknowledgments; Note on the Text; Introduction; "Howard's Fantasy" by Fritz Leiber; "Robert E. Howard: Frontiersman of Letters" by Donald Sidney-Fryer; "Barbarian Bard: The Poetry of Robert E. Howard" by Steven Eng; "Through Black Boughs: The Supernatural in Howard's Fiction" by Dennis Rickard; "The Western Fiction of Robert E. Howard" by Ben P. Indick; "Robert E. Howard: Hard-Boiled Heroic Fantasist" by George Knight; "Robert E. Howard: Professional Writer" by Glenn Lord; "The Dark Barbarian" by Don Herron.

———. *The Barbaric Triumph: A Critical Anthology on the Writings of Robert E. Howard*. Holicong, PA: Wildside Press, 2004. Contents: Acknowledgments; Note on the Text; Introduction; "A Voice from the Past: An Overture from 1943" by Paul Spencer; "Conan the Existential" by

Charles Hoffman; "Fists of Robert E. Howard" by Mark Finn; "The Shadow from a Soul on Fire: Robert E. Howard and Irrationalism" by Edward A. Waterman; "Heritage of Steel: Howard and the Frontier Myth" by Steven R. Trout; "Barbarism and Decadence" by Lauric Guillaud; "Twilight of the Gods: Howard and the Volkstumbewegung" by Scott Connors; "Gigantic Gulfs of Eons: Kull, Conan, and Tyrant Time" by Steven Tompkins; "Lands of Dreams and Nightmares" by George Knight; "The Reign of Blood" by Leo Grin; "The Barbaric Triumph" by Don Herron.

Van Hise, James, ed. *The Fantastic Worlds of Robert E. Howard*. Yucca Valley, CA: James Van Hise, 1997. Contents: "Queen of the Black Coast" by James Van Hise; "The Valley of the Worm: A Gathering of Howard's Essential Creative Themes" by Rick McCollum; "Conan, Kull and Bran Mak Morn: The Kings of the Night" by Patrice Louinet; "De Camp vs. Howard: Rewriting Conan" by Rusty Burke; "De Camp vs. Howard: Research Methods" by Rusty Burke; "Robert E. Howard: One Character Writer?" by Richard Toogood; "Robert E. Howard: Cross Plains Outsider" by Rick McCollum; "The *Weird Tales* Readers' View of Robert E. Howard: Comments from 'The Eyrie,'" compiled by Rusty Burke; "Skull-Face: A Closer Look" by James Van Hise and Rick Lai; "'Pigeons from Hell': Classic Howard Horror" by James Van Hise; "The Expurgated Solomon Kane" by Steve Trout; "A Solomon Kane Chronology" by Richard Toogood; "Robert E. Howard: Poet in Prose" by Charles A. Gramlich; "'The Frost-Giant's Daughter': A Deeper Look" by Rick McCollum; "*Almuric*: The Saga of Esau Cairn" by James Van Hise; "The Scarlet Citadel: A Portfolio by Roy Krenkel"; "Robert E. Howard's Book of Heroes" by Charles Gramlich; "Lin Carter and J. R. R. Tolkien: Problems" by Rick McCollum; "Lin Carter: The Inept Pasticheur" by Morgan Holmes; Covers of the 1973 German Conan Paperback Editions; *The Whole Wide World* reviewed by James Van Hise (contains interviews with Michael Scott Myers, writer, Dan Ireland, director, and the stars Vincent D'Onofrio and Renée Zellweger).

Journals

The Dark Man: The Journal of Robert E. Howard Studies. Edited by Rusty Burke (issues 1–4), Frank Coffman (issues 5–6), Mark Hall (issues 7–present). [Later *The Dark Man: The Journal of Robert E. Howard and Pulp Studies*.]

Issue 1 (August 1990). "Swords at the Academy Gates: or, Robert E. Howard Is There, Where Are the Critics" by Don Herron; "King Conan and the Aquilonian Dream" by Steven R. Trout; "Toward Other Lands: An Approach to Robert E. Howard" by Rusty Burke; "The Howard Complex" by Dan Stumpf; "Herbert Klatt" by Glenn Lord; "The Frost-Giant's Daughter; An Early Draft" by Robert E. Howard.

Issue 2 (July 1991). "The Horror Fiction of Robert E. Howard" by Steven R. Trout; "Solomon and Sorcery" by Michael Kellar; "The Old Deserted House: Images of the South in Howard's Fiction" by Rusty Burke; "'Come Back to Valusia Ag'in, Kull Honey!': Robert E. Howard and Mainstream American Literature" by Marc A. Cerasini; "On Howardian Fairyland" by Don Herron; "Bill Smalley and the Power of the Human Eye" by Robert E. Howard; "Cultural Trends in Literature" by Thomas R. Reid; "Barbarian Aftermath" by Don Herron; "The Expurgated Solomon Kane" by Steven R. Trout with Vernon M. Clark.

Issue 3 (April 1993). "From Cross Plains to the Stars: Robert E. Howard's Science Fiction" by Fred Blosser; "Cosmic Filth: Howard's View of Evil" by Charles Hoffman; "What the Nation Owes to the South" by Robert E. Howard; "The Active Voice: Robert E. Howard's Personae" by Rusty Burke.

Issue 4 (1997). "The Birth of Conan" by Patrice Louinet; "The Origin of Cimmeria" by Rusty Burke; "*The Star Rover* and 'The People of the Night'" by Fred Blosser; "Howard Publishing in Eastern Europe" by Glenn Lord; "Conan & Robert E. Howard on the Internet" by Edward A. Waterman.

Issue 5 (Winter 2001). "When Kull Rode the Range" by Fred Blosser; "'All Fled, All Done'" by Rusty Burke; "'The Tower of the Elephant': A Modern Fable" by Gary Romeo; "Escape from Eden: Genesis Subverted in 'The Garden of Fear'" by Charles Hoffman; "James Allison's Incarnations" by Joe Marek; "Soldiering for Fortune: Robert E. Howard's Kirby O'Donnell and 'The Treasures of Tartary'" by Gary Hoppenstand; "Dating Wolfshead" by Edward Waterman.

Issue 6 (Summer 2001). "Notes on Two Versions of an Unpublished Poem by Robert E. Howard" by Frank Coffman; "Spartacus to the Gladiators at Capita" by Elijah Kellogg, Jr.; "The Lives and Deaths of Three Writers: A Speculative Essay on London, Howard, and Hemingway" by Charles Gramlich; "Higashi, Masao. Kutourû Shinwa Jiten (Dictionary of the Cthulhu Mythos)" by Dr. Mark Hall; "A Short History of the Kull Series" by Patrice Louinet; "*The Last Celt* REH Letter Citations" compiled by Rusty Burke, Patrice Louinet, and Edward Waterman; "There's a White Wolf on the Ottoman, or, Another Revolt in the Desert" by Steven Tompkins.

Issue 7 (Spring 2004). "The Robert E. Howard Collections Found in the University of California at Berkeley's Bancroft Library" by Edward Waterman; "Bibliography of the Robert E. Howard Collections Held by the University of California at Berkeley, Bancroft Library" by Glenn Lord; "The Past Is Dead, the Past Is Deadly: Three

Dragons in One Hour" by Steven Tompkins.

Issue 8 (Winter 2004). "Texas as Character in Robert E. Howard's Fiction" by Mark Finn; "Robert E. Howard in the Gothic Tradition" by Charles Gramlich; "Two Views of *The Barbaric Triumph*" by Fred Blosser and S. T. Joshi; "Adventures—Imperial and Otherwise" by Mark E. Hall; Review of *Power of the Writing Mind* by Scotty Henderson; Review of *Graveyard Rats* by Charles Hoffman; "Through a Prism, Darkly" by David Robbins.

Volume 2, Nos. 1 and 2 (Spring 2006). "Robert E. Howard and Poetic Narrative: The Bardic Tradition and 'Popular Modernities'" by Frank Coffman; "Robert E. Howard: New Deal Heroic Fantasist" by Rusty Burke; "Crash Go the Civilizations: Some Notes on Robert E. Howard's Use of History and Anthropology" by Mark Hall. Reviews.

Volume 3, No. 1 (December 2006). Introduction by Mark E. Hall; "The Mysterious Isle" by Patrice Louinet; "Isle of Eons," Draft a1 (c. July 1925); "Isle of Eons" Outline (c. April 1926); "Isle of Eons" Draft a2 (c. April or May 1926); "Isle of Eons" Draft a3 (c. Spring 1928); "Isle of Eons" Draft b1 (c. second half of 1929); "Isle of Eons" Draft b2 (c. second half of 1929); "Tallyho!" (c. second half of 1928).

Volume 3, No 2 (2007). Editorial comments by Charles Gramlich; "The Influence of Joseph A. Altsheler's Young Trailers Series on Howard's Pictish Wilderness Fiction" by Robert M. McIlvaine; Review of *The Black Stranger and Other American Tales* by Ian Nichols; "Mind-Forg'd Manacles? Back to School with Robert E. How- ard" by Steve Tompkins; "Conan the Shakespearean / Hamlet the Barbarian" by Jeffrey Kahan; News contributions by Paul Herman and S. T. Joshi.

Volume 4, No. 1 (2009 [i.e., 2008]). Editorials. Reviews: "James Braddock: From Dockhand to Cinderella Man" by Chris Gruber; "Howard's Eastern Adventures" by Brian Taves; "Blood, Sweat, Tears and Oil" by Steven Tompkins; "From the Klondike to Cross Plains" by Steven Trout; "A Comparison of the Ideology of Robert E. Howard's Conan Tales and J. R. R. Tolkien's *The Lord of the Rings*" by Ian Nichols.

Volume 4, No. 2 (June 2009). "Elements of Sadomasochism in the Fiction and Poetry of Robert E. Howard" by Charles Hoffman; "Giant Intelligent Crabs, Oh My! Haggard and Howard" by Robert McIlvaine; Review of Sumathai Ramaswamy's *Time Lost Land of Lemuria: Fabulous Geographies, Catastrophic Histories* by David R. Werner; Review of *Night Voices, Night Journey: Lairs of the Hidden Gods* (ed. Ken Asamatsu) by Charles Gramlich; "An Honorable Retreat: Robert E. Howard as Escapist Writer" by Brian Murphy.

Volume 5, No. 1 (March 2010). "'The Shadow of the Beast': A Closer Look" by Charles Hoffman; "'Marchers of Valhalla,' Creation and the Cult of Castration" by Jeffrey Kahan; "Celtic Influences in the Works of Robert E. Howard" by Philip Emery; "A Second Look: *The Lost Land of Lemuria*" by Morgan Holmes; "Visualizing Howard's World: *The Savage Sword of Conan*" by Charles Hoffman; "The Good, the Bad, and Howard in Cross Plains Universe" by Morgan

Holmes; "Remembering *Wolfshead*" by Charles Hoffman.
Volume 5, No. 2 (August 2010). "Editorial" by Mark E. Hall; "The Man Who Helped Conan: An Interview with Roy Thomas" by Jeffrey Kahan; "Fandom at a Crossroads: Jonathan Bacon and the Legacy of Robert E. Howard" by Lee Breakiron.
Volume 6, Nos. 1 & 2 (November 2011). "Prefatory Remarks" by Mark E. Hall; "Jeffrey Catherine Jones (1944-2011)" by Charles Hoffman; "Ode" by Charles Hoffman; Letter: "Howard's Escape?" by Barbara Barrett; Letter: "Castration Anxiety" by Jeffrey Shanks; "Faction and Fiction in *Barack the Barbarian*" by Jeffrey Kahan; "Gloria" by Rusty Burke and Rob Roehm; "Theosophy and the Thurian Age: Robert E. Howard and the Works of William Scott-Elliot" by Jeffrey Shanks; Reviews: "Howard's Horror" by Jason Ray Carney; "Black Wings: Lovecraft's Widening Gyre" by John Goodrich; "Malygris, Malnéant, and Malinbois, But No Malfeasance" by Steve Tompkins; "Briefly Noted" by Mark Hall.
Volume 7, No. 1 (December 2012). "Prefatory Remarks" by Mark E. Hall; "The Writer's Style: Sound and Syntax in Howard's Sentences" by David C. Smith; "'I'n'I A-Liberate Zimbabwe': Motifs of Africa and Freedom in Howard's 'The Grisly Horror'" by Patrick R. Burger; "Robert E. Howard and the Lone Scouts" by Rob Roehm; Reviews: *Sword Woman* by Charles Hoffman; *Solomon Kane and the Castle of the Devil* by Charles Gramlich; John Carter of *Weird Worlds* by Charles Gramlich; Reflections on Le Fanu by Charles Gramlich.

Volume 7, No. 2 (December 2014). "Prefatory Remarks" by Mark E. Hall; "In Memoriam: Larry Richter (1949-2014)" by Rusty Burke; "The Least of Bob Howard" by Larry Richter; "Theosophy and the Thurian Age: Addendum" by Jeffrey Shanks; "The *Cromlech*ers: The Story of the First Scholarly Robert E. Howard Journal" by Lee A. Breakiron; Review: "Less an Archive, More an Agenda" by Mark Finn.
Volume 8, No. 1 (December 2015). "Twenty-Five Years Young!" by Mark E. Hall; "Reflections" by Rusty Burke; "On Editing Robert E. Howard" by Chris Gruber; "Mr. Robert E. Howard PhD Adventure" by Patrick R. Burger; Letter: "Comments of Finn's 'Less an Archive, Moore an Agenda'" by Todd Vick; Abstract: "On the Precipice of Fascism: The Mythic and the Political in the Work of Robert E. Howard and Ernst Jűnger" by Patrick R. Burger; "The Influence of Joseph A. Altsheter's *Apache Gold* on Howard's 'The Haunted Mountain'" by Robert McIlvaine; "Literary Gothicism in Robert E. Howard's 'Red Nails'" by Matthew Cirelli; "Berserker Synecdoche: Howard's Aesthetic of Violence" by Philip Emery; Papers from the Popular Culture Association Meetings: "The Outsider Scholar: Robert E. Howard, H. P. Lovecraft, and Scholarly Identity" by Karen Kohoutek; "Disintegrating Verse: The Poetry of the Shadow Modernists and the Ephemerality of the Ordinary" by James Ray Carney; Notes: Scott Connors, Mark Finn, Charles Gramlich, Mark Hall, Jeffrey Kahan, Gene Melton II, Jeffrey Shanks.

Volume 8, No. 2 (August 2017). "Notes from the Editor" by Mark E. Hall; Papers from the Popular Culture Association Meetings: "The Mistaken Identity of a Barbarian: Hero or Anti-Hero?" by Todd B. Vick; "Local Color and Underlying Meaning in Robert E. Howard's Weird Western, Southern Gothic Horror, and Detective Stories" by Dierk Günther; Review: "'The Trick of the Archive': A Review of Centipede Press's *The Best Horror Stories of Karl Edward Wagner*" by James Carney.

Volume 9 (January 2019). "Musings from a Cluttered Desk" by Mark E. Hall; "Onward, *The Dark Man!*" by Jason Ray Carney; "Where Shadows Linger: Comparing the Heroic Fantasy of Karl Edward Wagner and Robert E. Howard" by Charles Gramlich; "'I Was a Man Before I Was a King': An Examination of Conan's Kingship through the Political Theory of Giorgio Agamben" by Daniel Nyikosp; "The Outsider Scholar: Robert E. Howard, H. P. Lovecraft and Scholarly Identity, Part Two: A Complex and Baffling Question" by Karen Joan Kohoutek; "From the Days of Yore: An Interview with Andrew Offutt" by Mark E. Hall.

Volume 10, No. 1 (June 2019). Editorial; "By This Pen I Rule: Robert E. Howard as Gatekeeper in the Development of Weird Fiction" by Nicole Emmelhainz-Carney; "Faces of Kane: Exploring the Faces of Robert E. Howard's Puritan Swordsman" by Dierk Günther; "Texas Fists and Foreign Ports: Working Class White American Masculinity in Robert E. Howard's 'Sailor Steve Costigan'" by Jonathan Helland; "No Refuge in Idealism: Illusion Meets Reality in 'Xuthal of the Dusk'" by Karen Joan Kohoutek; "Heredity and Madness in H. P. Lovecraft's 'The Rats in the Walls'" by Julianna Gonzalez.

The Cimmerian. Edited by Leo Grin. Published 2004–2008.

Volume 1, No. 1 (April 2004). "Conan the Expensive" by Don Herron; "The One and Authentic Cimmerian" by Darrell Schweitzer; "Napoleon's Triumph" by Gary Romeo; "Hell Needs a New Devil" by Leo Grin.

Volume 1, No. 2 (June 2004). "The Great Game" by David A. Hardy; "The Runyonesque Raconteur" by Mark Finn; Reviews of *The Barbaric Triumph*; "Near the End of the Epic" (poetry) by Darrell Schweitzer.

Volume 1, No. 3 (September 2004). "Cross Plains Memories" by Leo Grin; "Sacred Ground" by Robert Weinberg; "A Spirit on the Wind" (poetry) by Frank Coffman; "He Was Deadly" by Don Herron.

Volume 1, No. 4 (October 2004). "Reverend Bob on Two-Gun Bob" by Robert M. Price; "The Last Temptation of Conan" by Robert M. Price; "The Ghosts of Fort McKavett" by Leo Grin; "Vengeance Quest" (poetry) by Richard Tierney.

Volume 1, No. 5 (December 2004). "After Twenty Years, a Landmark" by Darrell Schweitzer; "Hard-Boiled Heroic Critic" by Charles Hoffman; "Thirty Years as a Howard Critic" by Don Herron; *The Dark Barbarian*: Reviews 1984–1985.

Volume 2, No. 1 (February 2005). "Howard's Ruin" by Rob Roehm; "Inspiration from Life" by Gary Romeo; "Conquistadors of

Doom" by David A. Hardy; "The Companion's Tale" (poetry) by Darrel Schweitzer.

Volume 2, No. 2 (April 2005). "How the West Was Wondered" by Steven Tompkins; "A Gent Up Bear Creek" by David Gentzel; "A More Sincere Form of Flattery" by Rick McCollum; "Old Pickets Find New Homes" by Era Lee Hanke.

Volume 2, No. 3 (June 2005). "Born to Edit Boxing Stories" by Chris Gruber; "Frontiers of Imagination" by Rusty Burke; "Fight Stories Feeding Frenzy" by Donald Sydney-Fryer.

Volume 2, No. 4 (August 2005). "When You Wish upon a (Wandering) Star" by Steve Hall; "The Mystery of the Treasure Room" by Rob Roehm; "Bundling Inscribed" by Joseph Linzalone; "Crazy Son" (poetry) by Frank Coffman.

Volume 2, No. 5 (October 2005). "Blood Lust" by Charles Hoffman; "Asgard, Vanaheim, and Cimmeria" by Leon Nielson; "Trail of the Prophet" by David A. Hardy; "Small World" by James Reasoner; "That Bed Beneath the Stars" (poetry) by Anthony Avacato.

Volume 2, No. 6 (December 2005). "Robert E. Howard in the Necronomicon Press" by John Haefele; "In Defense of 'Little Boys'" by Donald Sydney-Fryer; "At the Mammaries of Madness" by Rick McCollum; "The Unseen Gods of Ancient Egypt" (poetry) by Stanley C. Sargeant.

Volume 3, No. 1 (January 2006). "The Note" by Rusty Burke; "Birth and Death" by Leo Grin; "REH and Guns" by J. D. Charles; "The Doom of Hyboria" (poetry) by Richard L. Tierney.

Volume 3, No. 2 (February 2006). "Birthday Bash at the Torch" by Rick Kelsey; "Lovecraft's Southern Vacation" by Brian Leo; "The Fire That Spread Around the World" by Arlene Stephenson; "A Vulture Comes Up Snake Eyes" by Glenn Lord.

Volume 3, No. 3 (March 2006). "The Shortest Distance Between Two Towers" by Steven Tompkins; "Once I Was John Wesley Hardin!" by Gary Romeo; "The Last of the Baker Kids" by Don Herron; "Plains Town Writer" by Robert E. Kane.

Volume 3, No. 4 (April 2006). "Indomitable Wilderness, Unquenchable Vitality" by David A. Hardy; "Curly Elkins of Bear-Tooth Creek" by Rob Roehm; "Two Barbarian Usurpers" by Darrell Schweitzer; "The Doom of Hyboria" (poetry) by Richard L. Tierney.

Volume 3, No. 5 (May 2006). "Viagra for the Soul" by Gary Romeo; "The Lancer Legacy of Frank Frazetta" by Anthony Avacato; "Long Ago and Far Away" by Richard Lupoff; "Pseudo Boom" by Leon Nielson; "A Vision of Atali" (poetry) by James Ruffini.

Volume 3, No. 6 (June 2006). "How Robert E. Howard Saved My Life" by Bill "Indy" Cavalier; "A Look at Blood and Thunder" by Mark Finn; "COnun and TarZAN" by Don Herron; "A Barbaric Song" (poetry) by Darrell Schweitzer.

Volume 3, No. 7 (July 2006). Coverage of centennial celebration of Robert E. Howard Days in Cross Plains, Texas.

Volume 3, No. 8 (August 2006). "Treasures of Our Own" by Danny Street; "Ur Gent" by Don Herron; "The Mysteriously Mysterious Jenkins Gent Mystery" by Damon

Sasser; "Chasing the Grail" by Edward Gobbett.

Volume 3, No. 9 (September 2006). "Skull-Face and Others at Sixty" by John Haefele; "It Is My Desire" by Don Herron; "Sailor Steve Meets Winston Smith" by Steven Tompkins; "Pulpcon 2006: Where's the Howard?" by Morgan Holmes.

Volume 3, No. 10 (October 2006). "Robert'll Be Famous Someday" by Don Herron; "Dog Brothers" by Steven Tompkins.

Volume 3, No. 11 (November 2006). "Beyond the Colorado River" by Leo Grin; "The Battle of Arsuf" (poetry) by Chris Gruber.

Volume 3, No. 12 (December 2006). "Robert E. Howard: Epic Poet in Prose" by Donald Sidney-Fryer; "Diary of a Bad Man" by Brian Leno; "Legacy" by Leon Nielson; "The Robert E. Howard Foundation" by Rusty Burke; "The Doom of Hyboria" (poetry) by Richard L. Tierney.

Volume 4, No. 1 (February 2007). "Underwood for the Ages" by Damon Sasser; "Adventure Days and Arabian Nights" by David A. Hardy; "The Would-Be Cimmerian" by Ben P. Indick; "On the Road to Cross Plains" by Chris Green.

Volume 4, No. 2 (April 2007). "I Suppose We Must Respect Him" by Rob Roehm; "The Statement of S. T. Joshi" by Morgan Holmes; "The Fouling of Robert E. Howard" by Brian Leno; "Our Labor of Love" by Leo Grin.

Volume 4, No. 3 (June 2007). "An Iron Harp Played through a Marshall Amp" by Scott Hall; "Worms of the Frontier" by David A. Hardy; "The Father of Sword-and-Sorcery" by Gary Romeo; "Raising Kane" by Paul Shovlin.

Volume 4, No. 4 (August 2007). "Sailor Steve and the Dane" (poetry) by Amy Kerr; "Down the Rabbit Hole" by Brian Leno; "A Tale of Two Pulp Shows" by Morgan Holmes.

Volume 4, No. 5 (October 2007). "In the Footsteps of Two-Gun and the Kid" by Rob Roehm; "The Other REH Days" by Bill "Indy" Cavalier; "Sword-and-Soul" by Steven Tompkins.

Volume 4, No. 6 (December 2007). "Lionization" by Fred Phillips; "The Thrill of it All" by Joseph Linzalone; "Enter the Barbarian" by Morgan Holmes; "Star-Studded Conan" by Rick Kelsey; "*Always Comes Evening*, for Fifty Years" by John Haefele.

Volume 5, No. 1 (February 2008). "Newer Barbarians" by Steven Tompkins; "How to Build a Better Barbarian" by Big Jim Charles; "A Statistical Analysis of REH's Vocabulary" by Rusty Burke; "REH at 102" by Rob Roehm.

Volume 5, No. 2 (April 2008). "The Feast Is Over" by Don Herron; "Jacques Bergier, or, The Man Who Also Discovered Robert E. Howard" by Joseph Altairac (translated from the French by Patrick Dusoulier); "An Unhallowed Ritual of Cruelty, Sadism, and Blood" by Michel Meurger (translated from the French by Patrick Dusoulier); "The Unnatural City" by Brian Murphy; "Conan and the Crusades" by Steve Trout.

Volume 5, No. 3 (June 2008). "In the Middle of the Street" by Rob Roehm; "Coins of the Cimmerians" by Joseph Linzalone; "Six Degrees to Cross Plains" by Barbara Barrett; "Robert E. Howard in *The Summit County Journal*" by

Ed Blohm; "Belad-el-Djinn" (poetry) by Richard Tierney.

Volume 5, No. 4 (August 2008). "Conan the Argonaut" by Morgan Holmes and George Knight; "Long Falls and Hard Climbs" by Steven Tompkins; "The Best Little Lore House in Texas" by Lee Breakiron.

Volume 5, No. 5 (October 2008). "When Yaller Rock Came to Chawed Ear" by Brian Leno; "Pigeons in the Darkroom" by Brian Leno; "Robert E. Howard in *Fantôme*" by Ed Blohm; "As Much Fort as Hotel" by Rob Roehm; "Tag-Ends, Snatches of History, and Disconnected Bits" by Leo Grin.

Volume 5, No. 6 (December 2008). "The Nietzschean Herd" by Nicholas Moll; "Strong to Save or to Damn" by Steven Tompkins; "The First Posthumous Collaborator" by Morgan Holmes; "Shadows and Light" by Donald Sydney-Fryer; "Sword-and-Sorcery" by Don Herron.

INDEX

Ace Books 42
Action Stories 7, 25, 234, 248
Adventure 19, 24, 237, 238, 239
Against Our Will (Brownmiller) 140
Almuric 213-16
"Altar and the Scorpion, The" 121
"Altars and Jesters" 252-53
"Always Comes Evening" 254
Always Comes Evening 40, 252
Annotated Guide to Robert E. Howard's Sword and Sorcery, An (Weinberg) 42-43
Aquinas, St. Thomas 177
Ar-i-e'ch and the Spell of Cthulhu (Blosser) 48
Argosy 7, 35, 237, 238, 239
Argosy-All Story Weekly 24
Arkham House 40
Arnold, Edwin Lester 213
Arthur, King 9, 195
Atlantis 7, 57, 101, 102, 134
Autry, Gene 221, 249

Baen Books 46-47
"Balthus of Cross Plains" (Scithers) 171
Bantam Books 42
Barbaric Triumph, The (Herron) 47-48
Baudelaire, Charles 253
Bearfield, Pike (character) 34, 248
Beast of Hollow Mountain, The (film) 148
Before Adam (London) 204
"Belshazzar" 253
Benét, Stephen Vincent and William Rose 251
Beowulf 9, 195, 208

Berkley Medallion Books 42
"Beyond the Black River" 135, 170, 171-77, 190, 198
Bible 68, 163,197
Bierce, Ambrose 251
Billy the Kid vs. Dracula (film) 221
Bison Books (University of Nebraska Press) 47
"Black Canaan" 139, 164, 224, 228-32
"Black Colossus" 135, 160, 191
"Black Country" 227
"Black Dawn" 253
"Black Hound of Death" 224
Black Mask 20, 44, 237
"Black Stone, The" 219-20
Blake, William 46, 126, 130, 132
Bloch, Robert 39-40, 218, 234
Blood & Thunder (Finn) 48
"Blood of Belshazzar, The" 241
Blosser, Fred 46
"Blow the Chinks Down" 234
Blue Book 237, 238
"Blue Flame of Vengeance, The" 78-79
Body and Soul (film) 244
Bohannon, "Aunt Mary" 217, 226-27
Bond, James (character) 10, 127, 148
Brackett, Leigh 213
Bran Mak Morn 7, 11, 12, 46, 47, 51-64, 65, 93, 101, 109, 131, 132, 172, 194, 196, 198, 202, 223, 248, 257, 259
Bran Mak Morn (play) 52-53
Brand, Max 248
Brando, Marlon 148, 195
Brave New World (Huxley) 186

Brownmiller, Susan 139-40
Brownwood, Texas 19, 20
Brule 57, 103, 104-5, 108, 110, 113, 114, 116, 117-19, 120
Buccaneers of Venus (Kline) 213
Bunyan, Paul 9
Burke, Rusty 37, 46, 54, 224, 233
Burroughs, Edgar Rice 80, 82, 85, 123, 127, 131, 161, 195, 213, 214
"'By This Axe I Rule!'" 119-25, 126, 131, 135
Byrne, John F. 34

Cabot, Tarl (character) 213
Cain, James M. 203
"Call of Cthulhu, The" (Lovecraft) 218
Campbell, Joseph 10, 195
Carter, John 213
Carter, Lin 41
Cassidy, Hopalong (character) 249
"Cat and the Skull, The" 121
Celts 17, 51, 134, 198, 199, 203, 258
Chambers, Robert W. 17-18, 175
Chandler, Raymond 20, 44, 45, 153, 195, 246, 262
Chaung Tzu 115, 262-63
Chesterton, G. K. 251
"Children of the Night, The" 220, 221
Cimmeria 7, 30, 136, 172
"Cimmeria" (poem) 29, 252, 253, 258
Cimmerian, The 48
Circus of Dr. Lao, The (Finney) 221
Clanton, Wild Bill (character) 246
Clavell, James 169
Clontarf (battle) 199
Coffman, Frank 255
Comanche 14, 134. 175, 208, 209, 234
"Coming of El Borak, The" 239
Conan 7, 9, 10, 11, 12, 30, 31, 34, 40, 43, 45, 51, 59, 99, 118, 127-87, 190-95, 196, 198, 212, 217, 240, 257, 258, 259, 261
Conan Properties 43, 47
Conan the Adventurer 42
Conan's World (Schweitzer) 43
Conquest of Peru, The (Prescott) 123
Corbett, Jim 71
Costigan, Sailor Steve (character) 14, 245

Cowboy Stories 35, 238, 249
Cowboys & Aliens (film) 222
Cross Plains High School 18, 31
Cross Plains, Texas 14, 17, 20, 22, 23, 26
Cthulhu Mythos 218, 220
Culture Publications 246

Dark Barbarian, The (Herron) 44, 45
"Dark Man, The" 64, 201-3, 258
Dark Man: The Journal of Robert E. Howard Studies, The 46
Dark Tower, The (King) 221
Dark Valley Destiny (de Camp et al.) 26, 37, 38, 43, 210
Dark Valley, Texas 13, 14, 29
Darker Than You Think (Williamson) 106
"Dead Man's Hate" 252
"Dead Remember, The" 221, 233
Dean, James 148, 195
de Camp, L. Sprague 25-26, 38, 40, 41, 42, 43-44, 123, 201, 205
Del Rey Books 47
Deliverance (Dickey) 175, 176
Dempsey, Jack 244
Dent, Lester 131
Derleth, August 27, 39, 40, 59, 218, 250
"Devil in Iron, The" 161
Die Hard (film) 10
"Dig Me No Grave" 220
Dill, Dr. 36
Dime Detective 237
Dime Mystery Magazine 237
Dime Sports Magazine 238
Dirty Harry 10
Doc Savage (character) 11
Doc Savage (magazine) 237
Don Quixote (Cervantes) 198
D'Onofrio, Vincent 47
Dostoevsky, Fyodor 148
Dowson, Ernest Christopher 37
"Dream Snake, The" 227
Dunsany, Lord 10, 100, 251
"Dunwich Horror, The" (Lovecraft) 218
"The Dust Dance" 253

Easy Rider (film) 148
"Borak, El" 239

El Borak (character). *See* Francis X. Gordon
Elkins, Breckinridge 31, 34, 247–48, 259
Ellis, Novalyne Price. *See* Price, Novalyne
Ellison, Harlan 41
Equus (Shaffer) 50
Eric John Stark 213
Ervin, G. W. 17
"Exile of Atlantis" 101–2, 122, 124
"Eyrie, The" (*Weird Tales*) 28, 40
existentialism 12, 148, 165, 190

"Fall of the House of Usher, The" (Poe) 146
Faulkner, William 203, 226
FAX Collectors Editions 42
"Feud, The" 253
Fight Stories 7, 25, 238, 244
Finn, Mark 32, 46
"Fire of Asshurbanipal, The" 220
Fitzgeoffrey, Cormac (character) 17, 241, 248
Fitzgerald, F. Scott 40
Fleming, Ian 9, 195
"Footfalls Within, The" 94–97, 113
"'For the Love of Barbara Allen'" 210–13
Ford, John 251
Forrest, Nathan Bedford 212
Frazetta, Frank 11, 41
Frontier Stories 238
"Frost-Giant's Daughter, The" 136–40, 157, 160

G-8 and his Battle Aces 237
Game, The (London) 244
Gangs of New York, The (Asbury) 182
"Garden of Fear, The" 205
Garvin, Viola 37
"Gates of Babylon, The" 253
Gentzel, David 46
George, St. 9, 205
"Ghost of Camp Colorado, The" 228
Ghost Stories 24, 237
Gnome Press 40, 41
Gods of Mars, The (Burroughs) 82
Gogol, Nikolai 259

"Gold and the Grey, The" 253
Golden Fleece 242
Gordon, "Chinese" 239
Gordon, Flash (character) 213
Gordon, Francis X. (character) 42, 52, 239–40
Gordon, Robert W. 211
Gramlich, Charles 255
Grant, Donald M. (publisher) 42
"Grey God Passes, The" 199–201, 203
Grey, Zane 248
Grimes, Buckner J. (character) 35, 248
Grin, Leo 46, 48
Guillaud, Lauric 255
Gurdjieff, George Ivanovich 194

Haeckel, Ernst 112
Haggard, H. Rider 11, 17, 80, 161
Hall, Mark 46, 255
Hammett, Dashiell 20, 44, 246
Harrison, Steve (character) 246–47
Haunted Mesa, The (L'Amour) 221
"Haunting Columns" 253
"Hawks of Outremer" 241
Hawkline Monster, The (Brautigan) 221
"Heart of Darkness" (Conrad) 71, 151, 175–76, 196
Henry, Jim 17
Henry, John 9
Herron, Don 44, 46, 47
"Hills of the Dead, The" 85, 97
Hitler, Adolf 126
Hobbes, Thomas 187
Holly Springs, Arkansas 15
Hollywood Detective 237
Holmes, Morgan 46
Holmes, Sherlock (character) 45
Homer 197
homosexuality 159–60, 182–83, 255
Hood, Robin (character) 148
"Hop-Frog" (Poe) 147
"Horror from the Mound, The" 221
Horror Stories 237
Hour of the Dragon, The 31, 136, 165, 191–94
"House in the Oaks, The" 220
"House of Cæsar, The" (Garvin) 37

"House of Peril, The." *See* "Blow the Chinks Down"
"House of Suspicion, The" 224
"Howard boom" 41–42, 44
Howard, Dr. Isaac M. 13, 14–15, 16, 24, 28–29, 32, 35, 67
Howard, Eliza 217–18
Howard, Hester Jane Ervin 13, 14, 15, 32, 35, 36–37, 67, 203, 214, 259–60
Howard Payne College 19, 23, 40
Howard, Robert E.: death of, 35–36, 37–38, 244, 260; education of, 17, 18, 112; employment of, 20–22; religion of, 67–68; sex life of, 26
Howard, William Benjamin 17
Hyborian Age 7, 9, 51, 134–35, 137, 172, 196, 197
"Hyborian Age, The" (essay) 196–97, 198
"Hyena, The" 20, 228
"Hymn of Hatred" 253

"In Memoriam: Robert Ervin Howard" (Lovecraft) 39
"In the Forest of Villefere" 20
"Iron Man, The" 244–45

Jack Dempsey's Fight Magazine 238
Jakes, John 41
James, William 112
Jason 89, 192, 195
Jessel, Ace (character) 233
Jesus Christ 84, 164–65
"Jewels of Gwahlur" 161
Jonah Hex (comic) 221
Jones, Casey (character) 9
Jones, Jeff 42
Josephus 163
Joshi, S. T. 218
Jules de Grandin 33, 78
Jones, Gulliver (character) 213
Jung, Carl 10, 105, 139, 204
Jungle Lore (Corbett) 71

Kahan, Jeffrey 255
Kane, Solomon (character) 7, 11, 12, 14, 24, 46, 47, 65–97, 100, 101, 105, 107, 118–19, 129, 131, 132, 152, 155, 194, 196, 204, 217, 227, 233, 257, 259

Kant, Immanuel 112
Karloff, Boris 224
"Kelly the Conjure-Man" 228
"King and the Oak, The" 252
King Kong (1933 film) 179
"Kings of the Night" 55–59
Kipling, Rudyard 123, 166, 251
Kline, Otis Adelbert 30, 33, 35, 213, 214
"Knife, Bullet, and Noose" 248
Krenkel, Roy G. 41, 243–44
Kull 7, 11, 12, 46, 47, 51, 57–58, 59, 99, 101–26, 129, 131, 132, 141, 152, 194, 196, 198, 204, 252, 257, 259

Lamb, Harold 17, 239
Lancer Books 11, 41, 42, 166
"Land of Mystery" 239
Lardner, Ring 244
"Last Ride, The" 248
Lawrence, D. H. 203
Lawrence, T. E. 239
"Law-Shooters of Cowtown" 248
Leiber, Fritz 41, 99, 166
Leone, Sergio 250
Leviathan (Hobbes) 187
Lewis, C. S. 10
Lewis, Sinclair 40
Liberty 24
"Lion of Tiberias" 242
Little People 61, 64, 221, 222
"Little People, The" (story) 221
Little Red Foot, The (Chambers) 175
Locke, John 110, 112, 116
London, Jack 17, 108, 123, 148, 151, 203, 204, 244
Long, Frank Belknap 218
Longfellow, Henry Wadsworth 251
Lord, Glenn 40
Lord of the Rings (Tolkien) 45
"Lord of Samarcand" 241
"Lost Race, The" 49, 52
Louinet, Patrice 255
Lovecraft: A Biography (de Camp) 43
Lovecraft, H. P. 18, 27–28, 30, 34, 35–36, 38, 39, 55, 59, 68, 92, 126, 129, 132, 156, 168, 182, 198, 211, 217, 218–19, 228, 283, 234–35, 256

Mac Art, Cormac (characer) 17, 142
MacDonald, George 10

Machen, Arthur 61
Magic Carpet 7, 25, 242
Mailer, Norman 244
Man Called Horse, A (film) 209
"Man on the Ground, The" 221
Man with No Name, The 148
"Marchers of Valhalla" 83
"Marching Song of Connacht" 253
"Mark of the Beast" 253
Marlowe, Philip (character) 45
Martin Eden (London) 21, 108
Maslow, Abraham 50
"Masque of the Red Death, The" (Poe) 146
McAllen, Texas 29, 30
McClane, John (character) 10
"Men of the Shadows" 53-55, 56
"Mirrors of Tuzun Thune, The" 109, 114-16, 117, 119, 129
Miss Minerva on the Old Plantation (Sampson) 233
Mission, Texas 29, 30
"Moon of Skulls, The" 79-85
"Moon of Zembabwei" 224
"Moor Ghost, The" 252
Moorcock, Michael 41
Morris, William 10, 100
Mundy, Talbot 17, 161, 166, 239
"Murders in the Rue Morgue, The" (Poe) 146
Mussolini, Benito 126
"Myth of Sisyphus, The" (Camus) 260

"Nekht Semerkeht" 35, 210, 260, 261
Nietzsche, Frederick 112, 114, 152, 256
N'Longa (character) 71, 73, 85-86, 97, 233
"Non Sum Qualis Eran Bonae Sub Regno Cynarae" (Dowson) 37
Norman, John 213
Nouvelles Editions Oswald 44
Nyberg, Bjorn 41

Oates, Joyce Carol 244
O'Brien, Turlogh (character) 14, 17, 199, 200, 201-3, 258
O'Donnell, Kirby 240
Odysseus 9, 139, 148, 192, 195
Offutt, Andrew J. 261
"Oh Babylon, Lost Babylon" 253

"Old Deserted House, The" (Burke) 233
"Old Garfield's Heart" 221
"Old Songs That Men Have Sung" (*Adventure* magazine column) 211
One Who Walked Alone (Ellis) 45-46, 47
ophidiophobia 105-6
Oriental Stories 7, 241-42
"Out of the Deep" 218
Outsider, The (Wilson) 262

Paradise Lost (Milton) 67
Patch 28-29, 174
Peaster, Texas 13
Peckinpah, Sam 250
"People of the Black Circle, The" 165-70
"People of the Dark" 221
Petaja, Emil 258
Phantom Empire, The (film serial) 221
"Phoenix on the Sword, The" 124, 135. 190
Picts 7, 49-52, 53, 54, 56, 64, 103, 134, 171-72, 173-75, 196, 198, 202, 203, 206, 208, 227-28, 258
"Piece of Steak, A" (London) 244
"Pigeons from Hell" 224-27, 233
Pioneer Western 238
Plato 110, 112
Poe, Edgar Allan 17, 114, 146-47, 208, 251, 259
"Pool of the Black One, The" 197-98
Post Oaks and Sand Roughs 21, 22, 23, 24, 232
Preece, Harold 198
Price, E. Hoffmann 28, 39, 40, 129
Price, Novalyne 31-32, 34, 38, 40, 45-46, 47, 111, 156, 187
Price, Robert M. 44
Private Detective 237
Pryke, Reginald A. 262
pulp fiction/pulp magazines 7, 11, 100, 109, 148-49, 237-38

"Queen of the Black Coast" 149-57, 194
Quick-Trigger Western 238
Quinn, Seabury 33, 39, 78, 234

racism 232-34
Raging Bull (film) 244

Railroad Stories 238
Rand, Ayn 7
"Rats in the Walls, The" (Lovecraft) 27
"Rattle of Bones" 77
Raymond, Alex 213
Rebel without a Cause (movie) 148
"Red Blades of Black Cathay" 241
"Red Nails" 34, 170, 177-87, 190, 210
"Red Shadows" 24, 68-77, 79, 99, 101, 105
Reid, Thomas 220
reincarnation 73, 203-4, 210
"Right Hand of Doom, The" 77
Rising Star, Texas 30
"Road to Rome, The" 253
Robert E. Howard: A Literary Biography (Smith) 48
"Robert E. Howard: Hard-Boiled Heroic Fantasist" (Herron) 44-45
Robert E. Howard Foundation Press 47
Robert E. Howard Guide, The (Louinet) 48
The Robert E. Howard Reader (Schweitzer) 48
Robertson, Lexie Dean 251
"Rogues in the House" 83, 144-47, 148, 149
Roland 9, 197
Romance 24
Romeo, Gary 46
Rousseau, Jean Jacques 132, 190

Sabatini, Rafael 11
Sampson, Emma Speed 233
Sappho 251, 259
"Scarlet Citadel, The" 135, 190, 191
Schopenhauer, Arthur 112
Schultz, Mark 8
Scithers, George H. 171, 174
Scott, Sir Walter 11, 17
"Screaming Skull of Silence, The" 109, 110-11, 112, 113-14, 116, 118
"Sea Curse" 218
Sea Wolf, The (London) 108, 123
"Servants of Bit-Yakin, The." *See* "Jewels of Gwahlur"
Service, Robert W. 251
Shadow, The (character) 11, 131
Shadow, The (magazine) 237

"Shadow Kingdom, The" 99, 100, 101, 102-9, 114, 116-17, 119, 121, 129, 131
"Shadow of the Beast, The" 224
"Shadow of the Vulture, The" 242
"Shadow over Innsmouth, The" (Lovecraft) 218
"Shadows on the Road" 253
Shakespeare, William 121
Shanks, Jeffrey 46
She Devil, The 42
Short, Luke 248
"Shunned Castle, The" 239
Shuster, Joe 195
Siegel, Jerry 195
Siegfried 9, 195, 205, 208
Singers in the Shadows 24
Skull-Face and Others 40, 41, 250
"Skulls in the Stars" 77
Smith, Clark Ashton 27, 39, 114, 129, 130, 168, 177, 218, 219, 251
Smith, Tevis Clyde 25, 31
"Solomon Kane's Homecoming" 97, 252
"Song Before Clontarf" 253
"Song for All Women, A" 253
"Song of the Bats, The" 252
"Sowers of the Thunder, The" 241
Speakeasy Stories 238
"Spear and Fang" 20, 49
Spencer, Herbert 112
Spicy-Adventure Stories 246
Spicy Detective Stories 246
Spicy Mystery Stories 246
Spicy Western Stories 246
Spider, The 237
Spillane, Mickey 9
Spinoza, Benedict 112
Sport Story Magazine 238
Stapeldon, Olaf 198
Star-Rover, The (London) 204, 210
Sterling, George 251
Sterne, Laurence 194
Strange Detective Stories 237
Strange Suicides 238
Strange Tales 29, 237
Street & Smith 35, 239
"Striking of the Gong, The" 109-11
Super-Detective Stories 238

Super Science Stories 239
Superman 195
Swinburne, Algernon Charles 251
sword and planet 213
"Swords of the Purple Kingdom" 121

"Tarantella" 253
Tarkington, Booth 233
Tarzan 85, 123, 127
Tarzan Triumphant (Burroughs) 82
"Teeth of Gwahlur." *See* "Jewels of Gwahlur"
Ten Detective Aces 237
Tennyson, Alfred, Lord 251
Terence X. O'Leary's War Birds 238
Terror Tales 237
Texaco Star 228
"Thing on the Roof, The" 220
Three Mesquiteers, The 249
Three Stooges, The 248
Thriller (TV show) 224
Thrilling Mystery 237
Thrills of the Jungle 24
"Thunder Rider, The" 35, 208-10, 216, 234
"To a Woman" 253
"To All Sophisticates" 253
"To Harry the Oliad Men" 253
Tolkien, J. R. R. 10, 41, 100
Tompkins, Steve 46
Top-Notch 7, 25, 237, 238, 239
Topo, El (film) 222
"Tower of the Elephant, The" 83, 135, 136, 140-44, 156
Trout, Steven A. 46
True Stories 24
Tully, Jim 18
Tunney, Gene 244
Twain, Mark 17
Two-Gun Bob: A Centennial Study of Robert E. Howard (Szumskyj) 48
Tyson, Lindsey W. 20, 23

"Vale of Lost Women, The" 140, 157-60
Valley of Gwangi, The (film) 222
"Valley of the Lost, The" 222-23, 261
"Valley of the Worm, The" 204-8, 227-28
"'Valley of the Worm': A Gathering of Howard's Essential Creative Themes, The" (McCollum) 204
Van Gogh, Vincent 262
Vikings 51, 56-59, 199, 201, 202
"Viking's Trail" 253
Vinson, Truett 25, 34, 40, 187
"Vultures of Wahpeton, The" 249

Wagner, Karl Edward 42
Wandering Star (publisher) 47
Warfield, Wayne 42
Waterman, Edward A. 46
Wayne, John 148
Weinberg, Robert 42
weird menace 246
Weird Tales 7, 8, 11, 20, 23, 24, 25, 28, 29, 31, 32, 33, 34, 39, 40, 41, 49, 54, 65, 69, 77, 99, 101, 109, 111, 119, 127, 129, 135, 156, 165, 168, 190, 213, 214, 217, 218, 228, 234, 237, 238, 241, 244, 252, 261
weird western 221-22
Western Aces 238, 249
Western Weirdness and Voodoo Vengeance (Blosser) 48
Whitehead, Henry S. 234
Whitman, Walt 256
Whole Wide World, The (film) 47
Wild West Weekly 238
Wild, Wild West, The (TV show) 221
Wilde, Oscar 251
Wildside Press 47
Wilson, Colin 262
Windsor-Smith, Barry 41
"Wings in the Night" 86-94, 153, 155
"Witch Shall Be Born, A" 161-65, 197
"Wolfshead" 21, 218
"Wolves Beyond the Border" 196
"Word from the Outer Dark, A" 253
"Worms of the Earth" 59-64, 93, 106, 117, 164, 213, 221, 258
Wright, Farnsworth 20, 27, 32-33, 34, 37, 40, 41, 54, 119, 182, 241, 258, 261

Yeats, W. B. 46

Zebra Books 42
Zellweger, Renée 47
Zeppelin Stories 238